"In the Rationalist Utopia of my dreams, Herb Silverman would be a Living National Treasure, if not Honorary President for Life."

—Richard Dawkins, author of *The God Delusion*

"These lively and thoughtful essays contain essential insights on how to advance a secular, humanistic worldview in a country and a world that is still dominated by religion. The discussions are invariably judicious, wise, and thought-provoking."

—Steven Pinker, Johnstone Professor of Psychology, Harvard University, and author of *The Better Angels of Our Nature*

"What I like most about Herb Silverman's eclectic collection of essays, on subjects ranging from holidays to the political clout (and weaknesses) of atheists and secular humanists in politics, is his emphasis on building coalitions with liberal religious allies when we agree on public issues and drawing the line when secular and religious values clash. There is uncommon good sense—sorely needed in this era of political incivility—in his insistence that it is both possible and desirable for atheists and humanists to proudly proclaim their values while seeking areas of common concern with the large number of liberal religious Americans who agree with secular Americans, not with the religious Right, on the separation of church and state."

—Susan Jacoby, author of *Freethinkers: A History of American Secularism*

"With wit, warmth, and insight, Herb Silverman deftly addresses a range of topics relating to religion, atheism, politics, and culture, and the sometimes uneasy relationships among them. His delightfully concise essays will bring enlightenment to your brain and a smile to your lips."

—Ron Lindsay, author of *The Necessity of Secularism: Why God Can't Tell Us What to Do*

"Herb Silverman has the unique gift of advocating atheism while simultaneously disarming his critics. He prefers intelligence over insults, prose over polemics, and conversation over conversion. He has spent his activist career bringing people together to advance our common goals and atheists everywhere owe him a debt of gratitude for it. In this book of essays, you get a taste of that Southern godless charm that has made him a popular draw for religious and nonreligious people everywhere."

—**Hemant Mehta, editor of FriendlyAtheist.com and author of *I Sold My Soul on eBay***

"*An Atheist Stranger in a Strange Religious Land* doesn't only give us the best of Herb Silverman. Its delightful mix of incorruptible reason, tolerance, and compassion—served with a deliciously saucy sense of humor—gives us the best of humanity."

—**Rebecca Goldstein, author of *36 Arguments for the Existence of God: A Work of Fiction***

"Whether you believe in God or not, you can have faith in Herb Silverman's ability to inform and entertain. He is an insightful and delightful conversationalist, as this collection of his columns confirms."

—**Wendy Kaminer, author of *Sleeping With Extra-Terrestrials: The Rise of Irrationalism and Perils of Piety***

"As America has been trending secular for the last two decades, nobody has been in the middle of the action more than Herb Silverman. Fortunately for us, in the midst of his activism he's always taken the time to provide written commentary that explains the secular position with eloquence and wit. *An Atheist Stranger in a Strange Religious Land* is a treasury of some of Silverman's insightful writings on atheism, religion, politics, and other hot-button topics from the culture wars. Silverman's clear, commonsense thinking on these issues is on display here, as is the personality of the happy warrior who has led the charge for a more rational and secular society."

—**David Niose, author of *Nonbeliever Nation: The Rise of Secular Americans***

"Whenever I see that Herb Silverman has written about something I care about, I drop everything and read it. This collection reminds me why. More than once, his clarity, intelligence, and easygoing wit have been the perfect antidote to the lunacy of our culture war, making me feel that things just might turn out fine after all."

—**Dale McGowan**, **author of** *Parenting Beyond Belief*

"Herb Silverman's writing is like listening to a favorite uncle give entertaining yet practical advice on how the world really is. Herb's mathematician side comes through in the flawless logic he uses to filet arguments in support of religion and against atheism. His puckish side comes through in the jokes and storytelling that make his enjoyable commentaries part cultural observation, part Borscht Belt routine. Herb's quixotic run for governor of South Carolina to challenge the state's prohibition on atheists holding public office made him the most famous nonbeliever in the state. He has used that fame to disarm his detractors through a series of clear-eyed commentaries. This volume of some of his best takes us inside Herb's mind—a place to linger only if you want to be challenged to think while chuckling."

—**Robyn Blumner**, **CEO of the Center for Inquiry**

"I've read many of Dr. Silverman's essays and expected merely to be going over old—good, but old—ground as I read this book. But this is far more and far better than that, since Herb has used selected writings to make a coherent and thoughtful case for a life well lived, and one that so carefully and logically promotes atheism and secular humanism. His stories are rich with wit and warmth, with great compassion for his fellow humans."

—**Ed Buckner**, **author (with Michael Buckner) of** *In Freedom We Trust: An Atheist Guide to Religious Liberty*

AN ATHEIST STRANGER
IN A STRANGE RELIGIOUS LAND

Selected Writings from the Bible Belt

HERB SILVERMAN

Foreword by Rev. Barry W. Lynn

Pitchstone Publishing
Durham, North Carolina

Pitchstone Publishing
Durham, North Carolina
www.pitchstonepublishing.com

10 9 8 7 6 5 4 3 2 1

Library of Congress Cataloging-in-Publication Data

Names: Silverman, Herb, author.
Title: Atheist stranger in a strange religious land : selected writings from
  the Bible Belt / Herb Silverman ; foreword by Rev. Barry W. Lynn.
Description: Durham, North Carolina : Pitchstone Publishing, 2017.
Identifiers: LCCN 2016052918 | ISBN 9781634311052 (pbk. : alk. paper)
Subjects: LCSH: Atheism—United States.
Classification: LCC BL2790.S55 A25 2017 | DDC 211/.80973—dc23
LC record available at https://lccn.loc.gov/2016052918

CONTENTS

Flavors of atheism include humanism, with a focus on being good; antitheism, with a focus on making fun of foolish religious beliefs; and even spiritual atheism, with a focus on ritual and community.

Sometimes dividing lines are not so much over religious beliefs, but over how to treat others. Liberal religionists who care more about this life than an imagined afterlife are natural allies for atheists, and we can frequently work together on issues and actions.

Educated people should know about the Bible: the good the bad and the ugly. It's important in our culture to be able to communicate with religious believers.

Significant numbers of women, Jews, and African-Americans have overcome electoral obstacles, along with some Muslim and gays. The nontheistic community is organizing politically to encourage open atheists and humanists to run for public office.

Theology often impacts foreign policy in problematic ways, with people willing to fight holy wars and die for heavenly rewards. In dealing with problems abroad, just as at home, we must emphasize human rights.

Purported wars on Christmas and other holidays by secular progressives benefit Fox News ratings, but also provide atheists with a much-needed forum to express their views.

Free speech protects unpopular speech, including hate speech and "blasphemy." Arguments against "political correctness," whether from the right or left.

Most Americans view god belief as a necessary component of patriotism, considering the godless to be second-class citizens. This view is harmful to a democracy, fosters hypocrisy, and repudiates the intent of our founders. In fact, it is downright unpatriotic.

Religious arguments against vaccinations create problems for children and the public, interfering with rights of individuals to obtain contraceptives, legal abortions, and end-of-life choices. Allowing people to use health services doesn't require them to do so.

Rather than celebrate what we have in common, manufactured holiday wars sometimes break out over religious differences. There are ways to minimize conflicts and improve communication during holidays and at other family gatherings.

It's problematic when people take literally any ancient, monotheistic "holy" book. More Muslims do today, but we must avoid Islamophobia, the hatred or fear of all Muslims.

Jews argue about who is a Jew, what it means to support Israel, and how or whether to celebrate Jewish holidays. Surprisingly, most Jews in the United States are atheists.

Ancient holy books continue to influence some people regardless of social and scientific evidence that gays are not inherently immoral. Despite religious objections, we all deserve equal rights in a secular society.

Religious people and institutions are free to decide who can marry and divorce within their houses of worship, but they may not discriminate against those who don't share their beliefs. People can easily find meaning in marriage without religion.

Most conservative Christians think Mormon beliefs are strange, but are they stranger than those of other Christian sects? Mormons have become more active politically and are trying to appear more mainstream.

Individuals have the right to pray, privately or publicly. However, government officials are wrong when they claim they can favor one religion over another, or religion over nonreligion. Prayer is especially problematic when it substitutes for solving problems.

South Carolina is unimportant in a general election because the state always votes Republican, but its early presidential primary is important. There is obvious religious pandering to South Carolina voters, along with unintentional humor and hypocrisy.

Books, churches, and movies significantly influence our religious culture, so it's worth discussing some of the good and bad influences in each category. Becoming aware of biases might help some people change their hearts and minds.

Countries whose citizens are scientifically literate tend to be less religious. Scientific discoveries become controversial politically when they conflict with religious beliefs. This often results in dumbing down our education system to the detriment of all.

We must continually fight against misperceptions that we are a Christian nation, that our government may favor religion over nonreligion, that taxpayer money may be used to privilege religion, and that we have freedom of religion but not freedom from religion.

Sorry, this is not an X-rated chapter. It's about how religious beliefs can turn healthy and natural sex into guilt-ridden and harmful sex, and how religious leaders use the political process to impose their religious views about sex on those outside the religion.

Sometimes it's easier to make a point with one pithy sentence. A few observations about God, morality, religion, Christianity, faith, and science, along with random thoughts.

There is still a lot of racism and religious privilege in South Carolina, but things are gradually improving and there are reasons for cautious optimism.

Many politicians and religious leaders use their holy books to justify treating women as second-class citizens, or worse.

FOREWORD

I have known Herb Silverman for over twenty years and was surprised to learn he is a mathematician as well as an activist atheist. Both vocations enable him to disprove certain tales in the Bible, like the biblical definition of pi as the number 3 found in 1 Kings 7:23. As a Christian clergyperson and a very frequent flyer, I'm thankful that religious engineers don't make circular airplane parts based on "pi" being exactly 3, which would have led to my untimely demise. Herb argues thoughtfully against any supernatural beliefs, but I'm relieved that he doesn't direct his most incisive commentary against liberal religionists like me. After all, we, too, ignore biblical passages that make mathematical, medical, or "scientific" claims.

Herb has made inroads into the thinking of religious people. Though I have no direct evidence that Pat Robertson faithfully reads Herb's pieces (though he should), even Robertson criticized Ken Ham, the young Earth creationist proprietor of the Kentucky Creation Museum. After Ham's debate with Bill Nye "the science guy," Brother Robertson said, "You have to be deaf, dumb, and blind to think that this Earth we live on has 6,000 years of existence. To deny the clear record that's there before us makes us look silly." The "us" would be "Christians."

Thanks to writings by Herb and others, every new poll shows the percentage of Americans who believe the Bible is literally true "word for word" continues to shrink. The most recent Gallup poll had it down to 28 percent, still much too high. Herb may be an atheist stranger in a strange religious land, but he's not quite as strange as he was in 1990, when he courageously ran for governor of South Carolina and successfully challenged the unconstitutional state provision that prohibited atheists from holding public office there.

Herb's book is a marvelous compilation of his thoughts on virtually everything that matters. His essays sometimes engage the reader in deconstructing particular biblical passages and contradictory claims, though that is not his main focus. He raises fundamental questions for people of all faiths (especially Christians) to ponder. They include significant discrepancies in the biblical text on the need to believe in a literal bodily resurrection, and why a loving god could value belief above behavior.

Many atheists, unfortunately, are reluctant to join in coalitions with theists. At a dinner with atheists following a lecture in North Carolina a few years ago, the woman next to me in this liberal university town was reluctant to reach out to local churches because she feared its members "would think (she) was going to Hell." I tried to assure her that most of those church members probably no longer believed that Hell ever existed. Herb is one atheist who looks for ways to collaborate with all nontheists. He also seeks common ground among religious believers, and urges cooperative actions to defend Constitutional rights, human dignity, and peaceful resolution of conflict.

Herb has never tried to "convert" me away from my Christian beliefs, perhaps because he recognizes the importance for those of all faiths and none to work together for absolute separation of church and state. I seek an American government that is both great and secular, but we have often failed on both counts. Fundamentalism in religion poisons almost every public policy debate, and it has throughout the centuries.

When I used to do a daily radio show interviewing authors, I really enjoyed chats with famous persons (Jesse Ventura, Mike Huckabee, John Irving, Patricia Cornwell, Peter Yarrow, Anne Rice, and Herb Silverman among them) and others who had spent decades contemplating big issues in physics, economics, or philosophy. Unfortunately, most Americans don't take lifetime learning very seriously. Herb is made of different stuff than those who have stopped thinking they need to think beyond formal education. Herb has an active and innovative mind, producing well-informed and entertaining opinions because he works at getting and keeping informed.

Someday, when Herb and I actually retire, I would welcome a time when we could sit by a river and discuss all kinds of issues that matter. For example, does "God" really need to be viewed as "omniscient"? (Former prosecutor and best-selling author Vince Bugliosi told me "yes" after he wrote his book on whether God exists—concluding that the evidence was insufficient, but conceding that the God of Genesis does lose Adam and Eve in the Garden of Eden.) Or how about, is "God" responsible for what happened on 9/11, or is this just one more horrible example of the "free will" of humanity? Such inquiries aren't "Breaking News" on cable networks, but they are worthy of healthy discourse for the next few thousand years.

In fact, having the opportunity to engage for hours with people like Herb about deep and important theological, philosophical, and humanistic issues is my idea of "Heaven," at least here on Earth.

—Rev. Barry W. Lynn

PREFACE

My life's journey has taken me from Orthodox Jew to apathetic atheist to activist atheist. But wait—that's wrong. I surely began as an atheist, for no baby is born a believer in anything more than a need for food, comfort and love.

I'll start again. My parents told me I was an Orthodox Jew when I was a child. But when I reached the age of reason and found Jewish myths unbelievable, I rejected religion and lived as a quiet, apathetic atheist. Years later when I moved to South Carolina and saw how important religion was to most people in the state, I became a more thoughtful atheist. And after a faculty colleague at the College of Charleston pointed out that our state constitution prohibited atheists from holding public office, I became an accidental, activist atheist.

Encouraged by the ACLU, I challenged the prohibition by running for governor of South Carolina in 1990. My surprisingly high profile in a losing campaign was followed by a South Carolina Supreme Court victory in 1997 that nullified the anti-atheist constitutional clause. It also led to unintended consequences: many people told me about their own problems living as public, or, usually, secret atheists. Hearing about prejudice, stereotypes, and even hatred for those of us who don't believe in any gods, I wished to educate religious people about atheists, agnostics, and humanists. I also wanted to organize our nonreligious community, make our viewpoints better known, and show we have a sense of humor. So I started writing locally and nationally about these issues, including *Candidate Without a Prayer: An Autobiography of a Jewish Atheist in the Bible Belt.*

In 2008 I began writing weekly for "On Faith," an Internet blog founded by Sally Quinn at the *Washington Post.* I have contributed regularly to the *Huffington Post* and a number of other blogs and magazines. In the process, I've developed a loyal following who regularly read my articles, forward them to others, and enjoy commenting (and sometimes arguing) about them.

I'm flattered that many people have suggested I publish all my freethought writings in book form, but that's a bad idea. First, my complete writings would be more than 1,500 pages. Even my loving wife wouldn't want to read so many pages of mine. Second, some of my writings are repetitive and outdated. So for this book I've cut and purged well over 80 percent of my published writings and grouped them topically rather than chronologically, making it easier to focus on specific issues.

Almost all articles are abridged, sometimes to a paragraph or two, and some have slight word changes. Each piece stands on its own without references that might interrupt the flow, but you can see the complete articles and references through the links provided in the Credits, which also includes links to all my articles for *On Faith*, *Huffington Post*, and *The Humanist*, as well as to some debates and talks.

While this is not quite a "best of" book, it's partly that. I've attempted to emulate two people I greatly admire: Thomas Jefferson and Paul Erdos. Thomas Jefferson literally took a razor to the Bible, cutting the supernatural and other passages he deemed ridiculous, and called what remained "diamonds in a dunghill." I've never produced any dunghills comparable to those in the Bible, but I hope you'll find a few metaphorical diamonds in this book.

Paul Erdos, an atheist and one of the finest mathematicians of the twentieth century, often referred to *The Book*, an imaginary scroll in which God wrote down the most elegant, clever, and beautiful mathematical proofs. Erdos's highest praise for a proof was, "This one's from *The Book*." He said, "You don't have to believe in God, but you should believe in *The Book*." With Jefferson and Erdos in mind, I've tried to make my condensed writings in this book more like *The Book*—short, relevant, aesthetically pleasing, informative, and entertaining.

I recently received a comment about one of my "inciteful" pieces. I asked the writer if he meant "insightful," which he did, but he acknowledged that either meaning of this homophone would apply. Whether you find my book insightful or inciteful, I hope it will lead you to engage in many provocative thoughts and conversations.

I
ATHEISM

General

Every era seems to have its preferred form of writing for the public. Thanks to our present immersion into cyberworld, listicles abound. So I'll start with a wishticle.

Ten Things I Wish Everyone Knew About Atheism

1. The prefix "a" can mean "anti" or "non." While some atheists are antitheists who enjoy ridiculing religion, most are nontheists who don't much care about religion.

2. Not many atheists are protesters, though that's how they are usually portrayed.

3. Atheists are not angry at God (or the Tooth Fairy), and we didn't become atheists because something bad happened. We just find no evidence to believe.

4. Atheists are not less trustworthy because we don't believe in a judging God. Does that imply religious people would be untrustworthy were it not for their fear of God?

5. We can find joy without belief in God and an afterlife. We may not see a cosmic purpose *of* life, but we find our own joyful purposes *in* life.

6. Most religious people are secular most of the time. Ask yourself how you would behave differently if you stopped believing in God.

7. Calling atheism a religion is like calling baldness a hair color. Atheism is the absence of a belief in any gods.

8. Most atheists don't go around proselytizing. For every open atheist you know, there are dozens of atheists you know who you mistakenly assume to be religious.

9. Atheists don't fit stereotypes. There are good and bad atheists just as there are good and bad Christians, Jews, Muslims, men, women, and any other category.

10. Most atheists I know have a good sense of humor, so I'll end with a joke: A Jewish atheist hears that the best school in town happens to be Catholic, so he enrolls his son. Things are going well until one day the boy comes home and says, "I just learned about the Father, the Son, and the Holy Ghost." The boy's father is barely able to control his rage. He grabs his son by the shoulders and says, "Joey, this is very important, so listen carefully. There is only ONE God — and we don't believe in Him!"

Varieties of Atheist Experience
Many atheists use different labels, including agnostic, humanist, secular humanist, freethinker, skeptic, rationalist, infidel, and more. Depending on context, I put myself in all these types and labels. Disbelief in gods doesn't describe individual atheists any more than disbelief in the divinity of Krishna and Zeus describes individual Christians. Monotheists *disbelieve* in all but one god; atheists just take that one step further.

Here are four terms some atheists use that I find inaccurate or misleading.

Nonbeliever: I believe in many things. I just don't believe in any gods.

Lack of faith or lack of belief in God: It's not a lack. I've gained freedom from religious superstition.

Abandonment of religion: I didn't abandon religion, as one abandons a child. I matured and put aside my childhood religious beliefs.

Atheist, but spiritual: I was on a three-atheist panel forum about atheist spirituality, with me the lone unspiritual atheist. The others said they were atheists—"but spiritual." I began, "Jonathan (the previous speaker) is a child molester, but . . ." I then paused. Since I qualified my comment with a "but," the attendees expected it not to be as bad as it sounded. I used this device to pronounce him guilty of distancing himself from "typical" atheists with his "but." Jonathan remains a spiritual atheist, except now without a "but."

Atheist or Agnostic—and Does It Matter?

I used to call myself an agnostic because I couldn't prove whether a god exists. I took the agnostic position that it's unknown, and perhaps unknowable. When I learned that an atheist is simply without belief in any gods, I became an atheist. My "conversion" was definitional, not theological. Agnostics don't give equal weight to belief and disbelief. For instance, I can neither prove nor disprove the following.

Claim 1: The universe was created 30 minutes ago and the creator planted false memories in all of us.

Claim 2: Infidels who don't believe in the Flying Spaghetti Monster are condemned to burn for eternity in a vat of hot pasta sauce.

Christians sometimes insist that I'm an agnostic, not an atheist, because I can't disprove God's existence with absolute certainty. I often respond, "If you can't prove with absolute certainty that Jesus is Lord, then you are an agnostic, not a Christian." I'm willing to call myself an agnostic atheist if they'll call themselves agnostic Christians.

The First Thing We Do, Let's Kill All the Agnostics

I've talked to atheists who (metaphorically) thought we should. If we are so convinced that our word is "good" and their word is "bad," then it's beginning to sound a lot like religion. I encourage and support those with no theistic beliefs to be open about it, help increase public awareness and acceptance, and protect that position in society. I'm more interested in getting this message out than in bandying words about. I once gave a talk to an organization whose leader, a proud atheist, was worried about her group being infiltrated and contaminated by agnostics and humanists. The group became so uncontaminated that it ceased to exist.

God Talk for Atheists

Many atheists try to avoid the kind of god-talk equated with belief in a deity. Although it's reflexive to say "God bless you" when someone sneezes, *Gesundheit* (good health) is more appropriate. A response to getting a wallet back with nothing missing could be "Thank goodness!" because we know goodness exists.

Some atheists use "God" as a metaphor, and are falsely assumed to hold a god belief. The most famous example is Einstein's "God doesn't play dice with the universe." The same kind of confusion arose when atheist Stephen Hawking said if we discover a "theory of everything" (reconciling general relativity with quantum theory), we would know the "mind of God."

When atheist physicist Peter Higgs proposed the existence of a particle now called the "Higgs boson," the media mislabeled it the "God Particle." Many scientists had been calling it the "Goddamn particle" because of its elusive nature. Confirmation of its existence has added a bit more evidence to our understanding of how our universe could have come into existence *without* the need of a creator.

Theists and atheists alike use god-talk in anger, like "God dammit!" or "Jesus Christ!" It's the theist, not the atheist, who might worry about the "sin" of taking the Lord's name in vain. Orthodox Jews go even further in the "not in vain" vein by writing *G-d* instead of *God*. We have many euphemisms for deities. "Holy Cow" replaces "Holy Christ," though I don't know how it plays in India where cows are sacred. "Holy shit" has nothing to do with divine defecation. But if you're an unrepentant sinner, Gosh might darn you to heck.

In closing, I'll share an admittedly immodest personal goal. I'd like my name to become a curse word—just like names of many deities. People might go around saying "Herb Dammit!" And imagine my pleasure when people shout "Jesus H. Christ!" as I assume the middle initial stands for "Herb."

(I know. That was a Herb-awful joke.)

Humanism

Positive Atheism

(Adapted remarks at the Unitarian Church in Worcester, Massachusetts on April 3, 2016)

As an atheist, some people assume I must be anti-religion. Not so. By one measure, I might be the most religious person in America. You see, I have not one, not two, but three different religions: I'm a member of the American Ethical Union, with Ethical Culture Societies; I'm a member of the Society for Humanistic Judaism, with atheist rabbis; and I'm a member of the UU Humanists. All three religions are nontheistic.

Still, positive atheism sounds like an oxymoron, doesn't it? After all, atheism really is a negative word. But negative isn't always bad. Other negative words are "independent," "nondiscrimination," and "antidote." Religious people even describe their deity in negative terms ("infinite," "unlimited," "infallible"). And 80 percent of the Ten Commandments (the eight "thou shalt nots") are negative. The two positives command you to honor your parents and remember the Sabbath day to keep it holy, though nobody can seem to agree on which day the Sabbath falls or exactly what holy means. And negative protesters founded the dominant religion in this country. They are known as *Protest*ants, or Protestants.

Some construe the mere questioning of faith or presenting alternatives to it as negative atheism, but being guided by reason instead of faith isn't negative. We want to maximize happiness, which usually involves making others happy, too. It's not true that atheists believe in nothing. An atheist has a naturalistic worldview (without supernaturalism). Science shows us the wonders of the world every day. As Albert Einstein said, "The most beautiful thing we can experience is the mysterious."

Many secularists are uncomfortable with the word "atheist" because it describes what we don't believe, rather than what we do believe. We don't go around calling ourselves A-Easter Bunnyists or A-Tooth Fairyists. Other labels include humanist, secular humanist, freethinker, skeptic, agnostic, ignostic, rationalist, naturalist, materialist, apatheist, and more. If you don't know what each word means, don't worry. Even those who identify with such labels often disagree on their meanings. Parsing words might be a characteristic of folks engaged in the secular movement. Though there are fine distinctions, which many of us like to argue about, it often comes down more to a matter of taste or comfort level than to deep theological or philosophical differences.

So what's the difference between positive atheism and humanism? I'm not really sure. I pretty much view them as two sides of a coin. I'm the same person whether I talk about what I don't believe as an atheist or what I do believe as a humanist. Atheists and humanists try to be "good without gods," though humanists might focus more on "good" and atheists on "without gods." For me, positive atheism is in the Goldilocks zone of the "good" / "without gods" spectrum.

I think the mathematician/philosopher Bertrand Russell summed up positive atheism nicely: "The good life is one inspired by love and guided by knowledge."

God, an Addiction

It's meaningless to ask whether we can be good without God because I think we are all without any gods. The question is whether we can be good without a *belief* in God. And by any measure, the answer is yes. Scandinavian countries, for example, are the least religious and have low crime rates, good social programs, and a high quality of life.

I question the morality of those whose behavior is based on perceived rewards or punishments from a deity. A caller on a talk-radio show said to me: "Since you don't believe in God, I suppose you can go out and rape and murder and do whatever you think you can get away with." My response was, "With an attitude like that, I hope you continue to believe in God."

I've even been asked how I can go on living without a belief in God. Such a level of dependency can turn God into a drug to which the believer is addicted. When Napoleon asked the mathematician Laplace what place God had in his theory of Celestial Mechanics, Laplace responded, "I have no need of that hypothesis." And I can say to a god-addicted believer, "I have no need of that drug."

Courting the "Values Voters"

The news story "Liberal Christians Challenge Values Vote" said values voters can be found on the religious left as well as the religious right, with a passing mention of religious moderates. That ignores the many secular voters whose moral choices are based on evidence rather than faith. Morality is not synonymous with religiosity. Morality should be based on how our actions affect others. Our creeds should not be more important than our deeds. Secular voters have values, too.

Atheist's Afterlife

The Faith & Values section had a story about how different religions treat their dead, all focusing on respect for and sacredness of the dead body. I preferred a heartwarming story in the same section about the generous act of a widow who saved four lives through donating her husband's lungs, kidneys, pancreas, liver, and heart. The heart recipient will be reading a poem at the upcoming wedding of the lung recipient. The family responsible for donating the organs will be guests of honor at the wedding ceremony, and the organ recipients are now volunteers for the Gift of Life Donor Program. Now that's the kind of afterlife an atheist like me can believe in.

All Humans' Rights
A letter requested true Christians to help Jews emigrate from Russia to Israel since Jews are the "chosen people" of God. I'm concerned that the writer singles out a specific group supposedly chosen by a god for favored treatment. It's dangerous to classify as special any community, whether with a positive or negative stereotype. Israel was recognized as a Jewish homeland because of atrocities committed by those who regarded Jews not as individuals with equal rights, but as a special population devoid of rights. A worthwhile and humanistic project would be for each of us to work toward improving the quality of life for everyone.

Peace with Tolerance
I hope the writer of "God's chosen people" is wrong that he speaks for the vast majority of Christians. He is appalled by suggestions that Israel offer land for peace, since "God made a covenant with Abraham's son Isaac to give Israel to the Jews." Many Muslims believe they are entitled to this same piece of property because God made a covenant with Abraham's other son Ishmael. Which interpretation of which holy book to believe?

For centuries, those who valued sacred land over human life have perpetrated Mideast turf wars. There will be no solution as long as people are willing to kill or be killed for the sake of a deity. The letter writer closed by asking readers to pray for "God's chosen people." He undoubtedly views me, a secular Jew, as one of those chosen. But I reject this preposterous, inflammatory, and divisive religious belief. Let's consider all people "chosen" and treat all humans with respect and dignity.

To Whom Much Is Given, Much Is Expected
I appreciate humanistic biblical passages like Luke 12:4: "To whom much

is given, much is expected." I'm fortunate to have had ample opportunities to attain a decent education and standard of living. What about those to whom much is not given? Americans who want to abolish estate taxes use the misnomer "death taxes," and have as a silent mantra, "To whom much is given, much more should be given." Passing tax-free wealth to the next generation of financially privileged family members is welfare for the rich. As bad as things are for our poorest Americans, they are worse for undocumented immigrants who live in the shadows. Many Americans claim to have pulled themselves up by their bootstraps. Let's at least give immigrants some bootstraps with which they can pull themselves up.

Institutional Apologies Fall Short

In 1992 the Catholic Church sort of apologized to Galileo for his 1633 heresy conviction, and acknowledged that the earth revolves around the sun. In 1995 the Southern Baptist Convention apologized for its past defense of slavery. In 2009 the US Senate apologized for slavery. Call me a cynic, but I think institutional apologies to those who have been dead for centuries are calculated to restore the reputation of the institution rather than the reputation of the departed. Instead of or in addition to apologies, I like to hear what individuals or institutions have learned from past mistakes. And also what steps are being taken to minimize the lasting damage and avoid the need for future apologies.

If you wrong someone, apologize to the person you wronged and seek ways to make restitution. If you are about to make a decision or take an action, ask yourself if it would embarrass your (imagined) great, great grandchildren. If you think it might, and that they would feel the need to apologize for your actions, don't do it.

Execution as Entertainment

Utah Attorney General Shurtleff brought up God when he tweeted about the execution of Ronnie Lee Gardner. I think capital punishment is wrong, whether we quietly execute a man or turn the execution into an open spectacle. It's wrong to have a volunteer firing squad shoot a convict, just as it's wrong for a mob to stone a half-buried prisoner. I became opposed to capital punishment as a teenager in 1960 after reading Shirley Jackson's classic short story, "The Lottery." In this chilling tale, villagers came to a festival each June to choose by lottery someone who would be stoned to death as a means to insure a good harvest: "Lottery in June, corn be heavy soon." We've mostly abandoned ritual human sacrifice to appease or please gods, but we still rationalize human sacrifice.

Dark Ages

There was a time when religion ruled the western world. It was known as the Dark Ages. Remarkably, the Reverend Father James Parker in his article, "Do I decide for myself?" seems to long for those good old days. He acknowledges, "Learning was not on a high plane. Men believed in God and hell, and they didn't question it." Then, alas, came the Enlightenment when people started to think for themselves. Reverend Parker adds, "Revelation is the source of knowledge, and the facts of the spiritual life are as objectively true as the facts of the physical life."

How do we settle disputes when people receive contradictory "revelations?" We could apply the Dark Ages standard and determine truth by the most powerful sword. Today, Reverend Parker and others can live according to revelations they receive, and people are free to practice non-revealed religions or no religion. I just hope we can avoid past mistakes (and present, in some countries) by so objectifying an internal revelation that those who raise questions about it are dealt with as they were in the Dark Ages.

Antitheism

Are Atheists Smarter and Humbler?

A recent study concluded that atheists are more intelligent than religious believers, but I'm more interested in perceived character flaws of atheists, perhaps related to intelligence. Some atheists come across as arrogant and smug when they gratuitously criticize and mock religious beliefs, occasionally quoting ludicrous biblical passages to those who don't interpret the Bible literally. Yet I can make a case for atheists being more humble and open to change than religious fundamentalists, illustrated by the T-shirt phrase, "Will Convert for Evidence." Richard Dawkins, the world's most famous atheist, supported a bus ad campaign with the relatively humble slogan, "There's probably no God." I've yet to see a comparable religious ad that says "There's probably a God."

Which of these worldviews sounds more arrogant?

Worldview 1. I know God created the entire universe just for the benefit of humans. He watches me constantly and cares about everything I say and do. I know how He wants me and everyone else to behave and believe. He is perfect and just, which is why we face an eternity of either bliss or torture, depending on whether we believe in Him.

Worldview 2. We're the product of millions of years of evolution. Most species are extinct, as humans will eventually be. I hope to make a positive difference because it's the right thing to do, not because of future rewards or punishments in an afterlife. When I don't know something, which is often, I say, "I don't know."

How Atheists Can Overcome a Reputation of Arrogance
I empathize with religious groups whose mission is to convert everyone, since I think the world would be better if everyone "saw the light" of secular humanism. But rather than seeking converts, atheists mostly want our worldview respected in a culture that dislikes us. Whether religious or secular, the best form of proselytizing is to lead by example.

Some atheists are arrogant intellectuals who belittle well-meaning Christians. We should respect the right of every person to believe what makes the most sense to him or her, which does not mean we need to respect the belief itself—or condone harmful actions based on beliefs. We should seek common ground with religionists and work on projects of mutual interest. We're more likely to be measured by what we do than by what we say.

Here's a personal example that led to common ground. In an op-ed in my local newspaper, the Charleston *Post and Courier*, I referred to our "Godless Constitution" and offered $1,000 to anyone who could find the words God or Jesus in it. I knew my offer would spark interest and that my money would be safe. The former religion editor, Skip Johnson, wrote an op-ed trying to make a case because the Constitution was signed "in the year of our Lord" (the standard eighteenth century way of signing important documents). He also argued that elected officials must take an "oath or affirmation" (not necessarily to God, but to uphold the Constitution). We went back and forth a couple of times and readers on both sides wrote letters to the newspaper about our exchanges. I then suggested to Skip that we write a joint op-ed about points of agreement.

I wrote the first draft, consisting of selected portions from the Principles and Values of my local humanist organization. Johnson, a liberal religionist, made only minor changes. (Our joint op-ed is in the full article.) I heard more positive reaction from local residents for this than for anything else I've written. Johnson reported a similar reaction. A number of Christians stopped me on the street saying what a wonderful idea it was to seek common ground. One writer said he followed our debate with interest, but found it to be no more than an academic exercise of little real consequence. In contrast, he found the joint letter to be "the most profound and uplifting to grace the Faith and Values section."

A New Atheist/Humanist Alliance

The words *atheism* and *bestseller* now regularly appear in the same sentence! Sam Harris (*The End of Faith*), Richard Dawkins (*The God Delusion*), Christopher Hitchens (*God Is Not Great*), and Daniel Dennett (*Breaking the Spell*) are best-selling authors who promote atheism. They are challenging the country's tradition of showing respect for all things religious, saying:

1. Religious belief should be treated like any other kind of belief, open to criticism.

2. People may innately deserve respect, but their ideas do not. We have the right to call foolish beliefs "foolish," and we are obligated to do so when such beliefs can be potentially dangerous to believers and innocent bystanders.

3. Liberal religionists have promoted a climate of tolerance that shields religious extremists with dangerous dogmas from the public condemnation they deserve.

4. Morality should be based on how our actions affect others, not on what we believe an imaginary deity expects of us.

Atheists are supposed to be respectful of religious beliefs, but religionists are not expected to reciprocate. Atheists often disagree about how or whether to react to religious beliefs we think are ridiculous. We know in a godless universe why bad things happen to good people, but we don't always know why unjustifiable beliefs infect good people (or whether we should use a more politically correct word than "infect.")

Zealotry: Good or Bad?

I've resisted the label "atheist zealot," but I understand the sentiments. I'm not like the original Zealots, first century Jews who advocated for violence against Roman authorities and against Jews who sought peace and conciliation with Romans. The greatest abomination was for Jews to convert to Roman paganism, so a terrorist faction of the Zealots (the Sicarii) assassinated both Roman and Jewish leaders, and sometimes directed their violence toward ordinary people in public places.

Throughout history, people have committed acts of religious terrorism because of a god-inspired hatred of those who worshipped differently, or not at all. So "zealot" is commonly associated with religious fanaticism. An updated notion of zealot is a person excessively devoted to a cause or an idea. The good and bad news about zealots is that they are the ones most likely to make a significant difference in changing the world, like Charles Darwin and Osama bin Laden.

While zealots are described as fanatics or extremists, it's not easy to come up with objective criteria. Extreme to some is moderate or mainstream to others. "Excessive" devotion to a cause says as much about the accuser as the accused. If we evangelize for atheism everywhere, we can seem as boring and irritating as religious fundamentalists. People understand why *religious* folks talk a lot about religion, but atheists have a harder case to make. We atheist zealots are sometimes viewed as non-stamp collectors who devote time and energy talking about why we don't collect stamps.

Eight Examples of How I Agree with Religious Fundamentalists

1. I agree more with fundamentalists than with Unitarian Universalists about heaven. Universalists say everybody goes to heaven, fundamentalists say very few, and I say nobody does.

2. I agree with Jerry Falwell when he says, "God doesn't answer the prayers of a Jew."

3. I agree with members of Westboro Baptist Church, best known for picketing funerals and its God Hates Fags website, when they claim to be true Christians. Christians pick and choose which parts of the Bible to emphasize. The Crusaders were "true" Christians, as were those who murdered abortion doctors, as were most Nazis.

4. I agree with Matthew 7:16: "By your fruits you shall know them." See number 3 above.

5. I agree with John 8:32: "The truth will set you free," as when I became an atheist.

6. I agree with fundamentalists who don't believe in evolution. Evolution is no more a *belief* than is gravity, with evidence for evolution stronger than for gravity.

7. I agree with Gen. William Boykin, a born-again Christian fundamentalist, who said during the Iraq War that Muslims worship an idol, not a real god, and that Islam is a false religion. In fact, I agree with anyone who calls any god or religion false.

8. I agree with the doctrine of Immaculate Conception. It refers to Mary's mom (Anne) who conceived Mary immaculately, meaning without the taint of "original sin." I was also conceived without the taint of original sin, and so were you!

Spiritual

On Religious Atheists
Some atheists go through the motions of prayer to preserve their place in family and community. I'm more puzzled by atheists who pray seriously and fervently to nobody. For instance, atheist Sigfried Gold followed a rigorous prayer routine to a made-up goddess. His prayers "worked," because he is no longer 110 pounds overweight. Obviously the pounds didn't miraculously melt away. Instead, he achieved a goal through strategies to replace bad habits with good habits. Atheist prayers sound like what I would call focusing or meditating, which some view as a transcendent or spiritual experience.

Many churchgoers, religious or not, are more interested in experiencing love and support within a community than in defining God or finding evidence for God's existence. They can feel joy in religious fellowship and tradition even if they think their official church doctrine is silly. Many put up with nonsense for the smell of incense.

Is Atheism Winning the Culture War?
Barking dogs chase cars, but don't consider the ramifications of catching

them. Many atheists have been barking at a mainstream culture wrapped in religion, and are getting closer to "catching" the culture. So they should consider strategies and ramifications. Atheists are known for criticizing religion and protesting the intrusion of religion into government. Such actions are warranted when a religious political agenda affects those who don't share those beliefs. We must confront and respond, and let the undecided judge who is more reasonable and fair.

Nontheistic groups have formed welcoming communities, with a variety of activities for individuals and families. Some are primarily interested in lectures and book clubs, some in socializing, some in good works, some in protesting, some in political action, and some in all of the above. Some are virtual and enjoy discussions with people they never meet. There are now even atheist churches for those who discarded the faith of their youth, but miss religious ritual and seek to replace it with the awe-inspiring wonders of science and reality. They find ways to address spiritual, emotional, intellectual, or community needs without supernatural beliefs. Such weekly "church" or congregational meetings may not be for me, but I appreciate and welcome these fellow travelers.

As we evolve into a country where deeds are more important than creeds, atheists will become part of a respected mainstream, along with progressive religious allies. If that happens, I will be glad to see the Secular Coalition for America (of which I'm founder) go out of business and call it "mission accomplished."

Honesty Is the Best Policy

Two professions in which leaders are expected to have strong religious beliefs are clergy and politician. They often have similar rationales for lying or evading questions about those beliefs: namely, that they can do a lot of good if they don't get sidetracked by superfluous issues. Translation: "I don't want to lose my job."

I'm only confident that religious or political leaders are being honest when they say something more likely to hurt than help their careers. Perhaps many parishioners would better be able to identify with and respect a preacher whose belief system has changed and matured. At my local Unitarian church, which has lots of atheists, a search committee invited congregation members to interview a candidate for minister. In a conversation with the candidate, I asked him about his personal theology and was quite surprised when he said he could "remember" eight of his past lives. I mentioned this later in a discussion with the congregation, and many were also surprised. But the search committee said he had met other important criteria, and they didn't feel it would have been appropriate to ask him about his religious beliefs. I didn't vote for this honest minister, but he was hired, confirming that honesty is the best policy.

Rest Is a Human Need

As a youngster, I wondered why an all-powerful God had to take a day off each week to rest. I no longer believe that "rest" was a commandment from God, but I appreciate the sentiment of the biblical writer. Occasionally the Bible gets it right. It's good to take time off from daily routines to refresh and rejuvenate. But even when religions get it right, they get it wrong. I was taught to rest on the Sabbath (Saturday, not Sunday, because I was Jewish, not Christian). I learned that "rest" meant we couldn't turn on the light ("work") to start the synagogue service, but we could ask a *shabbos goy* (gentile) to do it for us. We also couldn't rest in a moving car because that, too, was "work."

While religions are free to make rules for their adherents, they must not make rules for those outside the faith. Some communities still have "blue laws" designed to enforce religious standards for all, which include forcing merchants to prohibit the sale of alcohol on Sunday. How God went from resting on Saturday to becoming a teetotaler on Sunday requires a lot of faith. In any case, we don't need religion to tell us when to rest. Mother Nature lets us know when we need a break, and it's best not to mess with Mom.

A Case for Nothing

A man entered a small courtyard and saw an altar with a large zero in the middle and a banner that said NIL. White-robed people were kneeling before the altar chanting hymns to The Great Nullity and The Blessed Emptiness. The man turned to a white-robed observer beside him and asked, "Is Nothing Sacred?"

Karen Armstrong and I agree that nothing is sacred, but from opposite sides of this pun. She believes in a god about which or whom you can say nothing, and I see no thing worthy of worship. Our differences are less about supernatural beings than about supersemantical beings. Some liberal religionists define "God" in a way that blurs any distinction between theism and atheism: Nature, the Potential Within, Love, and so forth.

Believers in a nothing god create artificial barriers between themselves and atheists. The most common argument I've heard for why atheists and humanists are immoral is that we have no fear of a judging god. Shouldn't believers in nothing gods be equally "immoral"? To believe in a god beyond human understanding is to believe in a belief.

Faith in the Light of Science

I don't see how the Dalai Lama can talk about the "oneness" of all religions and also say, "If science proves facts that conflict with Buddhist understanding, Buddhism must change accordingly." Buddhism, or at least the Dalai Lama's version, is more in line with science than with faith-based religions. Here's the reason: if data conflict with a scientific proposition, scientists throw out the proposition. If data conflict with a faith belief, believers often throw out the data. Is the Dalai Lama at "one" with Judaism, Christianity, and Islam, which revere the mythical Abraham as a prophet who had so much faith that he was willing to kill his son because he heard a voice telling him to do so?

Most religious believers are guilty of wishful thinking, with their belief in an afterlife for which there is no credible evidence. The Dalai Lama is also guilty of wishful thinking when he assumes religions that preach love, tolerance, and compassion will also practice what they preach. Religions that focus on such values are close to humanism, which emphasizes being good without any gods. Along with the Dalai Lama, I wish all humans had this "oneness."

A Ghost Story Even I Can Believe

This is not one of those stories about supernatural events that turned a skeptic into a believer. I did not have a "road to Damascus" experience, but my worldview changed a little after hearing about ghosts from Will Moredock, a professional tour guide in my hometown of Charleston, South Carolina. Will, a secular humanist, is a Charleston guide for Ghost and Graveyard Walking Tours. Ghosts, like fine restaurants and antebellum houses, are among the many attractions in this historic city, but I thought Charleston ghosts, as in the film *Ghostbusters*, were created for laughs and commercial success. (Coincidentally, *Ghostbusters* star Bill Murray lives in Charleston.)

I was surprised to learn that most people who take ghost tours believe in ghosts. Many have "seen" or experienced ghosts. Charleston ghost stories are usually associated with people who suffered violent deaths and then "return" to fulfill a mission or take revenge. I asked Will how many ghosts are of black people, since revenge for enslavement and lynching might be in order. Will said most South Carolina ghosts were once wealthy plantation owners, undoubtedly with large slaveholdings. Just as slaves had been invisible in life, their ghosts are invisible in tales.

There are many fine reasons to visit Charleston. However, don't expect to see any ghosts—unless you believe in them. That's how faith works.

Discrimination Against Atheists

For Secular Americans, Lip Service Beats No Service
Just before the 2008 election, some progressives in South Carolina asked if I'd help Democrat Linda Ketner in her Congressional campaign against conservative incumbent Republican Henry Brown. They thought I was joking when I said I didn't plan to vote for her, and would leave blank that portion of my ballot. They ticked off issues on which Ketner was better than her opponent. I agreed, adding a couple more. My problem with Ketner was a thirty second TV ad in which she proclaimed her love of God three times.

I've gradually begun withdrawing support from otherwise acceptable candidates who make religious belief a focal point of a campaign. My friends said politicians may have thrown the Religious Right a few crumbs, but all it received in return was lip service. When my companions asked if I, an atheist, would settle for so little, I replied without hesitation: "YES! I'll take lip service!"

I would be thrilled to see politicians court us by accepting invitations to speak at atheist and humanist conferences, as they do at religious events. I would love to hear them say we were founded as a secular nation with no mention of any gods in our Constitution, and speak about the value of separating religion from government. I'd be delighted to hear them defend atheists and agnostics from our detractors, reminding Americans that freedom of conscience extends to citizens of all faiths and none.

Even if their words changed nothing about public policy, lip service would be a wonderful new dimension in the relationship between politicians and secular Americans. Such minimal recognition could go a long way toward changing the hearts and minds of people who assume god belief to be a prerequisite for morality.

The most scurrilous activity of the 2008 campaign season occurred in North Carolina when an ad put out by Elizabeth Dole accused her senatorial opponent Kay Hagan of associating with known atheists. The ad implied that Hagan herself might be "godless." Hagan's campaign responded that she is an active Christian, not an atheist, and then she filed a lawsuit claiming defamation of her good name and reputation.

To understand why atheists might be saying, "A plague on both your houses," what would happen if Candidate A accused Candidate B of consorting with Jews and possibly even being one, and Candidate B filed a defamation lawsuit because of the damage to her reputation? Substitute just about any other minority for "Jew" to get a sense of the secular community's reaction.

Secular Americans are a significant and growing part of every politician's constituency. They deserve and are beginning to insist on the same consideration politicians give to other citizens. Lip service is where it begins. Perhaps, one day, respect will follow.

An Atheist Invocation and Its Aftermath

Since the Charleston City Council starts meetings with an invocation, usually by a minister, our local secular humanist group asked if they would be more inclusive and occasionally invite one of our members. A council member invited me to give the invocation on March 25, 2003. But as Charleston Mayor Joe Riley introduced me, half the City Council members walked out because they knew I was an atheist. They returned for the Pledge of Allegiance, turning toward me as they recited "under God."

Nobody who heard my invocation, including the mayor, was offended by it. When councilmen were asked why they walked out, one quoted Psalm 14:1: "The fool says in his heart there is no God. They are corrupt, their deeds are vile, there is not one who does good." He then told me it wasn't personal. In other words, his religious beliefs compelled him to ignore or demonize an entire class of people he was elected to represent. Frankly, I would rather it had been personal. Another councilman said,

"He can worship a chicken if he wants to, but I'm not going to be around when he does it." My response was, "Perhaps the councilman doesn't realize that many of us who stand politely for religious invocations believe that praying to a god makes no more sense than praying to a chicken. At least you can see a chicken." (Invocation included in full article)

Value Judgment

A writer was upset that the Faith & Values section included an article about the billboard sponsored by the Secular Humanists of the Lowcountry: "Don't believe in God? You are not alone." He thought the article inappropriate because secular humanism has "no values by its very nature." One of our purposes for putting up the billboard was to let people know how false that stereotype is. Check the website (lowcountryhumanists.org) to see our principles and values, and the charitable and community service in which we engage. Secular humanists do not accept moral authority based on the supernatural. Our humanist ethics come from critical reasoning, and we test our moral principles by their consequences. We, like many religious people, try to be kind and compassionate to our fellow human beings, want to end racial discrimination, and work for social justice.

Another purpose for our billboard is to let other atheists and humanists know a community like ours exists. Many atheists remain in the closet because of unwarranted claims by people like the writer that we are inherently immoral. The more we become open about our beliefs, the sooner we will change this stereotype. Such a change can benefit us all as we work together to improve the quality of life in our society.

Bias Against Pomposity

You can tell how biased the media is against Christianity by the number of broadcasters who ridicule it and speak openly about how their lives improved after becoming atheists. Well, there's Bill Maher. And then there's Bill Maher. Coming out as an atheist is not generally viewed as a career enhancer. I find it difficult to drum up much sympathy for discrimination against Christians in this country.

There is a media bias, but it has more to do with advertising revenue than with religion or politics. My favorite TV show in 1950 was "Howdy Doody," a puppet I trusted implicitly. When Howdy told us kids to try a delicious drink called Ovaltine, I nagged my mother until she bought it. The drink tasted terrible, and I learned a valuable life lesson about specialized abilities. Howdy may have been a talented puppet with an engaging sense of humor, but he had a lousy sense of taste. Howdy Doody, actors, and athletes may be superb in their chosen professions, but the public mistakenly grants them an inordinate amount of wisdom and respect in areas completely unrelated to the fields in which they achieved. At least Howdy Doody's personal life was impeccable, if somewhat wooden.

Superstar basketball player Charles Barkley reinforced in 1993 the early lesson I learned from Howdy. After spitting on fans and having run-ins with the law, he wisely said, "A million guys can dunk a basketball in jail; should they be role models?" So be careful about what you buy, no matter how accomplished the person or dummy pitching it.

Atheists Do Good Anyway

Roy Rogers, Gene Autry, and Hopalong Cassidy were okay, but my favorite TV cowboy in the early 1950s was the Lone Ranger. I'm not sure why I liked him when I was ten, but I now think he was a good role model for atheists. He would arouse suspicion because of his mask, as did his trusted sidekick, Tonto, because he was an Indian. People later changed their minds because of the Lone Ranger's good deeds, but he never hung around for reward money or praise. In each last scene a grateful person would ask, "Who was that masked man?" followed by, "Why, he's the Lone Ranger."

Atheists are also sometimes viewed with suspicion, as if they are masking hidden values and questionable morals. When religious believers learn that some of their friends, colleagues, or even family members are atheists, it often dispels former negative stereotypes. But life is not a weekly TV show with happy endings, so good works by a lone atheist aren't enough to change our culture. Here are recent examples from my home state, where atheists were barred from participating in charitable endeavors.

A Spartanburg, South Carolina soup kitchen excluded Upstate Atheists from volunteering. Its executive director said she'd resign before letting atheists be a "disservice to this community," adding that her Christian organization "stands on the principles of God." Apparently, allowing atheists to help the less fortunate goes against her Christian principles. In response, across the street from the soup kitchen, the atheist group raised over $2000 to give care packages to homeless people.

My local humanist group in Charleston has long been active in community building and charitable work. But when we applied to participate in the annual YMCA Flowertown Festival, the organizers refused because "We (the YMCA) are a Christian organization." The legal center at the American Humanist Association pointed out that South Carolina state law prohibits discrimination based on religion in places of public accommodation, and threatened a lawsuit. The YMCA soon reversed its stand "through prayer, consideration, and legal counsel." I leave it for others to decide whether prayer or a potential lawsuit played more of a role in the reversal.

I like to think that a modern day Lone Ranger would be a community builder to help rid towns of poverty, prejudice, and poor education. He or she would be happy to include all participants on worthwhile projects, regardless of religious beliefs. And so would Tonto. Both would value deeds over creeds, and change with the times as evidence warrants. Perhaps the Lone Ranger of today would be an atheist, or at least an atheist ally.

2

BELIEF VERSUS BEHAVIOR

No Two Christians Are Alike

Christians are a lot like snowflakes—almost no two are alike. I can think of only one common thread. They've said about some other Christian, "He's not a *real* Christian." That's because their Book is ambiguous and contradictory. Its followers decide what to take literally or figuratively, and which passages were falsely attributed to a man or god or man/god called Jesus. We know more about people by which portions of a purported holy book they follow than from which religion they claim. When I hear a televangelist say, "Let us pray," I think of Jefferson saying, "Let us cut." Reflecting Enlightenment thinkers, he cut all superstitions and miracle stories from the Christian Bible.

I Have a Dream, Too

Franklin Graham agrees with 20 percent of Americans who say President Obama is a Muslim. Glenn Beck considers Obama a Christian, but the wrong kind. President Obama has nuanced positions on Israel, so some conservatives think he is an anti-Semite. In 2008, Obama's mentor, Abner Mikva, quipped that people will say Barack Obama is the first Jewish president because he has a *yiddishe neshama* (a Jewish soul).

We can say President Obama is a Christian because he claims to be one. But if asked Obama's religion, I would say I don't know, the same answer I'd give for most presidents. I know what they say, not what they believe. I could make a case for Obama not believing in God. His mother, whom Obama credits for teaching him his values, was a humanist without any god beliefs.

Whether Obama is a Christian, Muslim, Jew, or atheist should not matter in a country that prides itself in having freedom of religion and conscience. We should judge our candidates on their political positions, not on their professed religious beliefs. But that may be a dream of mine more difficult to achieve than the dream of Martin Luther King.

Belief Versus Behavior

Daniel Patrick Moynihan famously said, "Everyone is entitled to his own opinion, but not his own facts." People offer countless arguments for an afterlife, but no facts. My worldview is based less on the Bible than on the title of a soap opera (that I never watched): *One Life to Live*. Atheists and humanists try to make the most of it in pursuit of happiness and fulfillment. This usually involves helping others to fulfill their needs, too.

Different religious believers quote contradictory passages from their holy books about an afterlife and who winds up where. Many Christians don't find the teachings of Jesus sufficiently meritorious to stand on their own, as is apparent in 1 Corinthians 15: "If Christ be not risen, then is our preaching in vain." It's difficult to believe that a loving and all-powerful god would condemn Mahatma Gandhi to an eternity of torture while Catholic Adolph Hitler might have an eternity of bliss as he looks down on Jews suffering in hell. Now there's a final solution for all Christians to think about, and discard as nonsense.

God in Papua New Guinea

I visited Papua New Guinea (PNG) in 1987, and again in 2013. Each time I saw many Christian missionaries along with some fruits of their labor (both sweet and sour, depending on your point of view). More than 96 percent of PNG citizens now identify as Christian. Here are some of my PNG observations, then and now.

Then: I was in PNG for six months as a visiting professor of mathematics at the University of Papua New Guinea (UPNG) in Port Moresby, the country's capital and largest city. About 800 languages were and still are spoken in PNG, reflecting the isolation of its many tribes. In the 1930s, Australian explorers discovered the Highlands of PNG, home to roughly one million people who had never before encountered Caucasians. In a video of this first contact, one PNG woman said they thought white men were gods, until they had sex with them.

I talked to a Catholic priest who objected to the "ungodly" sight of bare-breasted women. When I brought up serious problems like wife beating, which was legal at the time, he shrugged and said he couldn't change everything. Shortly thereafter, I attended a UPNG beauty pageant with five contestants representing different villages. My colleagues were impressed when I confidently predicted the winner. You see, the primary judge was the priest, and four of the five contestants were bare breasted.

Now: When I revisited PNG in 2013 with my wife, Sharon, we traveled to remote villages. Pigs are a valued source of income and wealth in PNG. Many men sleep together in dirt-floored huts, while women, children, and young pigs share other huts. It's not uncommon for a woman to nurse an orphan piglet along with her own baby. Both brides and pigs are sold or used for barter, the woman-to-pig ratio depending on the quality of both. Knowing how valuable pigs are, I asked our guide, "How many pigs could I get for Sharon?" He thought for a moment and said, "About 20." I couldn't tell if he was complimenting or insulting Sharon, but I'm pretty sure he was just playing along with my joke.

PNG Christians maintain practices and beliefs that sound nothing like what I expected. For instance, most believe that animals and plants have spirits (like human souls) that need to be appeased or respected. I met a revered spirit doctor in one village who treats illness by smearing pig's blood on his magic stones. When I asked his religion, he said, "Catholic. Pope John Paul." Though two popes behind, the spirit doctor was the only one to refer to a Christian leader.

I began to understand how indigenous beliefs blended with traditional monotheistic beliefs. Rival tribes ate their victims' bodies to gain strength over enemies. The practice is now illegal, but still occurs in remote areas. There were initiation rites for boys at about age 13 in a ceremony where elders cut each boy on his back, chest, and neck so the ritual blood can flow freely. I'm glad I only had to go through a bar mitzvah ceremony to become a "man." A circumcision ritual performed when I was eight days old sealed a covenant (Hebrew for "to cut"), without which my "soul" would be cut off from my tribe.

The PNG blood sacrifices and cannibalism seemed strange because I was in an unfamiliar culture. But attaining magical powers by eating a body and drinking blood does not seem much different from the Catholic practice of Holy Communion, where communicants believe they are eating the body and drinking the blood of Jesus. Blood, a life force for all, is important symbolically for Judaism, Christianity, and PNG spirit practices.

Boy Scouts, Unitarians, and Atheists

Robert Gates, former defense secretary and president of the Boy Scouts of America, called for an end to the ban on gay leaders in order to avoid potential court action that might force the BSA to radically modify its positions. He was especially worried that a court order might overturn the policy of banning atheist scouts and troop leaders.

The Unitarian Universalist Association took a principled stand and disaffiliated from the BSA in 1998 because of its discrimination against gays and atheists. Unfortunately, the UUA re-affiliated in 2016 because the BSA ended its ban on gay leaders, though it continued to ban atheists. This decision is particularly perplexing because the tolerant Unitarian Church counts many atheists and agnostics among its members. The nontheistic UU Humanists organized a session at an American Humanist Association conference with UUA President Peter Morales, who told participants that the UUA cherishes and respects the humanists, agnostics, and atheists among its members, and that he feels the best way to change BSA policy is from the inside rather than from the outside.

After his brief talk, I asked, "Would you have supported UUA affiliation with the BSA if they had excluded Jews, Muslims, African-Americans, or any other minority but atheists and humanists?" Another question was why the UUA had disaffiliated from BSA over the gay issue instead of working for change from the inside. Morales indicated that these are judgment calls on which reasonable people can disagree. Many of us are especially concerned with the BSA equating God with morality. Though Morales expressed sympathy with our concerns, most in the audience were disappointed that the UUA has not strongly repudiated the requirement that scouts or leaders must sign a document that says, "The Boy Scouts of America maintains that no member can grow into the best kind of citizen without recognizing an obligation to God."

What most disheartened me was Rev. Morales's attempt to placate humanists and atheists by telling us we can simply make up different definitions of "God" in order to pass the religious test requirement. What he failed to understand is that we want to show we can be good without any gods, and help end the unwarranted prejudice against atheists.

A number of courageous and honest atheists have been kicked out of the Boy Scouts for rejecting God beliefs. Apparently, the BSA does not consider honesty a core value in becoming the best kind of citizen, and would rather that boys pretend to believe. This certainly would teach boys a lesson on how best to prepare for political careers, since open atheists currently have little chance of being elected to just about any public office. This situation is particularly sad because it teaches boys who are deemed moral enough to be admitted as Scouts that prejudice is OK.

Jimmy Carter, Oliver Sacks, and Me

In 2015, two people I've long admired revealed that they had terminal illnesses: Dr. Oliver Sacks and Jimmy Carter. Both have lived consequential lives and are role models for me on how to behave during my last months of life (many years from now, I hope).

In a February 2015 op-ed in the *Times*, Oliver Sacks announced that widespread metastasized cancer meant he probably had only months to live and he intended to live them in the richest, deepest, most productive way he could. And he did, dying at 82. In August 2015, Jimmy Carter, age 91, announced that cancer had spread to his brain. He also expected to carry on good works and live the rest of his life to its fullest. (Fortunately, at this writing in 2016, President Carter's cancer is in remission.)

Carter and Sacks expressed gratitude for having lived long, productive, and healthy lives. Carter takes solace in his faith, while Sacks, in a moving *Times* piece, said, "I find my thoughts, increasingly, not on the supernatural or spiritual, but on what is meant by living a good and worthwhile life — achieving a sense of peace within oneself." Though their theologies differ, Carter and Sacks focused on important and practical things that matter.

My background and beliefs are a lot more like those of Sacks than Carter. Raised in an Orthodox Jewish family, Sacks became a Jewish atheist. I'm sorry I never met Oliver Sacks, but I know from reading his books that he was a great and inspiring humanist.

Jimmy Carter is the only president I've known on a first-name basis, if only for a week. In the summer of 1988, I volunteered at a Habitat for Humanity project in Atlanta, where Carter also participated. I knew that Habitat was a Christian organization that did good works. I was happy to engage with such Christians, but I didn't know how Christian it was. There were prayers to Jesus before breakfast, lunch, and dinner, along with inspirational sermons. Habitat founder Millard Fuller was a tremendous and forceful speaker. After one of his sermons, he asked Jimmy Carter to say a few words. Jimmy said that Millard was a tough act to follow, and he was. Had Carter been as inspiring and skilled a communicator as Fuller, he might have been reelected president.

I told Millard Fuller that he could attract more volunteers if his inspirational messages were inclusive. "After all," I said, "we're all here to build houses for poor people." I was shocked by Fuller's response: "Not me. I'm here to build houses for Jesus." He even told me he would stop building houses if he believed Jesus didn't care. I preferred Jimmy Carter's brand of Christianity.

During one of our workdays, a reporter from a Jewish newspaper interviewed me about what it was like for a Jew to work with a Christian organization. As she was asking me a question, Jimmy Carter passed and said, "Hi Herb." The reporter stopped mid-question and asked, "Wasn't that Jimmy Carter?" She then lost interest in interviewing me, though she dutifully carried on.

Workers for Habitat ate lunches and dinners at different black churches in the region. Once I walked with Jimmy into a church auditorium for dinner, and the church members stood and applauded enthusiastically. I whispered to Jimmy, "I hope you don't mind. This happens to me wherever I go." My comment did not elicit a smile from him. I still think Jimmy Carter is a wonderful person, even though he didn't laugh at my little joke.

3

BIBLE TALK

General

For Atheists, All Religion Is Superstition

The "Good Book" is seriously flawed. Which book? Every book, because no book contains the truth, the whole truth, and nothing but the truth. All have errors (including this one) and should be read skeptically. The older the book and the more it asserts about the universe, the more skeptical we should be. Mathematician Paul Erdos once claimed to be 2.5 billion years old. His reasoning? He was told as a child that the earth was 2 billion years old. But many years later, in 1970, scientists said the earth was 4.5 billion years old. That was Erdos's humorous way of saying we don't have all the answers and, with new evidence, we must discard some beliefs learned in childhood.

Creationists would say that Erdos couldn't have lived billions of years because the earth is only 6,000 years old—and Methuselah lived for 969 of them. I wish such irreconcilable faith and science worldviews didn't matter. Unfortunately, we live in a world where a politician's faith can affect us all. Anti-science arguments from politicians are nothing new, like this one from former Georgia Rep. Paul Broun: "All that stuff I was taught about evolution and embryology and the Big Bang Theory, all that is lies straight from the pit of Hell." He added, "As your congressman I hold the Holy Bible as being the major directions to me of how I vote in Washington, D.C., and I'll continue to do that." Broun chairs the House Science Committee.

It's easy to wave a Bible or other holy book to justify political positions, though I'm troubled when rational people also give biblical justifications.

I've heard many theological debates about whether God supports gay rights, women's rights, and evolution. I find it a lot easier to take the homophobic, misogynistic, anti-science side when we only use the Bible as evidence. Liberal religionists often try to interpret as metaphor passages about stoning homosexuals and blasphemers, man being created 6,000 years ago, man being the head of woman (or even men beheading women), and countless other passages that we should either laugh about or ignore.

Who's Afraid of a (Mostly) Fictional Bible?
A piece by an anonymous pastor at a mainstream evangelical church asked, "Who's Afraid of a (Partly) Fictional Bible?" I understand why the pastor wanted anonymity. Religionists have had heated arguments and even wars over holy book interpretations, but our secular government does not condone killing for blasphemy. However, Christians may certainly fire sect leaders and shun family members for "incorrect" biblical interpretations. Literalists often disagree on what the Bible literally says, while non-literalists disagree on which parts to take literally.

I agree with Pastor Anonymous when he criticizes people for reading "our twenty-first century lives into a book composed in an ancient and wholly different world." However, we part company when he says that the made-up stories "tell us the truth about God and his purposes." How can that be when the Bible tells us the views of scientifically ignorant, misogynistic, and homophobic writers who were a product of their times? If an all-knowing God inspired the Bible, why are some parts so ambiguous or obviously wrong as to inspire people to behave badly? How does "Thou shalt not suffer a witch to live" tell us the truth about God and his purposes?

Pastor Anonymous says he is absolutely thankful for much in our scriptures that is literal. This includes the story that Jesus rose from the dead and will come again in glory to judge the living and the dead. I suppose Pastor Anonymous can take this literally because science can't disprove it. Nor can science disprove the Flying Spaghetti Monster.

A liberal religious friend who favors gay marriage pointed out that the Bible has many passages about social justice and only five that condemn homosexuality, but he couldn't tell me how many condemnations of homosexuality it would take for him to reverse his position. The Bible also has many passages in support of slavery, with nary a verse that condemns it. If the Bible is the inspired word of God, then it should only take one passage to condemn an action or an entire class of people. If it isn't, then a reader should choose only what make sense from the Bible or any other book.

An Atheist's Three Favorite Bible Stories

While atheists might make fun of some passages accepted by biblical literalists, it's important to distinguish between the quality of a book and the behavior of its adherents. The Bible and the religions it spawned have deeply influenced our culture and the world. For that reason alone, it's worth reading. Atheists rank highest in religious knowledge, and should try to understand why so many love the Bible even if they haven't read it.

Conservative theists mistakenly treat the Bible as all good, and some atheists mistakenly treat the Bible as all bad. The Bible contains many horrific, anachronistic, contradictory, and repetitive sections, but it also has passages with rich and diverse meanings. The same can be said for Greek mythology—fictional tales once considered religious texts.

As a child, I enjoyed reading Aesop's fables and biblical stories. Both have talking animals, moral lessons, and universal truths. Leaving aside which imparts better advice (though no Bible story was as consequential for me as Aesop's "The Boy Who Cried Wolf"), at least Aesop's stories are recognized as fables. One of the most productive ways to read the Bible is by identifying and discussing its fables. Here are just three examples from well-known stories in Genesis, followed by my moral lessons.

1. **Snake fable.** God tells Adam he may eat anything in a garden but the fruit from one tree, and that he will die on the day he eats it. A snake convinces Eve that she will gain knowledge after eating the forbidden fruit. Eve eats, likes what she learns, and encourages Adam to partake. They discover many things, including sex, and God banishes Adam and Eve from the garden and tells them they need to work for a living.

   My moral: God makes blind obedience the supreme virtue, assuming ignorance is bliss. God lied when he said humans would die on the day they received knowledge. So don't blindly believe, even if you pay a price for independent thought. It's better to have freedom without a guarantee of security, than to have security without freedom.

2.   **Cain and Abel fable.** Adam and Eve's two sons bring offerings to God, and God gives no reason for accepting Abel's while rejecting Cain's. Cain gets jealous and kills Abel. When God asks Cain where Abel is, Cain responds, "Am I my brother's keeper?" God curses Cain, who must then wander the earth, but God places a protective mark on Cain.

My moral: The first worship ceremony is followed by the first murder, which shows we must not put our love and worship of a God above our love for human beings. Cain belatedly learns that humans should look out for one another, making each of us our brother and sister's keeper. God recognizes his culpability in the first murder and puts a mark on Cain, as a sign to those he meets not to do to Cain what Cain did to Abel.

3.   **Binding of Isaac fable.** God commands Abraham to kill his son Isaac. Abraham unquestioningly agrees to do so, but God stops Abraham as he lifts his knife, and provides a lamb to take Isaac's place.

My moral: God tests Abraham, who fails the test. Nobody should commit an atrocity, no matter who makes the request. It is better to do good than to have faith.

God's behavior is particularly egregious in Genesis, but God learns from early mistakes and improves. There are hundreds of biblical fables, and atheists might find some in which to "praise God." Such praise would show that atheists don't hate God any more than they hate Zeus.

A biblical fables book could stimulate conversation between atheists and theists. An atheist's insights would be different from those of either liberal or conservative religionists. But if we assume that the Bible is an important book, this common bond might help atheists articulate their differences more effectively with some theists.

One Nation, Undereducated

With poetic passages that have greatly enriched our language and literature, ideally I would like to see the Bible taught in public schools, but only if done the "right" way. Of course, my right might differ from yours. Any course that does not include the good, the bad, and the ugly would not pass my objectivity test. If I were teaching a course on the Bible, I would ask my students to compose an essay giving evidence from the Bible to support fundamental American ideals like individual rights (including those for women and blacks), democracy, freedom of speech, and freedom of religion. I would also assign other necessarily short essays on scientific statements in the Bible *not* contradicted by modern science.

Since politicians exert so much influence over what goes into a public school curriculum, it would be better to drop Bible teaching entirely. Students should learn the importance of religious liberty, and why it is threatened when the government endorses a religious view. Many students falsely believe that the original Pledge of Allegiance contained the words "under God," words added in 1954 during the shameful McCarthy era. We are legally one nation under the Constitution and geographically one nation under Canada, but we are not theologically one nation under God. In fact, given how the religious right opposes the teaching of evolution or any scientific or social view that conflicts with a literal interpretation of the Bible, we are really becoming one nation undereducated.

The Constitution and the Bible

What can be more different for atheists than a godless Constitution and a god-awful Bible? Lots, actually. Each document is open to interpretation, with conservatives more likely to focus on "original intent," and liberals on societal changes. Though we don't always know original intent, we know political and social climates that inspired portions of the Bible and Constitution. Both were built on earlier works, modified to suit the times, and written for present and future generations. Before final approval, committees debated and voted on passages to include or exclude. Most Americans believe both documents were inspired and blessed by God. Religionists deify their holy books for obvious reasons. Liberals and conservatives "deify" those who wrote the Constitution, and quote selectively from founders when it suits their purposes.

Agreed-upon interpretive bodies make binding decisions about both documents. The US Supreme Court is the decider on constitutional law, while each religion determines who (if anyone) will decide belief and interpretation. Constitutional and biblical leaders often choose citations to justify preconceived outcomes. We expect secular judges to be more objective than biblical judges, but how do we explain the spate of five-to-four Supreme Court decisions? Some constitutional interpretations remind me of a quote from William Blake: "Both read the Bible day and night, but thou reads't black where I read white."

Like all analogies, the Constitution/Bible one is flawed. Writers of the Constitution understood it to be an imperfect document and made provisions for future generations to amend it. Alas, conservative religionists permit no such biblical escape clause, and I think I know why. By allowing amendments to so-called holy books, we would recognize them to be products of fallible humans, not an infallible deity.

Let's Give the Bible a Second Chance…By Changing It
Neither the Constitution nor the Bible included equal rights for women, prohibition of cruel and unusual punishment, or abolition of slavery— but our amended Constitution does. Many religious people would prefer an amended bible devoid of passages that are impossible to justify. Who should write it? Perhaps a committee of believers who view the traditional Bible as inspired, but not inerrant, along with scientists and ethicists as advisors. After discussion, they could vote on what to include, exclude, and modify.

Is this heresy? No, it's tradition! Roman Emperor Constantine in the fourth century brought church leaders together at the Council of Nicaea to vote the "word of God" into existence. And so it could be with my proposed second-chance bible for progressive believers who have informally been amending the Bible with their thoughts and behavior.

Here's how I might start a bible from the perspective of a scientifically literate God believer. Replace "In the beginning, God created the heavens and the earth" with "In the beginning of time, about 13.7 billion years ago, God created our universe with a big bang." I don't believe the "God" part, but at least this bible can begin more accurately and move on to God's "creating" the earth some 9 billion years after the big bang. The traditional Bible represented views from a pre-scientific and misogynistic era. Scientists and humanists can improve on ancient misconceptions.

Any second-chance bible would be far from perfect. Future generations would look back and laugh about some of our current misconceptions and prejudices, which would inspire them to write a more perfect bible. And so on. Maybe a day will eventually come when people accept a godless bible, just as they accept our godless Constitution.

To Talk or Not to Talk (About Religion)

I grew up hearing that it was impolite to discuss the three most interesting topics—politics, sex, and religion. Discussions about politics and sex are omnipresent today, with religion often used to justify views on both. For instance, many liberals promote a social agenda with passages like Mark 12:31, "Love your neighbor," while many conservatives promote a different social agenda with passages like Leviticus 18:22, which refers to male homosexuality as an abomination. But you rarely hear them cite other abominations in Leviticus, like eating pork, having tattoos, mixing seeds, or wearing a garment made from two kinds of material.

A recent piece in the *Atlantic* categorizes Americans according to the frequency with which they talk about religion in public, with only a third doing so at least once a month. Evangelicals do it most frequently, minority religions less frequently, while atheists and agnostics are the least inclined to talk publicly about religion. Many atheists are quiet about their religious views, especially in the Bible Belt, not wanting to appear impolite or offend others. Being polite by avoiding conflicts has never been a guiding light for me. After becoming the "village atheist" in South Carolina, strangers who had seen me on TV or in the newspaper would stop me in the street to discuss my religious views. Some thanked me for being open about my atheism, some had trouble understanding how anyone could be an atheist, and some attempted to convert me. My personality, along with job security, enabled me to thoroughly enjoy religious conversations with those whose beliefs were considerably different from mine.

As with many vocal atheists, I initially thought I could apply logical arguments and biblical contradictions to show religious people that there probably is no god. I've since learned that you can't reason someone out of a belief that they didn't come to through reason. We can listen and try to understand one another, find points of agreement, and perhaps even become friends. But at the very least we should be able to reach a point where we agree to disagree, and move on without hostility.

I've become more sympathetic toward religious fundamentalists who want to convert me because I now understand why it's so important to them. Since I came to atheism through following what I consider to be a sensible evidence-based path, it doesn't much matter to me whether others adopt my position. For fundamentalists, on the other hand, eternal life is at stake. And for many of them, that's more important than life itself. I find such a worldview odd at best, and potentially dangerous. But for those who believe in a god who wants them to love their neighbors, help the less fortunate, and follow the Golden Rule, I can happily cooperate on doing good works with them. There is one thing I won't compromise on, though. I will continue to fight nonviolently against those who try to force their religious beliefs on people who don't share such beliefs.

Slavery and Bible

A writer pointed out that slavery did not begin with the Civil War and is condoned in the Bible. I agree with him that we should not always judge people from different eras by today's standards and values. It behooves us to learn more about their history and culture. A group of slavery-supporting Bible believers disagreed with the liberal antislavery attitudes and activities of other Baptists and left the church over this issue. They organized their own sect at an 1845 Convention, and are now known as Southern Baptists. Today slavery is viewed as reprehensible, and biblical fundamentalists either ignore or reinterpret embarrassing passages that condone it. When we hear advice, whether written yesterday, a century ago, or 2,000 years ago, we should not accept it blindly, and we should be especially wary of proclaiming it to be a rule for all time.

God Is Opposed to Food Stamps? Let's Try an Evidence-Based Approach Instead

Biblical arguments are commonplace in politics, but this one's special. Tennessee Rep. Stephen Fincher quoted from Matthew and Thessalonians that the poor will always be with us and those unwilling to work shall not eat. Fincher complained about Washington stealing taxpayer money from some and giving it to others, but he had no problem with Washington giving him $3.48 million of taxpayer dollars since 1999 for farm subsidies. Fincher should have found a word or two in his Bible about hypocrites. Interdisciplinary courses, especially those that can lead to good jobs, are popular at universities. So I propose one that combines political science with religious studies.

Here's the syllabus: Choose about a dozen political issues such as taxes, healthcare, education, science, environment, gay rights, women's rights, immigration, war, foreign aid, religious freedom, church/state separation, climate change, gun control, capital punishment, drugs, etc. Write papers for and against each issue using only biblical arguments.

Then do the same using arguments based solely on evidence.

The course could lead to placement as an intern or political consultant, and maybe even a political career. Speechwriters regularly insert biblical phrases to justify political positions. It's easy to cite biblical passages for anything, but I hope students who can't find good secular arguments for a policy will embrace an alternative policy. Otherwise, they might consider ministerial careers.

Godless Faith in Social Justice

Glenn Beck thinks Christians should leave their churches if they hear preaching about social or economic justice, which he says are code words for Communism and Nazism. Over 90 percent in Nazi Germany claimed to be either Lutheran or Catholic, and these Christians wore Nazi belt buckles with the slogan, "Gott Mit Uns," meaning, "God is with us." As far as Communism goes, Hitler hated Communists even more than Glenn Beck does. And how fast would Beck run from Commie Jesus, whose followers said in Acts 2:44, "All the believers were united and shared everything." Glenn Beck may consider himself perfect, though he ignores the rather extreme social justice in Matthew 19:21: "To be perfect, sell your possessions and give the money to the poor."

Social justice may fit into some churches' theology, but social justice does not need a theology to be a desirable goal. Humanists understand that it is humane to help people who can't help themselves. It goes back to the simplest basis for interaction among humans: Treat others as you would like to be treated.

And finally, how does social justice fit into my faith? Social justice *is* my faith.

Education or Indoctrination?

Cal Thomas expressed dismay over the views of a theology graduate student at Emory University. Mr. Thomas said, "One might ask what good it does to study theology if the subject doesn't point the student to an authority higher than his or her own mind?" Perhaps Thomas can't distinguish between education and indoctrination. A rational inquiry into transcendent religious questions like the nature and existence of a deity leads people to different conclusions. There is more to education than memorization of facts or catechism. Those who close their minds to ideas and evidence that conflict with preconceived prejudices discover little that is new. We are better equipped to deal with the problems in a complex and technologically advanced democratic society if we emphasize how to think rather than merely what to think.

Lord of the Snickers: My Mount Sinai Revelation

In June of 1999, two years before Bruce Feiler's book *Walking the Bible*, I took a somewhat similar trek. A faculty member from the Jewish Studies Program at the College of Charleston arranged for a small group of faculty and students to take a Hebrew Bible study trip to Israel, Jordan, and the Sinai area of Egypt. We read about the history, culture, and religion of ancient Israel and its neighbors as we visited archaeological sites and historic locations, and experienced the diverse physical environments reflected in biblical texts.

We began our readings from Samuel and Kings, the first books in the Bible for which there is evidence that some of those written about were real people. Even so, there is no archaeological evidence for any buildings erected by Solomon. All we can say about David and Solomon is that they likely existed and their legend endures.

Just as important as our text studies were biblical insights we gained from our travels. We visited the Dead Sea, the lowest point on the earth's surface and too salty to sustain life. Sodom is the first biblical story about an actual place. I had always wondered why Lot's wife turned into a pillar of salt, of all things. Standing at the Dead Sea, I understood why, noting that some of the salt formations could look like people. At least they more resembled human beings than Blessed Virgin sightings on pizzas.

Strolling down by the Jordan River, where Jesus was allegedly baptized, a man approached and told me I looked very spiritual. He said I reminded him of Jesus (perhaps because I had a beard, sandals, and not much clothing). He asked if I would do him the great honor of baptizing him there. He simply wanted me to throw a little water on him, so I obliged. He thanked me profusely, saying this was one of the most significant experiences of his life. I resisted the temptation to respond, "It wasn't as good for me as it was for you." In any case, I guess I can now be called "Herb the Baptist."

The high point of my trip, both literally and figuratively, was my climb to the top of Mount Sinai in Egypt. Just like another Jew with a white beard, I also had a vision, one that even the mythical Moses could not have imagined. At the very pinnacle, I beheld a Bedouin selling Snickers bars. This clash of cultures wonderfully illustrated the mixture of the sacred and the profane. I bought a Snickers bar and a bottle of water, and enjoyed the beautiful sunset over the stark and magnificent desert below.

I then bought three more Snickers bars from the Bedouin to share with and surprise my friends at the bottom. But while descending, I tripped on a rock and lost one. My Moses moment was not Charlton Heston's in "The 10 Commandments." It was Mel Brooks' in "The History of the World: Part 1." He descends the mountain with three tablets shouting "I have 15…" (he drops and shatters one tablet) "I have 10 Commandments!"

Heaven and Hell

Do Atheists Go to Heaven?
Atheists are the only people who say unequivocally that atheists don't go to heaven. Some heaven-believing religions seem to have a clause that allows atheists to integrate the neighborhood. The road, however, is usually narrow and littered with obstacles.

Mormons, for instance, baptize dead people. Many Jews, myself excluded, are upset that Mormons focused on Jewish Holocaust victims (perhaps even my dead relatives) for posthumous baptism. This practice, however ludicrous, is meant to be helpful and does no harm to my deceased relatives.

Another positive sentiment came from Pope Francis, who spoke of finding common ground with those outside the Catholic faith. He even implied that atheists who do good works are good people and might get to heaven without passing through the "Go" of Christianity. Perhaps Pope Francis forgot to run this concession by the papal censors, because the following day the Vatican announced a do-over when a spokesman said that those who are aware of the Catholic Church couldn't be saved if they refuse to join.

Anyone can make up stuff about heaven or quote from books made up by others. Unlike, say, biology or geology, there is no academic discipline called "heavenology" or "hellology," unless such topics are included in a course on mythology. However, there is scholarship documenting what different cultures believed about the afterlife and how such beliefs have evolved.

There's even a strain of Christianity that says my dog is more likely to wind up in heaven than I am. The gist of these arguments is that dogs don't reject Jesus, but many humans do. I'm okay with a theology that praises dogs. If more people loved their neighbor as much as they loved their pets, we would have a better and more peaceful world.

Nonhuman Animal Rights and Souls

I began thinking seriously about the rights of humans compared to that of other animals after I brought together two people whom I admire, Peter Singer and the late Harriet Johnson. Singer is credited with having started the animal rights movement with his 1975 book *Animal Liberation*. He became considerably more controversial for his position that suffering should be relieved regardless of species, which would allow parents and doctors to euthanize newborns with hopeless and terrible disabilities, like the absence of higher brain function.

Singer, a Jewish atheist, spoke on my College of Charleston campus in 2001 on "Rethinking Life and Death." Not surprisingly, Harriet Johnson got into a heated exchange with Peter Singer. She was a severely disabled member of our secular humanist group and a representative for *Not Dead Yet*, the national organization leading the disability-rights opposition to legalized assisted suicide and disability-based euthanasia.

Harriet, an attorney, presented her case well, and Peter Singer invited her to debate him in his class at Princeton University on March 5, 2002. Their encounters were the subject of a subsequent 8,000-word *New York Times Magazine* cover story written by Harriet.

When I accompanied Peter Singer around campus, a student from the College of Charleston came up to him and said, "Dr. Singer, do you think animals have souls and go to heaven when they die?" His diplomatic response was, "As surely as humans do." The student left with a big grin on her face. Singer and I were grinning for a different reason.

10 Questions About Hell from an Atheist

I like Mark Twain's quip: "Heaven for the climate, hell for the company." There are as many ways to think about hell as there are believers in hell. I think the right way to think about hell is also the right way to think about heaven—nonexistent. All this afterlife theology raises a lot of questions. Here are just 10 that I've wondered about:

1. Why is faith a deciding factor on who winds up in heaven or hell?

2. Why do the last 30 seconds of life matter so much more than the complete life?

3. If we have free will on earth, will we have free will to sin in heaven?

4. What moral purpose does eternal torture serve?

5. What happens to people who died before Jesus was born, or didn't hear of Jesus?

6. If we want people to go to heaven, shouldn't we baptize babies and then kill them?

7. How much more deserving is the worst person in heaven than the best person in hell?

8. How can we be blissfully happy in heaven knowing loved ones are burning in hell?

9. Couldn't God come up with a better method than torturing his son?

10. Wouldn't a loving God make it unambiguously clear how to get to heaven?

4

CANDIDATES WITHOUT A PRAYER

Does This Candidate Have a Prayer?

"South Carolina is too small for a republic and too large for an insane asylum," observed Congressman James L. Petigru, shortly after South Carolina seceded from the Union in 1860 and declared itself a republic. I've lived there since 1976, and stories about our politicians no longer surprise me. The comedy group Capitol Steps takes its name from the escapade involving our former congressman John Jenrette, who had sex on the steps of the US Capitol in the late 1970s. More recently, Governor Mark Sanford secretly visited his "soul mate" in Argentina, which he mistook for the Appalachian Trail. Perhaps South Carolina is not too large for an insane asylum.

Some might argue that I'm also a candidate for this asylum. Why would a liberal, Yankee, Jewish atheist like me run for governor of South Carolina? In 1990 a colleague at the College of Charleston pointed out that the South Carolina Constitution prohibited atheists from becoming governor. Since the US Constitution bars religious tests for public office, I asked a local ACLU lawyer how this obviously unconstitutional provision could be removed. He said that an open atheist could mount a legal challenge and become a candidate. He added with a smile, "The very best candidate would be you—in a race for governor of South Carolina."

So I ran (unsuccessfully), and also engaged in an eight-year legal battle with my state, finally resolved by a South Carolina Supreme Court victory that nullified the anti-atheist clause in our Constitution. As a math professor, I had been used to talking to students, but not the media or the public. After several interviews, I got to know the kinds of questions people would ask. Here is a sample, along with my answers.

Q: What do you think are your chances of winning the election?

A: I'm an atheist, not a fool.

Q: What would be the first thing you would do if elected?

A: Demand a recount!

Q: What would make you believe in God?

A: Perhaps if I won the election. It would take that kind of miracle.

Q: What will happen to you when you die?

A: I'll be going to medical school, just like my Jewish mother always wanted me to do. I want to use my body parts to their fullest while I'm alive, but I hope others will be able to make good use of them when I die.

Q: Why are you wasting all this time on something so frivolous?

A: I find it appalling to be ineligible for an office because of my religious beliefs. To challenge a law that gives credibility to religious intolerance and bigotry is not frivolous.

Atheists in Office: Déjà Vu All Over Again

I'm reminded of my South Carolina experience when I hear that some folks in Asheville, North Carolina want to remove Cecil Bothwell from City Council. What he and I have in common is that we are open atheists, and the constitutions of both North and South Carolina bar atheists from holding public office. Atheists are now eligible in South Carolina, which means the provision against atheists is unenforceable.

Both Bothwell and I were called "avowed" atheists, though neither of us had taken vows. I once asked a public editor why the newspaper always adjectived "atheist." She said because it only has the word of someone who says he or she is an atheist. I asked if it's more likely that a religious person would pretend to be an atheist or an atheist would pretend to be religious. She conceded I had a point. I've sometimes been introduced on radio as a "so-called atheist" or an "admitted atheist." I wonder what the reaction would be if were someone were introduced as a "so-called Jew" or "admitted Southern Baptist."

Last Leper in the Colony

A white doctor in the rural South is presumed to be a Republican and a Christian. Wynne LeGrow, a physician in Emporia, Virginia, was neither, but he kept his political and religious beliefs to himself. He felt that his liberal political views would turn off most of his patients, and his atheism would shock almost everyone. His book, *Last leper in the Colony*, is the fascinating story of how he transformed himself from a small-town doctor who shunned politics (except to vote), into a Democratic candidate for Congress.

LeGrow grew up as a "PK" (preacher's kid) and attended church regularly (if not faithfully) until he graduated from high school. His father, a liberal Congregational minister, never talked about God belief with his son, but noticed Wynne's skepticism. Wynne assumed that one sermon was directed at him when his father preached that those who have doubts about religion should continue to go to church. When young Wynne mentioned he was having trouble with the concept of Jesus rising from the dead after three days, his mother told him that Jesus's followers probably felt his presence emotionally after he had been dead a few days, a casual and natural dismissal of that defining supernatural event for Christians.

In 2010, LeGrow secured the nomination for the US House of Representatives, a role that brought with it many ups and downs as he tried to figure out how a political neophyte should conduct a campaign. In many ways, this book is a guide on how to run for public office—as an open atheist. It offers an insightful assessment of what worked and what didn't. He ran against incumbent Republican Randy Forbes, a traditional Christian conservative and also founder and chairman of the Congressional Prayer Caucus. Forbes asserted, "The concept of separation of church and state was not borne to establish freedom *from* religion, but to establish freedom *for* religion."

Political operatives told LeGrow that he needed to spend six to eight hours a day calling people for money, though he much preferred discussing issues. However, one event was even more uncomfortable for him than fundraising—a Democratic Women's Fashion Show where he tried to make small talk. (I can identify with his discomfort.) This story and others like it are in the book's funniest chapter, "Bumps in the Road." Some of those bumps were more like boulders.

LeGrow hoped that his opponent would want to debate an atheist and gain national publicity as a defender of the faith, but Forbes didn't want to give him any media attention. Nate Silver, the statistician who handicaps races at ESPN's FiveThirtyEight blog, initially placed LeGrow's chances of winning at 0 percent. After stories about his atheism broke, his chances shot all the way up to 0.1 percent on the site.

The bad news is that Dr. Wynne LeGrow lost the election. The good news is that he garnered 37.5 percent of the vote, more than any Virginia Democrat running against an incumbent Republican that year. LeGrow can be proud of the way he conducted his campaign, and proud of the honest, perceptive book he's written about it. I hope the book will inspire more open atheists to seek public office, encouraged by words of wisdom from the last leper in the colony.

Belief in the Almighty Dollar: Why We Need an Atheist PAC

I almost always vote for Christians, not because I'm impressed by their God beliefs, but because I usually have no other choice. The good news for secular Americans is that a Freethought Equality Fund has been created, a Political Action Committee (PAC) dedicated to expanding voter choices by backing the candidacy of open nontheists. The PAC supports candidates who share our goals of protecting the separation of religion and government and defending the civil liberties of secular Americans. Before issuing an endorsement, the PAC questions candidates about their views on issues where religious belief could influence public policy. The PAC hopes to dispel the notion that atheists are "immoral" and lack values. When people see respected atheists and humanists serving in public office, stereotypes will change. Though atheists and humanists don't believe in an almighty deity, we do believe in the almighty dollar. We've seen evidence of its power and influence in politics, so it's not beyond belief.

We've learned from the success of EMILY's List, a PAC founded in the mid-1980s to help increase representation by women candidates who share the list's views. We've also learned from the LGBT movement that the most effective way to change public perception is to come out of the closet. And so it can be with atheists, including politicians who would like to benefit from our PAC.

I'm hoping, but not praying, that someday we will regularly elect acknowledged atheists and humanists to public office, and that the public will be more interested in a candidate's political ideology than professed theology. Should that day come, the Freethought Equality Fund can happily go out of business and declare, "Mission accomplished."

Political Atheism: The Last Taboo

In "The Last Taboo: Why America Needs Atheism," published in the *New Republic* in 1996, Wendy Kaminer wrote, "Atheists generate about as much sympathy as pedophiles. But, while pedophilia may at least be characterized as a disease, atheism is a choice, a willful rejection of beliefs to which vast majorities of people cling." The situation has improved significantly, but not so much in politics. The complete history of open atheists in Congress is very short: Rep. Pete Stark (D-Calif.). He acknowledged being an atheist after the Secular Coalition for America sponsored a contest to find the highest-ranking politician who so identified. Stark left Congress in 2012, reducing the number of open atheists from one to zero.

This brings me to three politicians I assume are atheists, though they don't so identify.

Barney Frank, an openly gay member of Congress for many years, came out as an atheist on the TV show *Real Time with Bill Maher*, but not until he had left office. Unfortunately, he later had a do-over saying his theological views are complicated by his Jewishness and he doesn't know enough to have a firm view on atheism. Frank also advised politicians not to be frank about their atheism.

Bernie Sanders is an open socialist in the Senate and a former presidential candidate. He identifies as a secular Jew. When asked on *Jimmy Kimmel Live* whether he believes in God, Sanders replied, "What my spirituality is about is that we're all in this together and it's not a good thing to believe that as human beings we can turn our backs on the suffering of other people." What does God have to do with that?

Jamie Raskin won a congressional election in Maryland. He is a member of the American Humanist Association, and accepts its definition: "Humanism is a progressive philosophy of life that, without theism and other supernatural beliefs, affirms our ability and responsibility to lead ethical lives of personal fulfillment that aspire to the greater good of humanity." When described as an atheist, Raskin said he is 100 percent Jewish and doesn't use the "atheist" label. If you are "without theism and other supernatural beliefs," then you are an atheist, whatever your preferred label.

Barney, Bernie, and Jamie are secular Jews who don't like to talk about religion or call themselves atheists, and they act as if you need to choose between being a Jew and being an atheist. On the contrary, a Harris survey shows that the majority (52 percent) of American Jews do *not* believe in God.

I admire all three politicians for how they have championed minority rights and separation of religion and government. People are free to use their preferred label or labels, but I'm disappointed when otherwise courageous politicians don't have the courage to embrace the A-word, which is perhaps the last political taboo.

5

CATHOLICISM

General

Pope Herb I

The Catholic Church, so reluctant to change its absolutist pronouncements, looks foolish when reasons for its conclusions keep changing. It used to accept the wisdom of St. Bonaventure, "Since only the male was made in the image of God, only the male can receive the godlike office of priest." After such claims of female inferiority became a bit embarrassing even to the church, the story became, "Only males can hold positions of leadership in the church because all the apostles were male." Since all the apostles were Jews, most of whom were married, I'm more qualified to be pope than gentile popes. So either the church must again change its reason or I would like future consideration to become Pope Herb I. My first act would be to declare *ex cathedra* (invoking papal infallibility) that all future popes must be atheists, turning Catholicism into an evidence-based religion.

How to Elect a Pope and Get Higher Ratings

The Catholic Church sometimes changes when it's beneficial to do so. I propose blending the method of choosing a pope with one adopted by another venerable tradition that has been mostly scandal free—the Miss America Pageant. Throngs of adoring fans follow Miss America, just as adoring Catholics follow the pope.

Since the pageant began in 1945, there have been ninety-two Miss Americas creating annual excitement, but only four popes. Here is my proposed procedure for electing future popes. To maintain tradition, allow cardinals to narrow the selection to ten candidates. Then bring in a panel of outside judges to choose the next pope. Since papal attire is just as important and elaborate as Miss America attire, the ten finalist cardinals will parade in front of the judges wearing their traditional outrageous costumes. We absolutely want our next pope to look stylish in his uniform.

Then the finalists will display a papal talent. For example, one might perform an exorcism. Another might turn a bottle of water into wine. The judges then ask pope candidates a question, just as with Miss America candidates. For example, "How many 'Hail Marys' would you require for a priest who molests a child?" Or "How do you think you will feel the moment you are transformed from fallible to infallible?"

When the panel of judges retires to vote, the announcement will be a bit different from the traditional white smoke/black smoke procedure. We will instead display a smiley face if a pope is chosen and a frown face if he is not. The day after the new pope is chosen, he will go on all the morning TV shows around the world and take call-in questions from viewers, answering them infallibly.

To Life, Not Martyrdom

My harshest criticisms of religion go to those that intrude on the lives of people outside the religion, but I can't ignore practices I find ridiculous. This brings me to Catholic sainthood. How many "miracles" does it take to change a dead human into a saint? The Church says two, but no miracle has been as convincing as, say, a prayer that results in a light bulb changing itself.

It's bad enough that an organization wastes time and money "documenting" that someone was cured of an incurable disease solely by praying to a dead person. I'm more bothered by the church's fast track to sainthood called "martyrdom." A person who dies for belief in Catholicism can become a saint without performing two post-death miracles. This dual track puts belief above behavior. No matter how good a life you led by Catholic standards, you would still have to perform two miracles after death if you didn't die a martyr. Also, the Catholic Church claims to stand for the "culture of life." If someone puts a gun to my head and says he will shoot me unless I pray to Zeus, I'll pray to Zeus. Such a prayer would hurt nobody, and it would save a life.

Sin: Making Sense Out of Nonsense

First, the nonsense: *original sin*. A talking snake convinced Adam and Eve to eat a piece of fruit forbidden by God, who then got so angry that he condemned all humankind to be born with this "original sin." Then came the "good news" that God's sinless son, Jesus, who is also God, visited earth to redeem us for that sin. So God sacrificed himself to himself to save us from himself, and when we die we will be rewarded or punished for eternity based on whether we believe this unbelievable story.

In Orthodox Judaism I was taught that sin is violating any of the 613 commandments in the Hebrew Bible. Some are reasonable (don't murder, steal, or lie), some are silly (don't mix wool and cotton; don't eat meat with milk), and some are impossible (animal sacrifice at a nonexistent Temple in Jerusalem). At least we had some choice about whether to sin, rather than having been born with it.

Sin is sometimes described as an offense against God, which makes atheists sinless. My wife, Sharon, who grew up Catholic and is now an atheist, was frightened as a child when she went into a dark booth and a man told her to confess her sins. Sometimes she had to make them up, like saying she had lied to her mother. At the time, young Sharon failed to see the irony of committing the sin of lying to a Father (priest) about lying to her mother.

Pope Benedict

What Did He Know and When Did He Know It?

This question was more consequential when asked at the impeachment hearings of President Nixon than when asked now of Pope Benedict XVI. A secular United States has checks and balances to allow for removal of a leader guilty of flagrant abuses. According to Catholic Church law, the pope "possesses supreme, full, immediate, and universal ordinary power in the Church." Rev. Thomas Doyle said, "The only person who can fire him is God."

Covering up the Watergate break-in is mild compared to covering up sex crimes involving minors. For years, bishops have not only covered up such evidence, but also transferred to other parishes some priests who raped and abused trusting children. Pope Benedict XVI has refused to discipline any bishops or ask them to resign, perhaps because these steps might ultimately require the pope to ask for his own resignation.

If this pope is incapable of acting quickly and unambiguously to end current abuses, here's an alternate plan. Popes sometimes choose the name of a previous pope whose reign they wish to emulate. Pope Benedict XVI can take the same action as a morally challenged namesake. In 1045, Pope Benedict IX resigned. (Note: XVI took my advice three years after I gave it.)

Political Popery a Bad Idea

I thought I was reading George Orwell's *1984* when leaders in the Catholic Church referred to the "democratic ideal," and called voting a "serious moral obligation." When do Catholics get to exercise this "democratic ideal" and vote for popes, cardinals, priests, or any church-related issue? The Vatican theocracy has the chutzpah to call democracy an ideal for which all humans should strive. If so, Pope Benedict: Heal thyself.

Let's take a hypothetical case (not so hypothetical, actually):

Candidate A supports the Iraq and Afghanistan wars, opposes government money to help the poor, wants to build a fence around the country to keep immigrants out, favors capital punishment, and opposes abortion under all circumstances.

Candidate B takes the opposite side of Candidate A on all these issues, and favors the right of a woman to choose.

The Catholic Church agrees with all the positions of Candidate B but the last, yet would urge its faithful to vote for Candidate A. That's what happens when a church engages in politics. I wish Catholics would ignore the pontiff when he pontificates theologically, but even more so when he pontificates politically. At least the pope and I agree that voting is a good thing, though I'll never have the pleasure of voting against a candidate for pope.

Papal Exoneration of Jews

Pope Benedict XVI has exonerated Jews of responsibility for the death of Jesus. He now claims that years of anti-Semitism resulted from a misreading of Matthew 27:25: "The blood of Jesus is on all Jews and on all their children." He spins the passage to be comforting because the blood of Jesus washes away sins. This breaking news comes 2,000 years too late, after countless murders of Jews by zealous Christians.

While it's nice to know that my fellow Jews have been "exonerated," I'm disturbed that so many people still base their morality on an ancient book with many outdated and untenable beliefs. I await an interpretation on how Jews are put in a favorable light by John 8:44, "The Devil is father of the Jews."

Pope Francis

No Track to Sainthood

Part of me wishes Congress were as willing to craft political compromises as Pope Francis, who approved making Popes John Paul II and John XXIII simultaneous saints. The first was a conservative and the second a liberal. (I'm grading on a curve here because "liberal pope" is an oxymoron.)

Pope Francis is so anxious to elevate both of them that he put John Paul II on the fast track and waved a second miracle for John XXIII. Even if I believed in sainthood, I would prefer that the church take its time to declare saints. A long waiting period allows for a legacy to endure or scandals to emerge.

The Catholic Church demoted saints like Christopher from the official list after learning they never existed, but they've never reversed sainthood after discovering a horrendous scandal. Since Pope Francis seems to care about public relations, I would advise him to slow down. After all, with abundant evidence that Pope John Paul II shielded pedophile priests and organized criminal activity of the Vatican Bank, what's the rush? Sainthood is for an eternity, so a few more years shouldn't make much difference.

Pope Francis Divides Atheists

Here's my paraphrase of Winston Churchill's remark about democracy: "Pope Francis is the worst pope we ever had, except for all the others." I can't think of a less bad pope than Francis. True, I have nothing bad to say about Pope John Paul I, perhaps because he was pope for only 33 days. Although Pope Benedict XVI unified atheists whenever he made pronouncements on atheists, gays, pedophilia, and all matters sexual, his successor, Pope Francis, is a divider rather than a uniter within the atheist community. Some atheists see this pope glass as 1/10 full, while others see it as 9/10 empty.

For instance, Pope Francis said, "God's mercy does not have limits and therefore it reaches nonbelievers, too, for whom sin would not be the lack of faith in God, but rather, failure to obey one's conscience." He added that

God forgives those who do not believe and do not seek faith, as long as they follow their own conscience. Pope Francis even gave a limited shout-out to gays, asking, "Who am I to judge a gay person of goodwill who seeks the Lord?" But he conditions his benevolence on a search for the Lord.

I like the pope's emphasis on conscience, though I neither want nor need forgiveness for not believing in a nonexistent deity. I doubt that the pope would appreciate someone telling him, "Zeus will forgive you for not believing in him as long as you follow your conscience." Following one's conscience instead of a religious "authority" is what atheists and humanists do.

Perhaps Pope Francis is a liberal Christian trapped in a conservative Christian body (the Catholic Church). Whether you call it tradition or baggage, popes live mostly in the past. Pope Francis may be as good as it gets, but the Catholic Church just doesn't allow popes to get that good.

That's an Atheist Thing to Do

Many atheists and humanists have mixed feelings when someone compliments one of our good deeds by saying "That's a Christian thing to do." We know they mean well, but they falsely equate goodness with Christianity. Consequently, and because of Pope Francis' recent remarks, I'm tempted to compliment him with "That's an atheist thing to do." Pope Francis said "proselytism is solemn nonsense" and we should listen to and get to know each other, expand our circle of ideas, and improve our knowledge of the world. He added that we should encourage people to move toward what they think is Good (he did not say God!). Pope Francis referred to heads of the church as "narcissists," and that he will do everything he can to change a Vatican-centric view that neglects the world around us. He even called himself "anticlerical," and said "clericalism should not have anything to do with Christianity." This sounds as if he might be encouraging people to question church dogma and then do what they think is right. That really is an atheist thing to do.

A Dangerously Incurious Pope

Just as I was feeling somewhat warmly disposed toward Pope Francis, he burst my bubble with a statement reminiscent of his predecessors. He said, "The spirit of curiosity generates confusion and distances a person from the spirit of wisdom, which brings peace." He added that the spirit of curiosity distances oneself from God. The pope has a point. Curiosity did distance me from god belief, and I'm far from alone. Curiosity has turned many religious believers into atheists.

I also agree that curiosity can generate confusion. Scientific curiosity frequently creates confusion, which can lead to breakthroughs. Much to the dismay of the Catholic Church, Galileo's curiosity inspired him to discover and publicize that the earth revolves around the sun. Not until Galileo had been dead for over 350 years did the Church absolve him of this spiritual heresy. The Catholic Church does not oppose science as long as scientific discoveries don't conflict with church doctrine, which means the church fails to grasp the rudiments of scientific inquiry. Science is about trying to solve problems, with no religious test to limit or discourage inquiry. Curiosity should not be stifled nor dissenting ideas suppressed. The "spirit" of curiosity, inquiry, and testability brings us closer to scientific truths, while history is littered with discarded religious "truths."

Most troubling is Pope Francis citing Abraham as a role model, saying that God asked Abraham to "walk in my presence and be irreproachable." In the most noteworthy biblical story about Abraham, he hears what he assumes to be the voice of God. Without offering a reason or an explanation, God tells Abraham to take his son Isaac up a mountain and kill him. The incurious and unquestioning Abraham dutifully leads his puzzled son up the mountain, intent on fulfilling God's will. If Pope Francis ever thinks he hears God telling him to commit an atrocity, I hope he will be more curious and skeptical than Abraham. Fortunately, those who kill innocent people today in the name of God are more likely to be institutionalized as criminals than revered as prophets.

7 Family Issues Pope Francis Should—But Won't—Discuss
There's an elephant roaming through the Vatican, but Pope Francis hasn't noticed. Its name is Women. He called for a two-week meeting of Catholic bishops to consider "the family." The pope encouraged bishops (all men) to speak openly on family issues. Women's thoughts are irrelevant, though they are present in almost every family. Here are ideas we aren't likely to hear bishops discuss with Pope Francis.

Stop treating women as second-class people; end celibacy for priests; diminish family poverty caused by having too many children; recognize that masturbation is natural and healthy safe sex; bless unions of responsible and mature people of the same sex who are in committed relationships and love each other; do not view morality primarily through the narrow prism of sexual conduct.

During conversations with religious leaders, I sometimes think of a line from "Positively 4th Street" by Bob Dylan: "I wish that for just one time you could stand inside my shoes . . ." I expect that more than one Catholic woman will be thinking about this song during the pope's synod on the family.

Exorcisms

Why I Wish Pope Francis Was Joking About the Devil

In an unintentionally funny comment, progressive Catholic theologian Vito Mancuso said about Pope Francis's old-school interpretation of the devil and the need for exorcists: "He is opening the door to superstition." Where to begin when describing a Catholic door that has always been more open to superstition than the mythical Pandora's box?

In fact (really, in fiction), the Pandora myth deserves credit for a foundational myth in Catholic theology. Pandora, the first woman, was given a box (actually a jar) and told never to open it. Of course, the curious Pandora opened it, whereupon evil escaped and spread throughout the world. So Pandora committed the original "original sin."

This brings me to Pope Francis's belief in Satan as the cause of evil, which is why some progressive theologians are probably disappointed with Pope Francis's inordinate interest in the devil, even praising the International Association of Exorcists. Gullible and deranged people are being encouraged to believe they live in a "Demon-Haunted World," one that Carl Sagan so eloquently and scientifically debunked.

I'm not an exorcist, but I have a four-word solution to combat demonic possession that is more effective than anything an exorcist has in his arsenal: "Stop believing in demons!" It's more productive to develop a personal relationship with reality. Comedian Flip Wilson's character, Geraldine, always excused her bad behavior with "The devil made me do it." Flip got it right—attributing bad behavior to the devil is something to joke about. And we'd live in a happier and more peaceful world if we'd all embrace Flip Wilson's devilish humor.

Exorcist Training

I read with interest (and amusement) that Roman Catholic Church leaders are gravely concerned about a shortage of exorcists, especially in the United States. To combat the problem, the Vatican is sponsoring an intensive eight-week training course in Rome to help future priest-exorcists tell the difference between demonic possession and psychological or physical trauma. I suggest, instead, a two-second course you can take in the comfort of your living room: Rational Thinking. Have you noticed that demons and devils never possess people who don't believe in them? No Vatican-sanctioned exorcist can claim such a 100 percent success rate.

An Invitation to Exorcise an Atheist

The phrase "More Catholic than the pope" refers to someone more religiously strict than the Catholic Church requires. Gordon Klingenschmitt, Republican nominee for the Colorado House of Representatives, is not Catholic, but I'd add him to the club. He falsely assumed that atheists were responsible for a court decision against a school district holding graduation ceremonies in a local church. His solution? Do an exorcism on atheists and cast the devil out.

Klingenschmitt had previously claimed that President Obama's support for gay marriage showed that he's possessed by demonic spirits. It's bad enough that Pope Francis and other Catholic clergy perform exorcisms on the gullible in their own church, but Klingenschmitt wants to exorcise the devil from everyone who disagrees with his theological views.

Here's my offer to Klingenschmitt: I invite you or the exorcist of your choice to perform an exorcism on me. You may use as much holy water, magic words, incantations, and ritual objects as needed—but no violence, please. If you see me smiling during the ceremony, don't think it's because the exorcist has successfully cast out any demons or that it's the devil smiling back at you. Instead, it will just be me smiling about my participation in such an absurd activity.

6

COALITIONS

Secular Coalitions

Atheists. Humanists. Freethinkers. Americans.
When I became engaged in freethought activities in 1990, I discovered a number of fine organizations that promoted causes I supported. However, each group was doing its own thing with little backing for worthwhile efforts of others. So in 1998 I contacted the national nontheistic organizations I knew, noting that none was large enough to make a significant impact. I suggested we begin to cooperate, show our strength in numbers, and more effectively counter the political and social threats coming from the religious right.

People with considerably more experience in the movement warned me that getting freethinkers to cooperate was akin to herding cats. My cats put aside personality differences, past grudges, and turf protection when I fed them cat crunchies. I assumed people like Pat Robertson and Jerry Falwell would be freethought crunchies around which we could all enthusiastically rally. After some delicate negotiations and ground rules, leaders from several national organizations met for a weekend in 2000. Afterward, all thought that first meeting had been worthwhile, focusing on the 95 percent we had in common, rather than arguing about the 5 percent that set us apart.

We had trouble choosing a coalition name acceptable to a diverse group of atheists and humanists. "Atheist" gets more attention and "humanist" sounds more respectable. We agreed that either both or neither word would be in our name. (Organizations within our freethought community

74

even disagree on whether to capitalize A(a)theist and H(h)umanist.) We considered Freethought/Atheist/Humanist Coalition, but the acronym (FAHC) sounded a bit unseemly. (This was before the movie, "Meet the Fockers.") We finally settled on the Coalition for the Community of Reason (CCR).

Though talk is good, I was hoping talk would lead to action. But an inordinate amount of time was spent on whether CCR should be publicly visible or simply a forum to exchange ideas. Even though CCR formed as a cooperative body, some leaders began to view it as a competing organization and withdrew support. The coalition died, which turned out to be a "blessing" in disguise. In 2002, CCR evolved into the Secular Coalition for America. Instead of a loose confederation, it became a formal organization with an activist mission: to increase the visibility of and respectability for nontheistic viewpoints, and to protect and strengthen the secular character of our government. The Secular Coalition filed under a section of the IRS code that allows unlimited political lobbying. Finally, atheists and humanists had a voice in the nation's capitol.

Our Secular Coalition Visit to the White House

Representatives from the Secular Coalition for America met with White House officials on February 26, 2010 to discuss issues of concern to secular Americans. We were grateful to have a place at the table, with a chance to hear from Obama administration representatives, and for them to hear from us about issues that affect all Americans. This historic meeting marked the first time a presidential administration met for a policy briefing with our nontheistic community.

Here are some grossly unfair but predictable media comments. The advocacy group, "In God We Trust," ripped the Obama administration "for meeting to plot political strategy with 60 atheist activists." Its chairman, Bishop Council Nedd, said we represent "some of the most hate-filled, antireligious groups in the nation." Sean Hannity claimed on Fox News that the Obama administration is giving special treatment to atheists, and that religious groups "have not received this treatment from the Obama White House." In Hannity's America, a two-hour meeting with Secular Americans is "special treatment," but not a recent two-day meeting sponsored by the White House Office of Faith-Based and Neighborhood Partnerships.

The Catholic League for Religious and Civil Rights sent a press release saying "Obama Aides Host Catholic Bashers." Bill Donohue, its president, ended his diatribe with "It is important that the public learn of the contents of this meeting. We will do what we can to find out what happened." Apparently, their crack investigative team never thought to contact any Secular Coalition representatives. So for the Catholic League and others who would rather opine than investigate, I'll make it easy by telling what issues we addressed at the meeting with administration officials.

Childhood medical neglect and abuse: Close loopholes for religiously based medical neglect of children, because no child should suffer from lack of medical attention.

Military proselytizing and coercion: Ensure that men and women who risk their lives to protect American values are not coerced into religious participation, subjected to proselytizing, or discriminated against because of their beliefs.

Fixing faith-based initiatives: Make certain that religious organizations receiving federal funding for social welfare programs cannot discriminate in hiring, that beneficiaries are not proselytized, and that secular options are made available.

These secular values are also American values. It's not religion bashing to mention that government neutrality is not government hostility, that the government should not favor one religion over another or religion over nonreligion.

Secular Coalition for America and Clinton Foundation
As with all non-profits (and non-prophets), the Secular Coalition relies on generous donations. If Pat Robertson or a Saudi sheik offered to donate a million dollars, I would happily accept as long as we could use the money to promote our mission (no such donations, yet). Donald Trump, if you are listening, we would like a major contribution so we, too, can help build a wall that will make America great again—Thomas Jefferson's wall to separate church and state.

While the Secular Coalition for America appreciates all donors, the "secular angels" ($10,000 or more) usually have greater access than supporters who contribute $100. For instance, if a donor were to offer us money to advertise in major media, we would thankfully accept the generous contribution to do something we can't now afford to do. On the other hand, we would not accept money to promote a donor's car dealership.

When it comes to the Clinton Foundation, I'm more interested in whether donors have influenced public policy, and, if so, how. As we know, problems arise when a legislator supports an issue solely to please a donor even though the legislator realizes it might harm other Americans. The bottom line for me is not just who the contributor is, but also what the recipient does for the contributor.

Compete or Cooperate? Endorse, Ignore, or Oppose?
The atheist/humanist community frequently disagrees about what kinds of issues are worth its time, money, and involvement, with whom to cooperate, and whether cooperation will be productive or counter-productive. While a big-tent alliance produces more influence overall, it also gives less influence and control to each group or individual within the alliance. The reasons for a reluctance to work with like-minded groups may include slight philosophical differences, turf protection, and personality conflicts.

One artificial barrier to cooperation is what I call the "fixed-pie syndrome," the false notion that the growth of a "rival" organization must be at the expense of others. In game theory terminology, poker is an example of a zero-sum game: one person's gain is another's loss. However, collaboration among nontheistic organizations isn't a zero-sum game. For every humanist or atheist in any organization, there are thousands who have never heard of any organization. Our players can cooperate to create a bigger pie that benefits all, because many who find out about one organization often wind up joining others. This mix of cooperation and competition is known as *coopetition*. In cooperative games, players form coalitions and reach agreements to create a bigger pie. They can continue to compete a bit, with each group getting a bigger slice than it had before.

Still, some humanists don't like working with aggressive atheists and some atheists don't like working with wishy-washy humanists. Ronald Reagan wasn't one of my favorite presidents, but he did unify his party with what he called the Eleventh Commandment: "Thou shalt not speak ill of a fellow Republican." I propose the following principle to help unify our movement: "Thou shalt not speak ill of anyone's nontheistic label."

Trailblazers Wanted: Perfection Not Required

A way to insult an atheist, as I'm about to do, is to compare him or her to a religious fundamentalist. Atheists, like fundamentalists, believe in perfect beings. Not in deities, mind you, but in honorees. Our flawed (human) laureates never live up to the perfection we expect. There were protests over giving Bill Maher an Atheist Alliance award because of his pseudo-scientific, alternative health claims that led him to oppose some vaccinations. I agree with Maher on most issues, and he should certainly understand why almost all atheists disagree with his vaccination position—the preponderance of evidence that vaccines are safe and effective. Fortunately, Bill Maher neither wants nor has children. I wish the same could be said of religious antivaccinationists.

Stephen Jay Gould was a "controversial" Humanist of the Year in 2001, awarded by the American Humanist Association. The problem can be summed up in an acronym, NOMA. Gould coined the phrase "nonoverlapping magisteria," claiming science discovers matters of fact and theory (the "what and how"), while religion is concerned with purpose and moral precepts (the "why"). Most humanists, myself included, disagree with NOMA. But I don't find Gould's position totally indefensible, just mostly so. In any case, Gould was a worthy recipient for many reasons, NOMA not being one of them.

We should recognize perceived flaws of awardees, but also consider the overall body of work. So here's my proposal, which won't insult any recipients and will acknowledge imperfections in the winners. Under lists of awardees, add one more. "Perfect Human of the Year: No winner."

What Atheist Groups Learned from the Christian Coalition

Here's an interesting distinction between Christians and secularists: Christians have the same unifying word, but fight over theology. Secularists have the same unifying theology, but fight over words. (At least our wars are only verbal.)

Though I disagreed with everything they stood for, I give credit to the Christian Coalition. They had a terrific model: put aside theological differences, work together on important political issues, and grab media attention. That was their plan to change the culture and make politicians take notice. Their strategy of demonizing atheists and secular humanists, while moving this country closer to a theocracy, worked all too well.

For too long our nontheistic community has been considered politically inconsequential, and the Secular Coalition for America now advocates for those millions without god beliefs. Discrimination still exists against blacks, women, gays, and Jews, but neither as overtly nor permissibly as it once did. Politicians pay attention to these groups because they have well-organized advocates and constituencies.

Now it is our turn to seek that respect. We may be the last minority against whom intolerance and discrimination are not only permitted, but also sometimes promoted by political leaders at every level. Improving the public perception of secular Americans is as important to many of us as pursuing a particular political agenda. Politicians think they are being tolerant when they express support for all faiths; instead, we expect to hear them publicly express support for all faiths and none, freedom of conscience for all.

What Atheists Can Learn from the Gay Rights Movement
How did homosexuality shift in public opinion from less respectable than atheism to more respectable? And what can the atheist movement learn from the LGBT movement? The psychiatric community considered homosexuality a mental disorder until 1974, and not until 2003 did the Supreme Court declare sodomy laws unconstitutional. When the public is polled about a willingness to vote for a well-qualified person for president who happens to be gay or atheist, gays are now ranked ahead of atheists.

The most obvious and effective lesson atheists are learning from LGBTs is to come out of the closet. Attitudes changed rapidly when people learned that friends, neighbors, and even family members were gay. Attitudes about atheists are slowly changing as atheists are slowly coming out. Gays are more likely to come out because it's easier for atheists to remain in the closet. There aren't many good excuses on why you've been living for years with someone of the same sex and not dating.

Here's an evidence-based case for why many religious people are less accepting of atheists than gays. Most don't worry about homosexuals "converting" heterosexuals, but do worry about arguments from atheists that might resonate with their flock. You're more likely to stay with your childhood religion if no one ever questions those beliefs.

The LGBT movement deserves enormous credit for framing and publicizing their issues, forming a big tent that allows for cooperation between activist and laid back gays, and developing a well-organized community with a constituency recognized by politicians. And so it should be with atheists, which is a goal of the Secular Coalition for America and its member organizations. I've heard a number of gays acknowledge that they were atheists, but wished to remain quiet about it because they were trying to appear "normal" in our culture. With continued success of both the LGBT and atheist communities, I expect it will become easier for gay atheists to emerge from both closets.

Secular and Religious Coalitions

Faith in Reason

Jon Stewart in 2010 held a "rally to restore sanity" on the Washington Mall, two months after Glenn Beck's religion-infused "Restoring Honor" rally. Beck said he was called by God to hold his rally. Atheist groups used Stewart's event to promote "reason," and many atheists view taking religion out of political debate as necessary to restore reason. Government should not be in the religion business, even if Glenn Beck believes God told him it should. Many people think secular Americans are insulting those with religious beliefs when we mention we don't believe in any gods. We may have different views on religion, but I hope we can agree on one fundamental good—the marketplace of ideas. Some may think reason and sanity are the opposite of religion, and some may not. Let arguments be heard, not stifled. That, to me, is the most sane and reasonable way to act.

Interfaith(less) Dialogue

There are two types of people who sometimes object to participating in interfaith ceremonies: religious and irreligious.

First the religious. After the Sandy Hook massacre, local clergy sponsored an ecumenical prayer service. However, the Lutheran Church-Missouri Synod denomination reprimanded Rev. Rob Morris for participating. They bar interfaith worship for fear of giving the impression that it doesn't matter who God is, how to worship Jesus, and what we need to do to get to heaven.

After the rebuke raised a public outcry, I was hoping to hear an apology, and there was one. Unfortunately, the apology did not come from the president of the church for having criticized Pastor Morris's attempt to comfort grieving people. It came from Pastor Morris, who humbly acknowledged that his participation was offensive to his church. He also promised never again to take part in such ecumenical activities.

Some irreligious people won't participate because of the word "interfaith." Atheists and humanists have no faith in deities, and would like to see a more inclusive term: Inter-worldview? Interbelief? Faith and values? Something else?

Most of us collaborate with religious people to achieve common goals. An added bonus is that negative stereotypes sometimes change when people get to know one another. I've participated in interfaith dialogues, mostly with progressive religionists who are comfortable working with people of other faiths and none.

I think it's terrific when interfaith groups invite atheists to participate. Even if gatherings start and end with a prayer, some participants know we are there despite what we view as meaningless prayers, and they often try to accommodate us in other ways. Sometimes they acknowledge in their prayers that good atheists are working alongside them.

Us Versus Them

So who is "Us" and who is "Them?" Often we treat "Us" as if we were "Them." We divide over words: atheist/agnostic, humanist/secular humanist, rationalist/naturalist, and the list goes on. We waste too much time and energy arguing over such narcissism of small differences. I'm reminded of the phrase from the cartoon character Pogo during the divisive Vietnam War: "We have met the enemy, and he is us."

So let's say that "Us" are nontheists who want to increase visibility and respectability for our viewpoints and protect and strengthen the secular character of our government. Is "Them" the theists? Not necessarily. We are often more effective when we cooperate with religious people. Here's an example from my home state.

The South Carolina Progressive Network is composed of more than 50 organizations, including the Secular Humanists of the Lowcountry. Most groups have no theological position or have members who are quite religious. All groups are outside the mainstream and opposed by the Religious Right. People are more likely to listen to a network of groups than to one lone group.

For instance, our group sought Network support for a Charleston Day of Reason, coordinating with national freethought organizations across the nation. I expected opposition from some religious members because it was on the same day as the National Day of Prayer. I told them the day was picked because reason is a concept all Americans can support and that we wanted to raise public awareness about the persistent threat to religious liberty posed by government intrusion into the private sphere of worship. To my pleasant surprise, the support was unanimous and the Progressive Network asked Mayor Joe Riley to issue a proclamation in support of a Charleston Day of Reason, which he did.

The Network and others joined in a local park to celebrate a day of reason, tolerance, democracy, and human rights. The celebration began with a member of Charleston City Council reading the mayor's proclamation. Others, both secular and religious, then contributed freethought statements or comments in support of reason.

When we associate faces with organizations, it is much easier for these groups to support each other's causes. It's also a great way to make new friends. And when "Us" combine forces and become influential within our community, then we can more effectively go after "Them." Just make sure that "Them" is not "Us."

7

COLLEGE OF CHARLESTON

My Beginnings

I started teaching at the College of Charleston in 1976, my first trip below the Mason-Dixon line, and in a city known for gracious living. I've never been known as a gracious liver. This formerly segregated college in a very conservative state was in the process of changing, sometimes upsetting administrators and frequently upsetting legislators.

The College is a public institution with academic freedom, so I was never asked to tone down my personal activism. Periodically, the administration received requests from disgruntled Charlestonians to fire the "atheist professor." In 1998, College President Alex Sanders showed me a letter demanding he either fire me or repent for allowing me to continue. His response: "I repent for a lot of things, but Professor Silverman is not one of them. He is a fine professor of mathematics. His personal beliefs, or lack thereof, have nothing to do with his teaching ability. Even if his views did carry over into the classroom, no harm would come of it. The Gospel of our Lord Jesus Christ does not need my protection or yours from Herb Silverman. To suggest that it does is the ultimate blasphemy. Fearing the Lord, as I do, I would not dare suggest any such thing. Why don't we instead pray for Herb? After all, God loves him just as he loves you and me."

Militant Atheism vs. Militant Christianity

Atheists are often accused of being "militant" because of anti-religion stances. Here's an example. The College of Charleston purchased a church building with a cross on top. I sent an email to Alex Sanders, president of the College, requesting that he remove the "plus sign" from what had become a public building. Sanders did, and then described our exchange in a local newspaper: "I will just assign the building to Herb Silverman as his office. With the cross at the top and Herb Silverman at the bottom, that would be an equalizing force. I told him that if he kept quiet about the cross, no one would be nailed to it." I wasn't offended by Sanders' public humor, but the community was outraged that I referred to the cross as a "plus sign." Indignant writers fumed about my offending Christians, but not Sanders' allusion that I might be nailed to the cross.

Charity Doesn't Require Religion

I like to know how legislators vote, and why. Voting based on religious faith is the wrong reason, though I might have good secular reasons to agree with the vote. If a politician focuses on portions of ancient religious texts to justify a vote, I think the politician either has no rational argument or is pandering to voters of that faith. Sometimes a politician with sound arguments feels compelled not to use them. When Alex Sanders was president of the College of Charleston, he spoke to our local ACLU in Charleston and gave solid arguments for opposing capital punishment. Sanders later became a candidate for the US Senate in 2002, and his opponent Lindsay Graham relentlessly attacked him on that issue. When candidate Sanders was asked for his rationale, he said only that capital punishment is "contrary to the will of God."

A Religious and Secular Studies Major

"They can send me to college, but they can't make me think," bragged a bumper sticker in my hometown. Unfortunately, this is often true. Many students want courses where they can get good grades without being critically challenged. The religious studies program at the College of Charleston affords students "the opportunity to explore diverse cultures and religions, while providing them with important tools to understand and interpret these worldviews critically." Good, so far. Some students even come away confused when they learn about religions diametrically opposed to their own. Questioning previously unquestioned assumptions is an integral part of education, even (or especially) if students begin to question what they have been previously taught is the one "true" religion.

I've heard it said half-jokingly that the difference between philosophy and religion is that philosophy is questions without answers and religion is answers without questions. A *secular* studies program would raise questions and provide some answers. I'd like to see a religious studies major at universities, including my own, evolve into a "religious and secular studies" major. Any credible religious studies program that incorporates a variety of worldviews should also include a growing secular worldview.

It's not enough to teach students about all world religions and ignore the perspective of millions of people who live happily and find meaning in their life without appeals to supernatural forces. There is a rich and important history of atheism and humanism that has been around as long as theism, though this history is rarely acknowledged. And yes, I agree that atheism should be examined as critically as all religions in an academic setting.

The bottom line is that if students leave college with the same beliefs and perspectives they had when they entered, then they have mostly wasted four years and many dollars.

College of Charleston Times, They Are a-Changin'

The College of Charleston, founded in 1770, recently received more publicity than in its first 244 years. While I think almost all publicity is good, the "almost" might be applicable because of the two controversies. Each involved a choice, of a new president and a new book.

The Board of Trustees chose state Lieutenant Governor Glenn McConnell as college president, despite strong opposition by faculty and students. A long time defender of the Confederacy, McConnell fought to keep the Confederate flag atop the Capitol dome. While a state senator, his Confederate memorabilia store sold items that included Maurice Bessinger's barbeque sauce, which lots of shoppers and stores were boycotting because of Bessinger's biblically justified pro-slavery tracts, and toilet paper with the image of Union General William Tecumseh Sherman.

The controversial book was *Fun Home* by Alison Bechdel, which a committee of faculty, staff, administrators, and students had picked as an option for students to read and discuss. After the College sent copies to incoming students, legislators vociferously objected to the book because of its lesbian theme, and voted to remove $52,000 in funding for the college, the cost of the books.

The good news is that the Board of Trustees and Legislature unintentionally activated and united faculty and students as never before. When I first arrived on campus, faculty and students were mostly apathetic about governance and social issues. The college had integrated less than a decade earlier, but there wasn't much intermingling between blacks and whites. While Bob Dylan might have inspired a generation with his 1964 song, "The Times, They Are a-Changin'," they didn't much in South Carolina. But better late than never, and the times are finally changing in South Carolina—at least for young people.

Glenn McConnell was a College of Charleston student back in the 60s when it was a segregated institution and students weren't even protesting the Vietnam War. However, students organized and protested against McConnell and the attempted censoring of book selections by politicians with social agendas that conflict with academic freedom. I was moved by the most recent student demonstration and speeches against suppressing *Fun Home*, as a female African-American student led a mixed group of black and white, straight and gay students. What most surprised and pleased me was how comfortable these students were with one another, including interracial hugs. It's no longer their grandfather's College of Charleston.

Because of the publicity, *Fun Home* author Alison Bechdel and members of the original off-Broadway cast performed a special concert of the musical at the College of Charleston. There were enthusiastic, standing ovations not only for the quality of the performance, but also for the cast's extraordinary support of academic freedom at the College. Many progressive and engaged students are questioning the custom of continuing to believe and do what has always been believed and done. I hope some of them will one day enter South Carolina politics. They've seen an abundance of role models for how not to behave in office.

8

DARWIN, CHARLES

Should Darwin Get His Day?

February 12, 1809 must have seemed like an ordinary day, but it is the day that two giants of humanity were born: Abraham Lincoln and Charles Darwin. Lincoln ended slavery in the United States in the nineteenth century, and Darwin made the greatest scientific discovery of the nineteenth century. Religious leaders vilified both men.

Slaveholders had economic incentives to maintain their abominable institution, encouraged by the blessing of southern clergy and politicians who biblically justified the morality of human slavery. Rev. Richard Furman, from my hometown of Charleston, was the first president of the South Carolina Baptist Convention and founder of the university that bears his name. Said Furman, "The right of holding slaves is clearly established in the Holy Scriptures, both by precept and example." Added Jefferson Davis, president of the Confederate States of America, "Slavery was established by the decree of Almighty God. It is sanctioned in the Bible, in both testaments, from Genesis to Revelation."

Today Abraham Lincoln is revered for what he accomplished, and the humanist principle that it is morally wrong for one person to own another is no longer controversial. Charles Darwin, on the other hand, is far from universally respected in this country, where some religious authorities treat the Bible as a science book. We wouldn't have expected scientifically ignorant biblical writers who lived thousands of years ago to have described the theory of evolution (or DNA, or any discovery of modern science), and they didn't. What we do find in the Bible is a flat, unmoving earth at the center of a 6,000 year-old universe. The scientific theory of evolution conflicts with Genesis, and describes how natural selection can explain our existence without need of a divine creator.

There is a growing movement to publicly celebrate February 12 as Darwin Day. With encouragement from the American Humanist Association, Rep. Rush Holt (D-NJ) in 2012 introduced such a resolution in Congress. While I'm thrilled to see it introduced, I'm not optimistic about its passage. Moral issues are more easily understood than scientific issues, which is why so many Americans who reject slavery still cling to a worldview that includes "scientific" creationism. Celebrating Darwin Day on February 12 won't eliminate all ignorance of and disrespect for the scientific method, but it's a positive step. Perhaps it will lead to a more enlightened era when even religious conservatives accept evolution, just as they came to accept an earth that revolves around the sun.

Groundhog Day and Darwin Day: My Favorite Holidays

Several years ago, the math department at the College of Charleston hired an administrative specialist in January. On February 2, Groundhog Day, I excitedly told her that Punxsutawney Phil had seen his shadow, which meant six more weeks of winter. When she laughed, I feigned disappointment and said, "It's not nice to make fun of a person's religious beliefs. I'm from Pennsylvania, where some of us consider Groundhog Day the holiest day of the year." She then apologized profusely. Now that she knows me better, we annually joke about my "holy" day. This year, she even presented me with an autographed (paw print) picture of Phil on February 2.

I thought I had made up a new religion until learning that Groundhog Day is beginning to look a lot like Christmas, which was originally a December 25 pagan holiday. February 2 was also a pagan holiday, when people lit candles to banish dark spooks. Christians appropriated that date in the fifth century and named it Candlemas Day, when clergy would light and bless candles.

However, February 12 is far more consequential. A resolution was again introduced in Congress in January 2013 to recognize that Charles Darwin's birthday is a "worthy symbol on which to celebrate the achievements of reason, science, and the advancement of human knowledge." The resolution also warned that the "teaching of creationism in some public schools compromises the scientific and academic integrity of the United States' education system." Though the resolution had a record number of 13 co-sponsors, it didn't pass in part because some House Science Committee members are getting their "science" information from the Bible.

It has been unseasonably cold in the South, so I often hear comments about the "myth" of global warming. I'm tired of explaining that the science behind climate change is more complex than what the weather is doing in South Carolina. That's why I now respond to faith-based global warning deniers that it's cold because Punxsutawney Phil told us we would have six more weeks of winter.

Hey Biblical Literalists, Stop Disparaging Darwin

When young Charles Darwin set sail on the Beagle in 1831 he was a firm creationist, but changed his mind when he observed contrary evidence. Even though we are living at a time of important scientific discoveries, 42 percent of Americans believe God created humans in their present form fewer than 10,000 years ago—dogma promoted by scientifically ignorant biblical literalists who disparage Charles Darwin. The religious right has waged a long and somewhat successful media campaign to persuade the public that the theory of evolution is both scientifically and morally flawed, and should be taught alongside so-called scientific creationism (or in its dressed-up form, "intelligent design"). But science is not democratic. As Anatole France said, "If fifty million people say a foolish thing, it is still a foolish thing."

Religious forces have been trying to water down science education since before the time of Darwin. We regularly hear politicians propose "creation bills" that pressure schools to "teach the controversy," meaning to provide evidence for and against evolution. (We never hear protests against the theory of gravity, which is not as well established as the theory of evolution.) In response, atheists and scientifically minded theists are joining forces to promote science and educate communities about evolution. Both sides accept the theory of evolution, but dispute its implications. Christian evolutionists try to show the compatibility of evolution and Christianity, fearing that those forced to choose will dismiss evolution. Atheists, on the other hand, see evolution as incompatible with the idea that humans are a special creation by a supernatural being. The more we know about evolution, the more it becomes clear that living things, including humans, come about through a natural process, with no indication of or need for a benevolent creator.

When I was a youngster, public schools closed on Charles Darwin's birthday, though the official reason was to commemorate the birthday of Abraham Lincoln. Today, instead of closing schools on Darwin's birthday, I'd like to see it become a day for students to study and explore the great scientific discoveries that continue to spring from Darwin's work.

Theistic Evolution

Atheists and scientifically minded theists sometimes form uneasy alliances to convince people that they should accept evolution. Christian evolutionists try to show the compatibility of evolution and Christianity, not wanting Christians to dismiss evolution. Atheists tend to agree with religious fundamentalists that scientific naturalism is incompatible with belief in an intervening deity. I once debated Dr. Karl Giberson (physics professor and vice president of the BioLogos forum founded by Dr. Francis Collins of the Genome Project) on "Does science make belief in God harder or easier?"

I asked Dr. Giberson if God arranged for an asteroid to hit the earth and wipe out dinosaurs so humans could evolve 55 million years later. He acknowledged that if the universe were again set in motion, humans in our present form might never exist, but opined that the laws were fine-tuned enough so that there would be some form of intelligent creatures. A few Christians in the audience cringed at the thought that God's plan might have led to a chimpanzee Jesus coming to save other chimpanzees from sin. Giberson agreed with me that science has proven many biblical miracles to be false, but he said Christians should believe in the resurrection miracle because it's essential to Christianity. Hmm. That's not an easy position to hold.

9

DAWKINS, RICHARD

I first met Richard Dawkins at an Atheist Alliance Conference in 2005. We talked briefly about the Secular Coalition for America, an organization I had founded. It happened to be Richard's birthday, and he created a meme to donate $1,000 to our fledgling organization and help us hire the first lobbyist to represent our constituency in Congress. His generosity and inspiration for many others became the best birthday present I ever received, even though it wasn't even my birthday. Since that time we've had two onstage conversations with overflow audiences (for him, not for me). Dawkins also endorsed me for the US Senate when our South Carolina Senator Jim DeMint resigned, which turned me into the top candidate in an online poll, even ahead of native son Stephen Colbert.

Richard Dawkins Visits the Bible Belt
I was thrilled when Richard Dawkins agreed to speak at the College of Charleston. But instead of a typical lecture, he suggested a format I liked even more: a conversation with him on stage. Anticipating a big audience, I reserved the largest campus auditorium, which seats 500. As local and regional enthusiasm grew, we began to worry that the auditorium might not suffice. So we reserved two overflow rooms with a capacity of 100 each, where the event could be streamed. As it turned out, some people had traveled to the event from as far away as Virginia. It was to begin at 7 p.m., but by 5:30 the auditorium was filled, and by 6:00 both rooms had overflowed. We opened a third room, with the same result, leaving many sitting or standing in the aisles. Finally, we allowed people to sit on

the stage floor, a few feet away from where Dr. Dawkins and I would be conversing. Although we managed to accommodate about 1200, at least a couple hundred had to be turned away. Fortunately, our discussion is now on YouTube.

Richard and I walked on stage to a standing ovation. When the applause finally died down, I thanked the audience for applauding *me*, indicating that I understood for whom the applause was really intended. After we had talked for about fifty minutes, the next hour belonged to the audience. While there were Christians in the audience, none asked pointed questions. I hope they didn't feel intimidated by the hundreds of passionate atheists around them. Richard Dawkins is a rock star in the atheist movement, and it was gratifying to see such large, mostly young and enthusiastic crowds of atheists, confirming that it's not your grandfather's South Carolina anymore.

Later, as Dawkins and I sat together for book signings, I was moved when so many told him that reading his books had changed their lives. People were thrilled to shake his hand, to chat briefly, and to have a picture taken with him. Of course, many more people bought Dawkins' books than mine. When one person playfully asked how it feels to play second fiddle to Dawkins, I said: "It feels great. First, I get to play the fiddle. And second, I get to play it with Richard Dawkins!"

Dawkins had recently completed the first of a two-volume autobiography. Two years later I would be on stage again, this time in Clearwater, Florida to discuss his second volume. I was pleased when Richard offered to write the foreword to my one and only autobiography. When he asked me for advice on how to remain humble when writing an autobiography, I said that I had a great advantage over him because I had so much more to be humble about.

As I walked away from the auditorium, I overheard a student who had not been present ask a friend who Richard Dawkins is. The reply was most revealing: "Richard Dawkins is really famous, but he doesn't act like he is." So true, and March 9, 2013 was certainly a big night in the Bible Belt— thanks to Richard Dawkins.

Herb Silverman for US Senate
By Richard Dawkins

My friend, Professor Herb Silverman is no stranger to amiably tongue-in-cheek runs for public office (see his lovely autobiography, *Candidate Without a Prayer*). A few years ago he ran for governor of the Palmetto State for the sole purpose of testing the constitutional stipulation of the state that no person could be eligible for the office of governor who denied the existence of "the" Supreme Being. When asked what would be his first act, in the unlikely event of his being elected, he characteristically replied, "Demand a recount."

Now Silverman is again seeking high office. He is asking Governor Nikki Haley to appoint him senator for the state. Joking though he may be, he is extremely well qualified. His presence would constitute a significant increase in the average IQ of the Senate, and he is also a man of unusual good humor and goodwill, far outclassing many in that august body.

However, beyond the chuckle of Silverman beating satirist/television host Stephen Colbert, as well as established GOP politicians in an informal poll, the real issue—the real purpose of his campaign—is to challenge the presumption that an openly atheist candidate could never successfully run for high public office.

Polls consistently suggest that atheists are the least trusted group in America. This presumably stems from the bizarre prejudice that you need to believe in a ("the"?) supreme being in order to be moral. Really? Are we really so cynical as to think that, without the threat of divine retribution—or without the promise of divine reward—we are unlikely to be good, unlikely to behave generously, altruistically or morally towards our fellow creatures? Herb Silverman is one of the most moral men I have ever met—genuinely and disinterestedly moral, for he expects no celestial payback for his righteousness.

In any case, the remarkable vilification of atheists contrasts oddly with the fact that people with no religious affiliation (the "Nones") are the fastest growing segment of the American population, hugely outnumbering religious Jews, Muslims and most Christian denominations. It is time for Americans who have given up superstition—and all belief in supernatural spooks – to make themselves felt as a strong political force. The "nones" have plausibly been given credit for the re-election of President Obama, while those "nones" who are of a conservative bent seem to offer the best hope for the Republican Party to detox itself of the Tea Party poison and put the grand back in the "GOP."

Humor can sometimes offer the best approach to open dialog on sensitive issues, and this was the purpose of Silverman's write-in campaign. But he also offers a serious strike to the heart of an important issue that America must face: the fact that religious radicals, ignorant of science and all that is best and most cultivated in our civilization, have succeeded in creating a climate of bigotry towards the millions of decent, usually intelligent and well-educated Americans who live their lives peacefully, morally and honestly, without the need for any god.

Silverman Concedes US Senate Race

It is with a heavy (10.5-ounce) heart that I tell my millions of supporters I am ending my campaign to become the first acknowledged atheist to serve as a US senator from South Carolina. While I didn't hear from each of the sixty million people in this country without any god beliefs, I've heard from enough of them (and even some religious believers) to know how proud and surprised they would have been to see South Carolina take a leadership role in such political diversity.

Special thanks go to the over 3,700 people who voted for me in the straw poll conducted by the *Charleston City Paper*. That's 85 percent of votes cast, which shows an increasing awareness and political engagement by secular Americans. Charleston native Stephen Colbert, who announced his candidacy on national television, finished second in this poll.

Before Gov. Nikki Haley made her disappointing choice, there was a plan for the top two vote getters in the *Charleston City Paper* straw poll (Colbert and me) to engage in a senatorial debate on Colbert's TV show. Regrettably, I was the only one with such a plan. Colbert apparently chose to duck the debate because he knew he would have had little chance of winning. Here is how I would have framed my senatorial case on his show:

> Al Franken and Stephen Colbert are among my favorite comedians. Franken lost his sense of humor after becoming a US senator, and he hasn't been heard from since. Our country cannot afford to take such a risk with a national treasure like Stephen Colbert, so he needs to stay where he is. As senator, I promise not to fall off the humor cliff—as most politicians do. I will report to my constituents every week on C-SPAN television about the many weird things I see and hear from members of Congress. I might not be as funny as Stephen Colbert, but the C-SPAN humor bar is set so low that even a mathematician like me can clear it with ease. Finally, I hope to start a much-needed trend toward shorter

political speeches by dropping the standard cliché ending, "God bless you and God bless the United States of America."

Despite receiving an endorsement from renowned evolutionary biologist Richard Dawkins, Haley preferred the endorsement from former Senator Jim DeMint who wanted Tim Scott to replace him. DeMint, as senator, wanted public school students to be taught that God created earth and put Christians in charge of America. Unfortunately, Tim Scott in many ways is a "spiritual" heir to DeMint. This fiscal conservative once insisted on posting a Ten Commandments plaque in the Charleston County Council chambers despite being told he would lose any legal challenge. Scott argued that the display was needed to remind residents of moral absolutes. But when asked to name all Ten Commandments, Scott couldn't. The court, as expected, declared the display unconstitutional, handing taxpayers a substantial legal bill.

Scott barely edged out Ricardo Montalbán, who died in 2009, for third place in the *Charleston City Paper* straw poll in 2012. Had Governor Haley appointed Montalbán to the Senate, South Carolina would have made history by having the first officially dead senator in office. I'll not comment about our late Strom Thurmond, the only senator to reach 100 while in office.

Despite losing by only one vote (Haley's), I'll be a good sport and not demand a recount. And I won't mount a campaign to see either Haley's or Scott's birth certificate.

10
DEBATES AND DISCUSSIONS

How to Debate Christians:
Five Ways to Behave and Ten Questions to Answer

1. **Give the Bible due praise.** It's an important part of our culture. Post-debate, I also offer the audience a list of books with different perspectives.

2. **Respect the audience**. They're more likely to hear what we say when we address them respectfully. We want to reach open-minded Christians who have never heard an atheist's point of view from an atheist.

3. **Seek common ground**. Show how much we have in common.

4. **Use a conversational format**. This creates a more comfortable atmosphere than a competitive mood, even for audience questions. And it helps to show a sense of humor.

5. **Smile**. Make good points in a reasonable and pleasant manner. I emphasize "pleasant" because many in the audience are affected more by personality than by arguments.

1. **What's an atheist?** A person without a belief in any gods, nothing more.

2. **What's a Christian?** Most believe in salvation by faith through grace, that Jesus died for our sins, rose from the dead, appeared to some before ascending to heaven, and that people go to heaven or hell depending on such belief. Sometimes audience members argue with one another about what a true Christian is, and I'm fine with that.

3. **What about morality?** As a secular humanist, I believe that ethical values are derived from human needs and interests, and are tested and refined by experience. Deeds and compassion for others are more important than creeds and dogmas.

4. **Does God explain gaps in our knowledge?** Mysteries in nature have been considered acts of gods, but scientific discoveries have changed many supernatural beliefs, and will continue to do so.

5. **Why is science more reliable than religion?** Scientists go where evidence leads, and rely on experimenting, testing, and questioning until a consensus is reached. Unlike religious dogma, scientific views changes if new evidence appears.

6. **How can we distinguish the "right" religious beliefs from wrong ones?** Most stay with their family's religion. Religious belief is based more on geography than theology. The many conflicting religious beliefs can't all be right, but they can all be wrong.

7. **What about evidence for the resurrection of Jesus?** The only "evidence" is in a Bible written by people who had never met Jesus. Are you aware that after Jesus was resurrected he went to Missouri, where he will return? Christians skeptical of this resurrection story in the Book of Mormon will understand why I'm skeptical of theirs.

8. **Why do you hate religion?** I don't. I prefer religions that focus on improving the human condition, not on those that view this life as preparation for an afterlife.

9. **If there is no judging God, why be moral?** Personal responsibility is a good conservative principle. We should not give credit to a deity for our accomplishments or blame satanic forces when we behave badly. I try to be good for goodness' sake, not because of future rewards or punishment.

10. **What questions do you have for Christian believers?** Why does God give the "gift of faith" to some, but not all? Is belief more important than behavior?

Those who "feel" the presence of Jesus and regularly "see" his miracles will not be swayed by scientific evidence or biblical contradictions. But some Christians and atheists might get to know one another and find ways to cooperate on issues of importance to both communities. Whenever that happens, I consider it to be a win-win debate.

Science Versus Bible: To Debate or Not to Debate?

The atheist community is divided about creationism, but not on whether such a preposterous claim has any validity. They disagree on whether scientists should debate about the "science" of the Bible. Sharing a stage with creationists lends them credibility, but if we don't defend scientific theories, we lose the battle of public opinion. Many fundamentalists might benefit from hearing a scientific theory explained by a scientist.

On February 4, 2014 a debate between Ken Ham, founder of the Answers in Genesis Creation Museum in Kentucky, and Bill Nye, known as the "Science Guy," took place at the museum. I watched the "Ham on Nye" debate streamed live on the Internet at the College of Charleston, along with students that included members of the Secular Student Alliance. Students laughed at claims made by Ken Ham, and laughed even more when Bill Nye described the implications of Ham's young-earth biblical world.

Audience members weren't concerned about a scientist debating a creationist. They were entertained, viewing Nye as an intentional comedian and Ham as an unintentional comedian. Some learned more about evolution from Nye, and I hope some in Ham's flock also did. The debate losers were Christians who accept evolution and don't want to be stereotyped as believers in either Ken Ham or in Ham, a son of the fictional Noah.

Silverman's Wager

In debates or discussions about the existence of God, I'm often asked, "What if you're wrong and there is a God?" Such questioners assume that God belief is of ultimate importance, and are perhaps unknowingly applying Blaise Pascal's seventeenth century attempt to defend Christian belief with logic. In his *Pensées*, Pascal said, "If there is a God, he is infinitely incomprehensible, since, having neither parts nor limits, he has no affinity to us. We are then incapable of knowing either what he is or if he is." But Pascal's seriously flawed conclusion, that it's safer to believe in God, became known as

Pascal's Wager: If God does not exist, we will lose nothing by believing in him, but if God does exist we will lose everything by not believing.

First, Pascal assumes people can choose to believe in a god or a tooth fairy. Second, Pascal acknowledges we can't know anything about an incomprehensible deity, but he assumes a god who exists would reward believers with eternal bliss and punish nonbelievers with eternal damnation. Moreover, it would be a god who either could not distinguish between genuine and feigned belief or would simply reward hypocrites for pretending to have faith.

That is not the kind of god I could respect. Nor could Bertrand Russell who, like Pascal, was a mathematician and philosopher. Russell, an atheist, hypothesized a less-vain deity when he said, "And, if there were a God, I think it very unlikely that he would have such an uneasy vanity as to be offended by those who doubt his existence."

I agree with Pascal that no god is comprehensible. But suppose I posit the existence of a creator who wants to spend an eternity with a chosen few. What selection criteria would such a supreme being adopt? I expect this divine scientist would prefer a "personal relationship" with intelligent, honest, rational people who require evidence before holding a belief. Pascal undoubtedly would have agreed with me that our most promising math students ask provocative questions until convinced by rational arguments, while our dullest students mindlessly regurgitate what they think we want them to say. Wouldn't a supreme teacher concur? My kind of Supreme Being would favor eternal discourse with a Carl Sagan, not a Jerry Falwell. This brilliant designer would be appalled by those who profess and glorify blind faith. With that kind of deity in mind, I modestly make my own wager. It's almost a plagiarism of Pascal's, except that his last "not" appears earlier in the wager. But what a difference a "not" makes!

Silverman's Wager: If God does not exist, we lose nothing by *not* believing in him, but if God does exist we lose everything by believing.

Evangelizing: The Good, the Bad & the Ugly

I've been called an "evangelical atheist" because I enjoy discussing my worldview when opportunities arise. I was raised an Orthodox Jew, and Jews don't proselytize gentiles. But Jews do proselytize other Jews. In a Shabbos (Saturday) walk in Philadelphia with my rabbi, a man asked where the nearest subway was. My rabbi asked if he was Jewish, and the man said he was. My rabbi refused to tell him because Jews are not permitted to ride on the Sabbath. Such a response was consistent with our weekly wait outside the synagogue on Saturday morning until a gentile passed who would turn on the lights for us. There is no pretense that such rules have anything to do with ethical behavior. We were simply separating our tribe from the gentile tribe.

My first exposure to Christian evangelism was at a Billy Graham Crusade in the early 1960s. At the end, he invited people to come forward. So I did, out of curiosity. After Graham mumbled a few words about being "saved," waiting pastors each chose one of us to indoctrinate further.

My pastor asked if I had accepted Jesus into my life, to which I said no. Further attempts (fire and brimstone included) were met with similar frustration for him. When he found out I was Jewish, he transferred me to a pastor with a Jewish background. I asked Pastor Two if his parents were alive, which they weren't, and then asked how painful it was for him to know that they were suffering the torments of hell. When he disagreed, I suggested we invite Pastor One into our conversation. The highlight for me was watching them argue about the afterlife of Pastor Two's parents.

I know I'm in a distinct minority, but I decided after this experience that being evangelized could be fun. I've invited Jehovah's Witnesses into my house, frequently to their surprise. More often than not, they leave before I want them to.

I consider myself a counter-evangelist. I don't usually initiate discussions with religionists, but I enjoy having them. I counter-evangelize evangelists until either they or I see the discussion becoming counter-productive. There are many opportunities to make people aware of our position without trying to force it on them. For me, in a culture replete with religionists, engaging impassioned participants in a conversation they never had before is the best kind of (counter) evangelism. But silent evangelism might be the most effective approach for all of us. People are more likely to respect our worldview for what we do than for what we preach.

A Rose by Any Other Name

Joe, my best friend in the third grade, was left-handed. Our teacher repeatedly moved his pencil from his left hand to his right. Joe tried unsuccessfully to write right, but he then began to blink more frequently and develop a stutter. I was left with the impression that lefties were prone to other idiosyncrasies and deficiencies, and I was thankful to be a "normal" righty. Fortunately, this discrimination has ended. The only pejoratives left for "left" are its "gauche" and "sinister" synonyms. Left-handers are a minority. We are sometimes slow to recognize the difference between being different and being wrong.

There are similarities and differences between hand, sexual, and religious orientations. I would argue that being an atheist, just like being left-handed or gay, is more an orientation than a choice. My reasoning abilities, based on observation, experience, discussions, and reading, have left me with no choice. I can pretend to believe in a deity, but can't truly believe extraordinary claims backed by not a scintilla of evidence any more than I can change my skin color, sexual orientation, or handedness.

Since people are more accepting of differences based on nature than on choice, the above argument might convince some to be more tolerant of atheists. Yet I don't agree with this choice/orientation premise. Even if gays (or left-handers) had a choice, I would still treat them as I do straights (or right-handers) since I would see nothing inherently wrong with such a choice. If a genetic component were found for child molesting (or murder), such acts would and should remain illegal. Whether we are atheists by choice or orientation, we can make a case to the general public for why our worldview is reasonable.

Winning by Losing
Then there was the guy who interviewed at a radio station for a job as a broadcaster, but they hired someone else. A friend asked, "Why didn't you get the job?" The guy answered, "B-b-b because I-I'm a J-J-J Jew." Discrimination exists against many minorities but, to quote Sigmund Freud, "Sometimes a cigar is just a cigar." Crying "wolf" when there is none is the quickest way to lose credibility and damage a cause. For atheists, a more interesting option is when to cry "wolf" when there really is a wolf.

We can't fight every battle, but I want to suggest ways to take advantage of the "Law of Unintended Consequences," where an action results in an outcome other than what was intended. To plan for the unplanned sounds paradoxical, but having Plan A squashed can make Plan B more effective. There are opportunities to take the "moral" high ground on wedge issues, creating a win-win situation. We can ask for our rightful place at the table and either get it or get others to share our outrage if we are denied.

Here's a classic example. Of the many heroes in the civil rights movement of the 1960s, my surprise choice for the top ten is Birmingham police chief "Bull" Connor. His use of fire hoses and police attack dogs against unarmed, nonviolent protest marchers in 1963 was broadcast on national TV. This incident shocked and moved the entire nation, and led to the most far-reaching civil rights legislation in history, the Civil Rights Act of 1964. Bull Connor's tactics hastened the change he had been opposing. As atheists, we should look for serendipitous opportunities to expose religious "Bull Connors." This can inspire Christians to support the moral position of an atheist over that of fellow Christians. Movements are most successful when they appeal to folks outside the group.

Here's another example. I've been in a number of public debates with fundamentalist Christians, but one of the more interesting was with Dr. Richard Johnson, religion professor at Baptist-sponsored Charleston Southern University. After the debate, Johnson asked me if he could speak to the Atheist-Humanist Alliance, a student group at the College of Charleston where I was faculty advisor. I agreed, and he tried unsuccessfully to bring some of those students to Jesus. In the Q&A after his talk, a student asked Johnson if he would invite me to speak to his religion class. He agreed, and the date was set. However, the day before I was to speak, Johnson called to tell me that he had to rescind the invitation because of "complications," and that his administration did not want him to devote class time to my appearance. I immediately recognized this as an opportunity to win by losing.

I told the religion editor at the Charleston *Post and Courier* that a Christian professor at the Baptist institution had broken his promise of allowing me to speak at his university, after I had kept my promise of allowing him to speak at mine. The reporter's article quoted me, "I think it reflects poorly on an academic institution that allows only one point of view. Had the administration at the College of Charleston objected to Dr. Johnson speaking at my institution, I would have fought it and engaged others on campus to help keep academic freedom alive."

The Chair of the Religion Department at Charleston Southern University told the reporter that the invitation was rescinded because their "students had heard quite enough from Dr. Silverman recently." I asked what that meant, since I had never been allowed to speak on their campus.

The religion reporter wrote that the provost of Charleston Southern University declined to explain how not allowing Silverman to speak in Johnson's classroom fits in with CSU's vision of academic freedom. Johnson also declined to comment on the situation. I felt sorry that his university had put him in such an untenable and embarrassing position. This is a case where many Christians acknowledged that atheists acted more reasonably than did their Christian counterparts.

II

FAITH

Many people think faith is good, regardless of the faith. But well-meaning people have done irreparable harm by imposing their faith on children and others. Surveys show that religious people know less about the Bible than do atheists.

Neglect in the Name of Love
What should be done when parents rely on religion instead of medicine to heal sick children? We don't always have easy answers for where the parental rubber meets the child road. Some parents act irresponsibly in the name of love—and religion. The American Academy of Pediatrics calls corporal punishment harmful psychologically and physically, and an ineffective behavioral strategy. Nevertheless, parents justify such measures because the Bible says to spare the rod is to spoil the child.

How bad is bad enough for the government to step in? Since our secular government must be neutral regarding religion, what we deem parental abuse should be independent of whether that abuse is for religious or nonreligious reasons. Both motive and mental stability should be factors in determining whether the abuse constitutes a crime and what kind of punishment, if any, should be meted to a parent.

Some parents reject modern medicine and pray that their child be healed, believing all things possible through God. But we know serious illnesses are not healed through prayer, regardless of the sincerity of the prayers. Adults may use prayers, crystals, tarot-cards, or exorcists to cure themselves, but society must step in to prevent such "cures" as the only treatment for children with serious illnesses. Compassion for parents who love their children goes only so far. Perhaps this is an example of what Nobel Prize-winning Physicist Steven Weinberg meant when he said: "With or without religion, good people will do good things and bad people will do bad things. But for good people to do bad things—that takes religion."

In Defense of Snake Handlers

An easily affordable health care plan is offered in Mark 16:17–18: "These signs will follow believers: In my name they will cast out demons; they will speak in tongues; they will take up serpents; and if they drink anything deadly, it will not hurt them; they will lay their hands on the sick, and they will recover." (X-rated note: Adults only.) In reality, snakes are more effective in reducing over-population than in healing the sick. Kentucky Pastor Jamie Coots, who was also a reality TV star on "Snake Salvation," recently died after refusing treatment for a bite he received while handing snakes during a service. To paraphrase Matt 26:52: He who lives by the snake, dies by the snake.

Nonetheless, I side with the religious freedom of snake handlers who practice their religion without imposing it on those of us who live in the real world and decline to play with poisonous snakes. What I admire (sort of) about Coots is that he was no hypocrite. He died for his beliefs. Contrast that with televangelists who ask poor people for love offerings, financial or otherwise.

Ignorance and Faith

I'm not surprised by a recent survey that showed atheists and agnostic surpass all others in knowledge of religion. Most atheists gave careful consideration to religions before rejecting them. I'm reminded of a quote from Isaac Asimov, scientist and prolific author who wrote a comprehensive *Guide to the Bible*: "Properly read, the Bible is the most potent force for atheism ever conceived." The words "Properly read" were key for me as a child. Raised as a religious Jew, I was taught to read the Torah (Hebrew Bible) exclusively in Hebrew. When I began translating it into English, I understood that the God of the Bible couldn't exist, and probably neither could any other gods. At a Freedom Foundation address on December 22, 1952, President-elect Eisenhower said, "Our government has no sense unless it is founded on a deeply felt religious faith—and I don't care what it is." This endorsement of ignorance prevails today, when many consider a "person of faith" admirable, regardless of how little that person may know about his or anyone else's religion.

Obama, Prayer, and Reason

President Obama made some reasonable remarks at the National Prayer Breakfast on February 3, 2016 and at a mosque the day before: Respect the right of every American to practice his or her religion, overcome unfounded fears, and speak up when any religious group is unfairly targeted. However, Obama ignored the growing elephant in our country, those of us who have no need for prayers. Though he claimed to be inclusive, he said nothing about the millions of nonreligious Americans who call themselves atheists, agnostics, humanists, secularists, skeptics and "nones." We know that it's easy to be good without a belief in God—just as President Obama's own humanist mother was.

Another problem with Obama's speech was his claim that faith is the great cure for fear. To the contrary, there is abundant evidence that religious faith often creates fear, including fear of outsiders, of hell, and of people with other faiths or none. Better cures for fear are evidence, education, experience, knowledge, and rational thought.

When President Obama said at the prayer breakfast, "My faith tells me that I need not fear death, that acceptance of Christ promises everlasting life and the washing away of sins," I thought of the ISIS "soldiers" who also have no fear of death because they believe that their faith and brutal actions will bring them an everlasting life of bliss. I'm more comfortable with people who prefer to live long and productive lives.

There might be a positive takeaway from President Obama's overlooking secular Americans. He spoke at the mosque in part to support Muslims who might help counter extremist Islamic groups like ISIS. He spoke at the prayer breakfast about the need for people of all religious faiths to cooperate instead of fighting wars with each other. There is no fear of this kind of trouble from secular groups. We disagree with religious faiths, and sometimes with one another, but our weapons of choice are pens, not swords.

12

FOREIGN POLICY

Avoiding Armageddon

It's no coincidence that the Middle East, birthplace of the three monotheistic religions, is ground zero for nuclear worries. Many religious fanatics believe that the destruction of the infidel will bring either a better life or better afterlife. How to deter or stop? Here's what doesn't work: empty words and prayers. My wife tells our cat how beautiful and smart he is, after which I tell him he is ugly and stupid. The cat seems not to distinguish our comments because we treat him equally well. Just as with our cat, it doesn't matter whether we pray for nuclear disarmament or nuclear war. There is no *there* there.

We must seek common ground with religious moderates and humanists. There are enough of us who want to cooperate in making this life as good as it can be. Recently, I walked through a lovely new park, but my moment of peaceful bliss ended when I saw a prominent War Memorial. Wouldn't it be nice to erect a Peace Memorial?

Not only must we work for world peace, we must do so in peaceful ways. Though we can't put the genie back in the bottle, we can focus on making constructive what might also be destructive. Alfred Nobel, inventor of dynamite, offered a Peace Prize that bears his name. "Atoms for Peace" was the title of a speech delivered by President Eisenhower to the UN General Assembly in 1953, perhaps as a counter to the 1945 horrors that occurred in Hiroshima and Nagasaki. We must now avoid using atoms for war.

Theocracy: Always a Problem, Never a Solution

Football coach Vince Lombardi said, "Winning isn't everything; it's the *only* thing." I disagree, but a comparable and more apt slogan about Afghanistan could be, "Religion isn't part of the problem; it's the *only* problem." After 9/11, the US understandably wanted to bring the al-Qaeda perpetrators to justice and prevent such future attacks. Since the Taliban in Afghanistan were protecting their al-Qaeda guests, it was reasonable in 2001 to find and punish responsible parties.

But an occupying force has at most a brief period to be productive rather than counter-productive. Eight years of US military presence in Afghanistan has far exceeded that statute of limitations. I'm pessimistic about a positive outcome anywhere without a fundamental separation of religion from government. There has never been a theocracy that resulted in a decent standard of living for its citizens or where minorities were treated with tolerance and respect. And the more theocratic the country, the more severe has been the abuse. Islamic beliefs and practices of the Taliban are akin to Christianity during the five centuries of the Christian Inquisition. Religion can only be part of the solution when those with a god belief are motivated by their god to treat everyone with respect and dignity. That's not what we see in Afghanistan.

Secular Nation, Secular Military

The US is a secular nation with a secular military. Its personnel take an oath of allegiance to the Constitution, which prohibits religious tests for any public office. Military officers are representatives of the US government and should not tell subordinates that the only way to salvation is through Jesus Christ. Mikey Weinstein, President of the Military Religious Freedom Foundation, has documented many such incidents. Military personnel who deem their comrades to be religiously inferior should seek employment elsewhere—preferably in an occupation where the cohesion of a diverse community is not essential. Stressful situations can bring out the best and worst in people. We've seen an abundance of both in the military. We should disqualify anyone from active duty who acts as if our country is engaged in a holy war.

Honor Tillman, Not McChrystal

General Stanley McChrystal should have been dismissed in 2004 as head of Special Operations command in Afghanistan when he aided in the cover-up of Army Ranger Pat Tillman's death. Those in charge knew from the beginning that Tillman did not die in battle, but they perpetrated this myth to make the former football star a recruitment tool and poster boy for soldiers willing to sacrifice their lives while fighting the enemy.

Pat Tillman died from "friendly fire," one of my least favorite euphemisms. Here's what Lieutenant Colonel Ralph Kauzlarich, under whom Tillman was serving, said about the grieving family: "These people have a hard time letting it go. It may be because of their religious beliefs." He added, "When you die, there is supposedly a better life, right? Well, if you are an atheist and you don't believe in anything, if you die, what is there to go to? Nothing. You are worm dirt. So for their son to die for nothing and now he is no more… I do not know how an atheist thinks, I can only imagine that would be pretty tough."

Kauzlarich was never disciplined for his insensitive and hurtful remarks.

Welcome to Holy War Land

No country goes to war thinking its cause is unjust, but more wars are viewed as "just" going in than going out. We can't bring back the lives of those who died in an unjust war. In close calls, it's better to err on the side of a war not being "just" enough to enter. The number of "just" holy wars is zero. Holy wars give "war" a bad name.

The holiest of holy wars in Western "Civilization" were the Crusades, typified by the Cathar Wars in France. Abbot Arnaud Amaury, representative of the ironically named Pope Innocent III, was a military adviser during the Crusades. His troops succeeded in carrying out the Abbott's 1209 battle orders, "Kill them all. God will know His own." Amaury was rewarded in 1212 for his holy war service by being promoted to archbishop.

For those who believe that the one true God is on their side and that the other side are infidels, that the world is black and white without shades of gray, that this life is a dress rehearsal for an imagined afterlife, that you get extra eternal benefits for killing and being killed in the name of God, then welcome to Holy War Land.

Foreign Policy + Religion = Recipe for Disaster

When any country's foreign policy gets religion, disaster usually follows. What US foreign policy should get is secular. This involves learning about religious and cultural beliefs of people in countries where we are engaged so we can more effectively communicate with them. Then we can determine what changes are both beneficial and doable and at what cost, and develop rational strategies to accomplish a mission.

We started a war in Iraq after President George W. Bush consulted a "higher" father, rather than his "lower" father, the former Bush president, who likely would have advised against it. I'm not sure if George W. Bush's reference to the Iraq War as a "crusade" was a sign of cultural illiteracy or a core belief. Some government officials interpret freedom of religion as the right to proselytize for Christianity, which could very well be why many other cultures view us as imperialists.

Here are our dilemmas. We should not act as cultural imperialists, but we must not condone horrendous human rights violations perpetrated by religious leaders, either. We can't ignore religion when dealing with world conflicts (since that's often the cause); however, making religion an "integral" part of foreign policy is fraught with danger and difficulties. When it comes to engagement overseas, it makes sense to follow many of the policies that have worked well at home. We try to avoid entanglements between government and religious agencies in the United States, and such entanglements are even more problematic abroad.

Land for Peace

During a visit to California in the mid 1990s, I showed my gentile wife Sharon a side of Judaism she hadn't seen from this Jewish atheist. We went to a free dinner sponsored by Chabad-Lubavitch, an ultra-Orthodox sect. She was surprised that men and women dined at separate tables. After dinner we saw a short film honoring the recently departed Rebbe Schneerson, whose return as the messiah many attendees were hoping to witness soon.

The film showed Schneerson, a so-called humanitarian, telling his sect never to make territorial compromise in Israel. Afterward, I asked one of the leaders, "Would you be willing to cede a little territory if there were somehow 100 percent assurance that there would be peace in the land?" He looked at me as if he couldn't believe a Jew would ask such a strange question, and said, "How can we give away a gift God promised to us?" Ever since, I've been pessimistic about peace breaking out in the Middle East. Unfortunately, my pessimism has been more than justified.

War's Peace

Shortly after moving to South Carolina in 1976, I saw the 1915 American movie classic, *Birth of a Nation*, a horribly racist film that portrays Ku Klux Klan members as heroes. There is, however, a heartrending two-word caption in this silent movie that stayed with me. At the end of the Civil War, the camera pans thousands of graves. Then appear the simple words, "War's Peace." What a poignant antiwar statement.

We've seen "War's Peace" too many times in the world. A peaceful negotiation instead of war usually requires compromise. However, Jewish, Muslim, and Christian fundamentalists tend to espouse an uncompromising and absolute worldview. It's not surprising that there have been Middle East wars for millennia, since a god allegedly promised this territory to three different monotheistic religions. Were I a believer, I would pray for God to finally get out of the real estate business.

Consistent Values for an Inconsistent World

Is freedom a religious or secular idea? I looked through my Bible and other holy books, but I couldn't find much about "freedom" other than when to free slaves or release prisoners. I saw nothing about religious freedom, tolerance for other points of view, or anything close to what Thomas Jefferson said: "It does me no injury for my neighbor to say there are twenty gods or no God. It neither picks my pocket nor breaks my leg." The word "democracy" was nowhere to be found, but kings appointed by God were omnipresent and necessary to rule over people.

I don't mean to imply that secular leaders are always benevolent promoters of human rights. For me, the most difficult situations arise when the choices are between a secular dictator and a democratic revolution likely to bring rule by religious fundamentalists. One is bad and the other is worse, but it's not always clear which is bad and which is worse. This is especially problematic in the Middle East.

If we want to be respected throughout the world, we need to be consistent on values we promote: the inherent dignity and inalienable rights of all humans; justice and peace in the world; equal rights for men and women; freedom of thought, conscience and religion, including the right to change or even denounce religion. Authoritarian leaders seem impotent when confronted with the Internet gods. Information and knowledge can be a force for freedom and democracy, more powerful than any imagined deities.

War Is a Last Resort, Not an Olympic Sport

I don't rejoice at Osama bin Laden's death, but I'm relieved that he is dead. He can no longer mastermind or inspire the deaths of others. However, I cringe when I see people waving American flags as they cheer and shout USA! USA! War is a last resort, not an Olympic sport. Many of Osama's followers believe he was engaged in a holy war, died bravely as a martyr, and is now enjoying the fruits of heaven along with the first of his 72 virgins. But by some unlikely chance, had Osama repented of his nefarious deeds and become a born again Christian just before he died, many Christians would believe that Osama is now in heaven, comforted by the Blessed Virgin.

I don't care what ludicrous beliefs people have except when those beliefs cause harm to innocent people. Our goal should be to prevent more deaths overall, not to "win" by having more of their people die than our people. At some level, I grieve whenever a life is lost. I'm pleased with the success of the operation and that the brave troops who carried out the mission returned safely with minimal loss of life. While we might have had a good day, we won't have a great day until we achieve peace in all the countries where we are at war.

13

FOX NEWS

The War on Christmas: A Holiday Tradition for All

The much-ballyhooed "War on Christmas" has become a predictable holiday tradition, with Fox News as both director and producer of this manufactured war, presumably for better ratings. Comedians also love the war material they have to play with, so both Fox and comedians have become war profiteers.

Atheists, who are usually marginalized or ignored by media, use this seasonal opportunity to join the war by supporting diversity. Christmas for some atheists is a time to promote freedom of expression on billboards and buses. Atheists put up signs that say "Be good for goodness' sake" or "This season, celebrate reason," and Christians protest.

Now we have the Christian war on "Happy Holidays" (instead of "Merry Christmas"), which includes boycotting stores that use the more inclusive term. This is a war against religious diversity. There is also a war by Christians and others against the consumerism that permeates the season, a war that even atheists, myself included, sometimes support. Unfortunately, this war seems to have been won—by commercial interests.

The warring makes many Christians miserable instead of joyful, some even claiming to be a persecuted minority. This is like saying there is a war on white, heterosexual males because marginalized groups have finally gained rights they've long deserved. My favorite Christmas memories were during the Vietnam War. I had hoped that Christmas truces would feel so good that the killing would not resume. Sadly, we gave peace a chance only briefly, and Silent Night soon returned to bombing nights.

No, atheists didn't manufacture the "War on Christmas," so I would like to wish all of you a Happy Holiday, whichever and however you celebrate.

Reza Aslan Meets Experts on God

Fox News personality Lauren Green unintentionally helped Reza Aslan's book reach the top of bestseller lists when she repeatedly asked him why a Muslim would write about the "founder of Christianity." Aslan mentioned his scholarly credentials and research, from which he drew conclusions independent of his religious beliefs.

I must confess to a fantasy that Lauren Green interviews me about my book, and substitutes "atheist" for "Muslim" to discredit anything I say about Jesus. And here's my fantasy response: "Jesus was born and died a Jew, knowing nothing of Christianity. The Bible refers to him as king of the Jews, not king of the Christians. Perhaps my Jewish background makes me more qualified to talk about Jesus, a fellow Jew, than someone like you with a gentile background. Just as we're both skeptical when members of the American Nazi Party praise Adolph Hitler, we should also be skeptical when Christians make claims about an infallible Jesus while literally worshipping the ground he walked on. So shouldn't we also have reason to suspect your biased accounts?"

My Jewish upbringing neither qualifies nor disqualifies me from writing about Jesus, Hitler, or anyone else. It's fair to ask how any author's background or beliefs might have influenced his or her writings, but the focus should be on whether the author justifies assertions. Students at public universities are often surprised that courses on religion are not designed to strengthen their faith, as they are in Sunday school.

Green's Fox News bio mentions her degree in piano performance, but nothing about scholarly religious credentials. Fox adds that she was Miss Minnesota in 1984 and third runner-up in the 1985 Miss America contest. Gretchen Carlson, another Fox News personality, seems to have followed in the same high heels as Lauren Green. Carlson was Miss Minnesota in 1988 and went on to become Miss America.

Wait a minute. Am I doing to Green what she did to Aslan—focusing on background and beliefs in an attempt to discredit? After all, winning a beauty contest neither qualifies nor disqualifies anyone from pontificating about religion or interviewing religious scholars. Are my comments about Green relevant? As Fox News is fond of saying, "We report, you decide."

Honest and Dishonest Bias

Though most of us have biases, not all biases are created equal. There are degrees of honest biases, and there are clearly dishonest biases. The most common kind of honest bias is Confirmation Bias: "The tendency to selectively search for and consider information that confirms your beliefs, and ignore or discount evidence that refutes your beliefs." We usually recognize at some level when we are being biased, but we genuinely believe our position is correct and try to make a strong case for it.

Perhaps a more honest and naïve bias is what I'll call Magic Bias: "The belief that supernatural forces intervene in our natural world." Magic bias includes belief in gods, demons, horoscopes, psychics, tarot cards, miracles, and lots of other superstitions. People who accept some of these beliefs usually consider other magic beliefs ridiculous. I'm with "ridiculous."

A third kind of honest bias occurs among people who are ignorant of essential facts. For instance, some believe that our founders intended America to be a Christian nation under a Constitution that favors Christianity over other religions, and guarantees freedom of religion but not freedom from religion. They are honestly wrong.

My "Dishonest Bias Award" goes to Todd Starnes, host of *Fox News & Commentary*, for his 2013 piece titled, "American Humanist Association Sues Teacher Who Prayed for Sick Student." It's the dishonest bias with which I'm most familiar because I'm a member of the American Humanist Association (AHA) Board of Directors. Starnes claimed that the AHA said it was unconstitutional for a Christian club to meet before the start of the school day, and accused the teacher of owning a Bible. He closed his commentary with, "This over-the-top attack on Christianity is just unbelievable. Then again, what do you expect from a bunch of humanists who don't believe in anything that really matters?"

The AHA press release presented the facts, which have nothing in common with Fox's report. AHA objections included weekly Christian "devotional" prayer sessions led by a teacher in her public school classroom during school hours, in which the teacher told students that God will punish them if they are not good; morning announcements by the principal over the school's public address system promoting the prayer sessions; and a prominent display of the book *God's Game Plan* in a classroom during class time.

The AHA sent a letter to the school administration outlining why school-sponsored and school-promoted classroom prayers are unconstitutional, but school officials ignored the letter. Fox News never bothered to contact the AHA for comment, or even link to the AHA press release. Had it done so, the folks at Fox News might at least have been true to its motto, "We report, you decide."

14

FREE SPEECH

Reasonable Speech

I agree with your editorial that the Charleston Board of Architectural Review should allow Rev. Parks to display his sign about Jesus's warning that September 11 was a wake-up call. However, I disagree with your purpose: "No local law can infringe on reasonable religious expression." My problem is with the word "reasonable." One person's reasonable speech is another's outrageous or heretical speech. I hope you would also defend the right to display a sign that said "Man created God," which I think is far more reasonable than the sign by Parks. The First Amendment does not restrict us to reasonable or popular speech. Nor is the right of religious expression any more precious than the right of political expression. I hope the editorial was not implying, to paraphrase George Orwell, "All speech is free, but some speech is more free than others."

Bad Neighbors

Jack Hunter claims that Christianity is part of South Carolina culture, so those outside the mainstream should accept state government favoritism and sponsorship in the form of Christian-themed license plates. Apparently, Hunter doesn't understand the difference between individuals expressing cultural views and government favoring a religion. The former is free speech protected by the Constitution, while the latter is an endorsement prohibited by the Constitution. We are free to express our beliefs, but we must not expect or allow the government to approve or disapprove of religious messages.

Hunter closes by calling someone like me who opposes government sponsorship of Christianity a "bad neighbor." I have neighbors who hang signs or promote causes I oppose, but they are not bad neighbors. A good neighbor does not try to impose beliefs on others or seek government assistance to do so.

Everybody's a Blasphemer

Under a new law in Ireland, a person can be found guilty of blasphemy if "he or she publishes or utters matter that is grossly abusive or insulting in relation to matters held sacred by any religion, thereby causing outrage among a substantial number of the adherents of that religion." Here's a paradox: religious believers may be required to blaspheme against other religions. Christians blaspheme against Jews when they recite Mathew 27:25: "The blood of Jesus will be on all Jews and on their children." Jews who read the First Commandment, "You should not have any gods but Yahweh," are blaspheming against those who promote Jesus, Allah, or any of the other 7,000 gods.

Blasphemy has little to do with what you say, and lots to do with whether others feel so insulted that they want you silenced and punished. It's acceptable to call atheists fools, as in Psalm 14:1: "The fool hath said in his heart, there is no God." Atheists don't insist on the right not to be insulted, just on the right to be treated as others. Many religions sprang from blaspheming other religions, from questioning or criticizing the "sacred." And if I said that blasphemy shouldn't be punished because it's a victimless crime, well that, too, could be considered blasphemous.

Free Speech Trumps Firearms

To paraphrase George Orwell, "All amendments are equal, but some amendments are more equal than others." For me, the First Amendment right to free speech is a lot more equal than the Second Amendment right to bear arms. I deplore the incendiary political language of Sarah Palin, Rush Limbaugh, and Glenn Beck, but I defend their right to use it. Without the millions of Americans who enjoy listening to these blowhards, they would become inconsequential. The best counter to bad speech is good speech, and I hope the public will reward those who want to change the uncivil political climate in this country.

Mentally disturbed people will do disturbing things, and I don't hold politicians or pundits directly responsible for the tragic shootings in Arizona of Congresswoman Gabriel Giffords and others. I don't oppose an action simply because it has the potential to incite. I admire brave civil rights advocates who marched in the South in the 1960s, knowing that their actions might lead to violence. We should not avoid criticizing religion because of threats of violence, as occurred with Danish cartoonists who drew the Islamic prophet Muhammad. The pen and the voice should be mightier than the sword; in an ideal world, we wouldn't need swords.

This brings me to the Second Amendment. In South Carolina, struggling to fund public education and Medicaid, legislators passed a law creating an annual tax-free holiday specifically for gun purchases. Why is anyone surprised when mentally ill and angry people use guns to kill? We had a ban on assault weapons from 1994 to 2004, which would have made it illegal and difficult for Jared Loughner to obtain the kind of extended clips to fire so many shots outside that supermarket in Tucson. The ban was lifted because of three powerful letters—NRA. Politicians fear the NRA's ability to mobilize one-issue voters who view any gun restrictions as unpatriotic. It's patriotic for those of us who want more gun restrictions and rational discourse to exercise our free speech rights in the public arena and at the ballot box. In fact, I would say it's our duty.

In Support of Draw Muhammad Day

There's an inspiring legend about Danes during World War II. When Germans ordered Jews to wear yellow stars, the king of Denmark and other non-Jewish Danes thwarted the order by doing likewise. (Unfortunately, I've recently heard that the legend is false, though its valuable lesson remains.)

Some 70 years after Nazis occupied Denmark, a Muslim group threatened violence to prohibit freedom of expression. In response, there was a call to make May 20 "Draw Muhammad Day." I have no interest in drawing Muhammad, but I support the idea of joining others to stop injustice. I was raised an Orthodox Jew, which took seriously the Second Commandment about not having graven images. Though I think it's a silly prohibition, there is a significant difference. Such Jews don't draw, but they don't prevent others from drawing. Religious belief moves from irrelevant to evil when belief inspires harm to those who don't share the belief.

Freedom to Hate

I think crimes motivated by hatred of the victim's sexual orientation should be treated no differently than crimes motivated by rage or anything else. I don't want to hold the accused guilty of having an opinion. We have the right to hate, but not to commit crimes.

A crime is a crime, regardless of the victim's race, color, religion, national origin or sexual orientation. A murdered white heterosexual male is no less dead than a Hispanic, gay Christian. Suppose three murders occur: one for money, another out of jealousy, and a third because the victim is a black, gay Wiccan. If the third murderer is given a longer sentence than the first two, I don't consider this to be equal justice under the law.

I'm somewhat conflicted, because I support laws that prohibit discrimination. A hotel owner should not be allowed to deny accommodation to blacks, women, or gays, even if the owner claims a faith exemption. A more serious problem in criminal cases is that race, color, religion, or sexual orientation may sway a jury. For example, an atheist who refuses to swear an oath with his hand on the Bible would undoubtedly prejudice some on the jury. I don't see what we can do about such legal injustices, other than to use our free speech right to dissuade those who discriminate.

We Have a Religious Right to Be a Bigot

"In Indiana, Using Religion as a Cover for Bigotry" was the title of an editorial in the *New York Times* on March 31. It reminded me of a line by Captain Renault in the movie *Casablanca* as he accepted a bribe: "I'm shocked, shocked to learn that gambling is going on in here." I'm also reminded of lyrics in "National Brotherhood Week," Tom Lehrer's satirical song: "The Protestants hate the Catholics, and the Catholics hate the Protestants, and the Hindus hate the Muslims, and everybody hates the Jews." Conclusion: Religious bigotry is as old as religion, itself. We have the right to hate anyone, but not the right to commit crimes. It's OK to hate gays, but not to kill them. Perhaps that's why Bob Jones III, former president of fundamentalist Christian Bob Jones University in my home state of South Carolina, recently apologized for his 1980 remark that we should follow the biblical injunction of stoning gays to death.

Religions may make rules about whether to sanction same sex or mixed race marriages, whether women are permitted to sit next to men in their houses of worship, who to shun for not appropriately following rituals or doctrine, and who to excommunicate. But religions may not impose their views on others. If the only argument for a public policy is that a person's religious doctrine says it's bad, why should such a policy apply to everyone? We are a secular country with secular laws that apply to all citizens.

Equal treatment under the law is not a radical idea. Same-sex couples should have the same rights, benefits, and protections as opposite-sex couples. Those who wish to make civil laws compatible with a particular interpretation of a so-called holy book might think about moving to one of the many theocratic countries.

Bad/Good Teachers

My best and most influential teacher was someone I once considered the worst. Dr. Hamm was my English teacher in my senior year of high school, and also our class advisor who wanted us to demonstrate school spirit. So he declared that our graduating class would wear a tie each Friday. When I came to school tieless, Dr. Hamm asked me to sit in the back and write an essay explaining my behavior. I incorporated in my essay some unsolicited advice from another student. I began, "This jerk sitting next to me just told me to write that I forgot the tie. Well, I didn't." I then explained how "team spirit," if it was important, which I didn't think it was, couldn't be forced.

The following Friday, I again came without a tie and Dr. Hamm said nothing. He didn't admit I was right, but the Friday tie seemed to turn from a requirement to a request.

This incident must have been significant since I remember it many years later, but we had another conversation that changed my life. He asked all seniors to write short essays, and he would choose the best three to be read at graduation. I wasn't surprised that he didn't choose my essay. As I was leaving class, Dr. Hamm told me to go to his office after school. I assumed he wanted to tell me how furious he was by my essay. When I got to his office, he closed the door and said, "I wish I had the courage to choose your essay. You see, I'm in a responsible position, and you're not. I hope someday, when you are in a responsible position, that you will have the courage to do the kinds of things I don't do."

Dr. Hamm's remarks both angered and elated me. My first thought was about his being a coward. My second thought was about his liking my essay. My third thought, which should have been my first, was that I had just talked to a very special teacher. He was my first teacher who had been honest enough to admit his foibles and regrets. He was also confident that I would someday be in a responsible position, something I had doubted about myself. I made up my mind that whenever future conflicts arose for me between respectability and self-respect, I would opt for the latter.

Before giving you my rejected essay, a little background is in order. It was 1959, during the Eisenhower years, and I was at an all-academic public high school for boys in Philadelphia. What follows would not be nearly as shocking or as original today, though it would likely still be rejected at most graduation ceremonies.

Words are neither clean nor dirty. I still believe one of the sayings I learned in kindergarten, "Sticks and stones may break my bones, but words will never hurt me." Morality should be based on how we treat each other, not on our choice of words. What is so wrong with saying the word "fuck" in public? For those who do not know its meaning, there can be no harm. For those who know that "fuck" is a synonym for "sexual intercourse," why is one term acceptable and the other not? Why are we not allowed to see people fuck (or, if you prefer, have sexual intercourse) on television or in the movies? Are we afraid that this will inspire others to do likewise? On the other hand, we can see plenty of violence and killing on television and in the movies. For my part, when children grow up I would rather that they fuck than kill.

15

GODLY PATRIOTISM

General

Patriotism, Religion, Obama
Some Republicans continually ask if President Obama is a Christian and a patriot who loves his country. I'm more interested in why people ask these questions, and how their answers ("No" or "I don't know") reveal more about the questioners than about Obama. In the movie *Head of State*, Chris Rock ran for President against a flag-waving patriot who ended all speeches with "God bless America, and nowhere else!" I can no longer hear "God bless America" from a politician without thinking of that three-word ending. Many Americans want all countries to emulate America, but create considerable barriers to people desperately seeking a better life here. That President Obama is viewed as soft on immigration is another reason some think he is unpatriotic and doesn't love America. Perhaps they would like to see the phrase on the Statue of Liberty changed to: Keep your tired, your poor, your huddled masses yearning to breathe free.

Is President Obama a Christian, and Does It Matter?
My answer about whether President Obama is a Christian is the same as for most politicians: "I don't know." I can take professions of faith at face value or hypothesize that they are making a political calculation by publicly embracing Christianity. I'm probably more skeptical than most Republicans about whether Obama is a Christian. He had an atheist father and was raised by a secular humanist mother whose values he embraced. He became a Christian when he ran for public office.

However, why does this matter? We elect a president who will be Commander-in-Chief, not Pastor-in-Chief. I hope she or he will base decisions on good secular arguments, not faith-based beliefs. One of my favorite political quotes comes from Jamie Raskin, Maryland State Senator and law professor, who testified at a Maryland State Senate hearing in 2006 about gay marriage. At the end, Republican State Senator Nancy Jacobs said, "Mr. Raskin, my Bible says marriage is only between a man and a woman. What do you have to say about that?" Raskin replied, "Senator, when you took your oath of office, you placed your hand on the Bible and swore to uphold the Constitution. You did not place your hand on the Constitution and swear to uphold the Bible."

Do the Right Thing
During President Obama's first trip to India, he chose not to visit a Sikh Golden Temple because it required a head covering that his advisors feared would fuel speculation about his faith. Nearly 20 percent of Americans believe the president is a Muslim. My advice to President Obama about where to visit and what to wear is similar to my advice on policy issues: Do what you think is right. If Obama wants people to believe he is a Christian, he should bring back his old pastor, the Rev. Jeremiah Wright. Some Obama haters will then move from Obama being a Muslim to Obama being the wrong kind of Christian. Of course, a few will find a way to double hate, calling Rev. Wright a secret Muslim.

With so much support for Obama being a Muslim, here is my case for Obama being a Jew. Rabbi Capers Funnye, in an Ethiopian Hebrew Congregation of Chicago, is known as "Obama's rabbi" because he is Michelle Obama's first cousin. Perhaps Obama's "real" birth certificate would show that he was born "Baruch Hayeem Obamawitz."

I think I've just presented enough evidence for Obama's Judaism to qualify me as a Tea Party organizer or a radio talk-show host.

Herb Tea Party
I checked the Tea Party positions and liked what I saw. They want to protect marriage, champion life, strengthen the military, limit government, control spending, and defend our freedoms. Me, too, and here's how I would do it.

Protect marriage: Allow people to marry, whether someone of the same or opposite sex.

Champion life: I oppose capital punishment.

Strengthen the military: War should be for defensive purposes only, never preemptive.

Limit government, control spending: Legalize all drugs. Violence would be significantly decreased, and we wouldn't waste so much taxpayer money on prisons. For similar reasons, legalize gambling and prostitution.

Defend our freedoms: To promote religious liberty, we need a high wall that separates religion and government, where people can practice or not practice without government interference or support.

But just as I was about to sign up with the Tea Party, I read their program more carefully and learned that they oppose what I support and support what I oppose. They definitely are not my cup of tea. So I'm toying with the idea of starting my own political party and naming it after myself: the *Herb Tea Party*. I would welcome all freedom-loving promoters of religious liberty, even coffee drinkers.

Exceptional Arrogance

I agree with Sarah Palin and Newt Gingrich (in a rather roundabout way) that America was formed as an exceptional nation because of a special relationship with God. Our founders wanted no part of the religious intolerance and bloodshed they saw in Europe, and wisely established the first government in history to separate religion and government. They understood the devastating nature of holy wars and formed a secular nation with no deity mentioned in the Constitution. The special relationship America has with God is God's complete absence in our founding document.

"Exceptional" does not mean "perfect," which is why I appreciate those who help improve our flawed country. Unfortunately, many politicians are exceptionally proud of their purposeful scientific ignorance on climate change, evolution, and whatever else conflicts with their holy books or displeases constituencies. Bragging about God blessing America is less impressive than working together to improve American life for everyone.

Under God

The Right to Blaspheme: For No God and Country

I could not have had a more patriotic beginning, or so I was taught to believe. I was born on Flag Day (June 14) in 1942, during World War II, at Liberty Hospital in Philadelphia, birthplace of the nation and the flag purportedly designed by Betsy Ross. On my twelfth birthday, President Eisenhower signed into law the addition of "under God" to the Pledge of Allegiance, saying, "From this day forward, the millions of our schoolchildren will daily proclaim in every city and town, every village and rural schoolhouse, the dedication of our nation and our people to the Almighty." Eisenhower made no mention of the Constitution, perhaps because it prohibits religious tests for public office.

This melding of God and country turned a secular pledge into a religious one, causing me to feel less patriotic when I no longer believed in God. The Pledge is not simply a passive reference to religion. It calls on every child in public school to affirm that our country believes in God. No child should go to school each day and have the class declare that she and her family are less patriotic than God-believers.

Though we tend to view our nation's founders as role models, we act more like them when we question the old order and try to improve it. Criticizing our country and working to eliminate faults is definitely patriotic—a lot more so than reciting pledges and prayers or waving flags. Patriotism for me includes criticizing public policies that need improvement, and living in a country where we are free to say and do unpopular things. I agree with the Supreme Court decision that the First Amendment allows flag burning as a protected form of political expression. Some believe burning the American flag is a form of blasphemy because it takes a symbol revered as sacred and desecrates it. That's why such acts should be protected, just as blasphemy is protected speech in a free country.

I recently enjoyed watching a patriotic 1939 cartoon starring none other than Porky Pig. The cartoon shows him saluting the American flag while reciting the original "one nation, indivisible" version of the Pledge of Allegiance. I consider it my patriotic duty to advocate for and support others who are working to restore the original pledge in a country that takes pride in recognizing freedom of conscience for all people.

Nothing Says "Divisible" Like "Under God"
As a baseball-loving elementary school student in the early 1950s, two apparently unrelated changes became part of my daily life. The Cincinnati Reds became the Redlegs and "under God" was added to the Pledge of Allegiance. Actually, they were related—to the fear of Communism. Both the Cincinnati team and the Soviet Union were "Reds," and we didn't want anyone in 1953 to believe participants in our national pastime could be card-carrying members of the Communist Party. It's a wonder we didn't remove a color and give two cheers for a new version of "Old Glory" in just white and blue. But by 1959 our national chromatic fears had diminished, so the team once again became the Cincinnati Reds, their original name when they joined the National League in 1876.

Besides being red, the Soviet Union was also godless. So in 1954 our politicians added "under God" to the "one nation, indivisible" Pledge of Allegiance, which was originally written in 1892, only two years after the Reds entered the National League. And we turned our unifying and inclusive secular pledge into a divisive and exclusive religious pledge that public school students are expected to recite every day.

Here my analogy ends. Professional baseball teams are private, and it's not the government's business what a team calls itself. The Reds changed their name for a silly reason and wisely returned to their traditional name. On the other hand, public schools are *not* private. The government cannot tell us we are one nation under God any more than it can tell us we are one nation under no gods.

"Under God" Is Not All That Needs to Change About the Pledge
The words "under God" added to the Pledge of Allegiance in 1954 didn't mean much to me when I was 12. Like most students, I mindlessly recited the Pledge. At the end of the public school day, I attended Hebrew school where I mindlessly recited prayers. The altered pledge just made it seem more like my Hebrew prayers.

Fortunately, not everything in public and Hebrew school was done by rote. A few good teachers in each inspired me to think about concepts and ask questions—a welcome transition from indoctrination to education. Public schools train students to say the pledge whether they understand it or not, because daily regurgitation is supposedly patriotic. That strategy succeeds if patriotism means following orders of those in power, equating patriotism with God belief, and implying that atheists can't be patriotic.

Here's how I would like to see public school teachers turn the Pledge of Allegiance into a meaningful patriotic exercise. First, assign each student to write a short essay on one of ten segments in the Pledge. For example:

1. **I pledge allegiance** (What does it mean to pledge, and what is allegiance?)

2. **To the flag** (Why to a flag? Should it be to someone or something else?)

3. **Of the United States of America** (How united are we, and what is America?)

4. **And to the republic for which it stands** (What's a republic, and why are we one?)

5. **One nation** (In what sense are we one nation?)

6. **Under God** (Are we all under God, under the same God, and the only such nation?)

7. **Indivisible** (How are we indivisible, and what might divide us?)

8. **With liberty** (What does it mean to have liberty?)

9. **And justice** (Do we all have equal access to it, and does it ever conflict with liberty?)

10. **For all** (Does that mean all people or only American citizens?)

Next, have students read their essays, followed by class discussions. Encourage each student to rewrite the pledge in a way that is more meaningful to him or her. Instead of daily group recitation, the class can discuss different student pledges. One thing for sure is that students would learn and understand the Pledge of Allegiance better than previous generations have, whether "under God" or not.

16

HEALTH CARE

Health Care a Priority, Not a Product

"If God had decreed from all eternity that a certain person should die of smallpox, it would be a frightful sin to avoid and annul that decree by the trick of vaccination." So said Timothy Dwight, president of Yale University from 1795 to 1817. He was speaking passionately against Edward Jenner's new medical invention called vaccination. Many religious leaders also denounced vaccination and inoculation, even though they were highly effective. Fundamentalists today will not say that God changed His mind. Most will find a different interpretation or verse, ignoring contradictory verses.

A controversy today is whether God condemns those who don't apply technology to extend lives of brain-dead people. Witness the multi-year political and legal struggles to remove a feeding tube from Terri Schiavo, a woman in an irreversible persistent vegetative state. We need to reconsider devoting most of our resources to the last few months of life, while many of our young never have the opportunity to grow old because they lack financial means for adequate health care. If medical experts agree on an irreversible loss of meaningful quality of life, I would put no more public money into it. Re-allocation of resources can transform a few extended weeks of life into a combined hundred years for several young people. Call it, if you will, rational rationing.

I find it odd that those who expect eternal bliss in an afterlife are so unwilling to let go of this life. It seems they want to go to heaven without dying. Atheists are more likely than religious fundamentalists to have end-of-life directives. For many atheists, "immortality" will be through organ donations and a will that benefits worthwhile causes. I don't know what the best heath care system should be, but I hope we come up with one where the poor, even if they will always be with us, are provided with decent health care.

Quality of Life Panels

A few years ago, there was a license plate war in my home state of South Carolina. The legislature wanted to authorize the department of motor vehicles to distribute plates with the antiabortion motto "Choose Life." When Planned Parenthood objected, a state representative from my county suggested that they sponsor a "Choose Death" plate. When it comes to end-of-life decisions, choosing death can sometimes be a good option. Such controversies didn't exist 1,000 years ago, when most believed the terminally ill were in "God's hands." With scientific breakthroughs, they are often in technology's hands, and it's up to humans to decide the extent to which that technology should be used. For me, the bottom line is about quality of life, not just length of life.

Spare Rods, Not Vaccines

There are religious reasons to decline a vaccine, there are valid reasons to decline a vaccine, but there are no valid religious reasons to decline a vaccine. An adult should have maximum decision-making freedom on issues that involve him or her, alone. However, since viruses are contagious, ethical considerations demand taking into account how declining a vaccine may affect others. Society has a special duty to protect children from abuse and physical harm, without regard to religious motivation. If a child dies from a burst appendix because parents neglected to seek effective and proven medical care, it makes no difference whether the parents preferred instead to pray or watch television. I don't doubt the sincerity and concerns of most religious parents, but abuse is still abuse. Children have died because a rod was *not* spared and because a vaccine *was* spared.

Separation of Church and Health

I feel the same about separation of church and health as I do about separation of church and state. Government money must be used for secular purposes. Church-related hospitals that don't receive public funds may make medical decisions for informed adults based on the advice of church leaders, but must not impose medical restrictions on uninformed patients. Unfortunately, there are communities with only one hospital, and it embraces religious restrictions on the quality health care a patient needs and deserves.

Our government tries to assure that nobody is denied emergency health care for financial reasons, and it should also assure that nobody be denied secular health care because of the hospital owner's religious beliefs. If hospitals don't publicize what they offer (or refuse to offer), patients probably won't know. I'd like to see some truth in advertising, where hospitals are required to prominently display religious restrictions. Perhaps we would see signs like "We are more likely to pray over you than give you a blood transfusion" or "Exorcism is among our psychiatric services" or "Our sexual advice comes from celibate priests."

Banning Circumcision Won't Change Reality for Children

A ban on male circumcision would outrage both Jews and Muslims who might even cooperate to oppose it. If cooperation starts with a piece, perhaps it will lead to peace. I oppose medically unnecessary operations, including circumcision, but a ban would bring more medical problems because the procedure would be performed underground by less qualified cutters. We rightly reversed an unenforceable ban on alcohol, but we haven't reversed the War on Drugs, started in 1971 by President Nixon, which has been as ineffective as alcohol prohibition. I prefer education to bans.

Were there strong medical evidence that circumcision caused considerable harm to boys, I would favor a ban. But I think circumcision is further from child abuse than current, perfectly legal procedures initiated by parents—like teaching children religious fairy tales as fact, and shielding them from evidence-based material that includes evolution and comprehensive sex education. That's where I worry more about the thin line between religious freedom and child abuse.

Religion and Health

If I believed in the existence of a god, I'd be tempted to say it was her sense of humor that inspired your paper to follow an article on the purported beneficial effects of religion on health with an article on the placebo effect in healing. Rather than attribute health benefits to divine intercession, it makes more sense to realize that friendship and advice on healthy lifestyles often accompany membership in a church, just as I expect many of my health benefits can be attributed to the camaraderie I enjoy with my Sunday morning runners' group, my monthly Secular Humanist meetings, and a loving wife.

17

HOLIDAYS, WAR, AND PEACE

Holiday Wars

Be Good, Accept Diversity, and Strive for Peace

Christmas has not *recently* become too secular. Christmas officially became a secular holiday on June 28, 1870 when President Ulysses S. Grant declared December 25 a legal holiday, along with January 1, July 4, and a day to be determined for Thanksgiving. Just so there is no doubt about President Grant's intent, in his seventh annual message to Congress on December 7, 1875, he said, "Declare church and state forever separate and distinct; but each free within their proper spheres."

Individuals may focus on whomever they view as the reason for the season: Santa, Rudolph, Jesus? My preference is a Santa who wants us to be good for goodness' sake, without fear of eternal punishment for not believing in him. From Rudolph we learn that it's OK to be different, and to stand proud even if others laugh at you. And though Jesus primarily wants us to give glory to God, I like that he also promotes peace on earth and goodwill toward men.

What a wonderful world we would have in any season if we followed these three lessons: be good, accept diversity, and strive for peace. I wish this holiday season would bring us closer to such important secular principles. Unfortunately, the Christmas season has become increasingly divisive. A manufactured "War on Christmas" by some Christians now forces people to choose between wishing a "Merry Christmas" or "Happy Holidays." It's ironic that some people boycott stores that wish customers "Happy Holidays," implying that the true meaning of Christmas for religious people must be "shopping."

Being Nice

One and a half cheers for Cal Thomas' column criticizing the charade of blending commerce with spirituality. I, too, would like to see people focus more on feeding the hungry and clothing the naked (good humanist values) than on buying unneeded items they can't afford. I part company with Thomas when he complains about Santa becoming a God-substitute who requires nothing more of children than that they be nice. What's wrong with that? I hope children will notice that being nice to others makes them feel good about themselves, and that this simple discovery will follow them into adulthood.

Santa doesn't ask children to worship him or to put love for him above love for family and friends. He asks only that we be good for goodness' sake. Three cheers for Santa!

Holidays for Everyone

Full disclosure: I'm a member of the American Humanist Association (AHA) Board of Directors. But even if I weren't, I would strongly support their godless holiday campaign with ads like, "Bias Against Atheists Is Naughty, Not Nice." The goal of such is to show that there is a humanist community for like-minded people, that our perspectives should become part of the fabric of public opinion, and that we are open to dialog with those whose views are different. Saying you don't believe in God is no more anti-Christian or anti-religious than saying you are black is anti-white, saying you are female is anti-male, or saying you are gay is anti-straight. In the words of that great philosopher, Popeye the Sailor Man, "I yam what I yam."

Unfair Comments

In addition to seven articles about religious faiths, I was pleased that the Faith & Values section reprinted an article from *The Wall Street Journal* titled "Nonbelievers get out their message, too." The article described nonreligious traditions, such as HumanLight, to celebrate the holiday season. It pointed out that humanists and atheists are not evangelizing. Instead, they hope to make the public more comfortable with atheism and give fellow atheists a sense of community. There was, however, one aspect typical of stories about atheists, but rarely found in pieces about religious believers. The article quoted people of faith who disapprove of atheists and mentioned a giant sign put up by a Christian group asking, "Why Do Atheists Hate America?"

It's a step in the right direction that positive voices on atheism are now being heard, even if countered by opposing voices, presumably intending to be fair and balanced. However, I doubt that any fair and balanced newspaper would print only positive articles about one political party while always countering positive quotes with negative quotes when writing about the opposing political party.

War on Thanksgiving

Many religious believers and atheists express regret at the crass materialism, when Thanksgiving now represents the prelude to a shopping spree for Christmas presents. I gained an appalling insight on the day after "Black Friday." First I saw frenzied crowds of Egyptian protesters in Cairo's Tahrir Square, risking their lives to demand freedom. Then I saw frenzied crowds of American shoppers trying to push others aside to save a few dollars on sale merchandise. Though their causes were significantly different, the crowds looked the same.

We've become accustomed to a media-manufactured "War on Christmas," but this year breaks new ground with a manufactured "War on Thanksgiving." It involved President Obama, who gave a three-minute Thanksgiving Day speech without the word "God."

Here is a portion: "We're especially grateful for the men and women who defend our country overseas. To all the service members eating Thanksgiving dinner far from your families: the American people are thinking of you today. And when you come home, we intend to make sure that we serve you as well as you're serving America. We're also grateful for the Americans who are taking time out of their holiday to serve in soup kitchens and shelters, making sure their neighbors have a hot meal and a place to stay. This sense of mutual responsibility—the idea that I am my brother's keeper; that I am my sister's keeper—has always been a part of what makes our country special. And it's one of the reasons the Thanksgiving tradition has endured."

Imagine that. President Obama gave an inclusive speech showing support for the men and women who serve overseas, and also praised those who help the less fortunate. However, many Christians would have preferred he thank an imagined God rather than the real people he did thank. Atheists and theists can agree on the value of setting aside at least one day per year to give thanks, though we may disagree over "to whom" and "for what." On Thursday, I thanked my friends who prepared a wonderful Thanksgiving meal and provided us with the opportunity to share one another's company.

Happy Halloween to All Who Aren't Afraid of Harmless Fun

After getting used to wars on Christmas and Thanksgiving, we now have a war on Halloween. Pat Robertson is the most famous opponent of Halloween, which he calls "Satan's night." Robertson claimed, without any evidence, that the original practice of trick-or-treating came from the Druids, who went house to house asking for money and threatening to kill an owner's sheep if he didn't pony up.

Robertson doesn't want children dressing as ghosts or zombies because he says they don't exist. But he believes the Holy Ghost exists. And since a zombie is supposed to be a human who died, was raised from the dead, and once more walked among the living, the Gospels seem to imply that Jesus was a zombie. Furthermore, Zombie Jesus offers the ultimate trick or treat: eternal torture or eternal bliss. To Pat Robertson's credit (I've never used *that* phrase before), he is merely spreading misinformation and advising Christians not to celebrate Halloween.

The ministry "Christians against Halloween" considers Halloween "the anti-Christ's biggest nightly congregation of hell and damnation on earth." They want Christians to "barricade their family in their home, with the doors locked and the shades closed, praying for Jesus Christ to protect them and stand guard around their home to keep them safe from all the wickedness (people and demons) that are crawling the neighborhoods."

And some churches use "Hell House" evangelism on Halloween to shock young people with graphic exhibits and frighten them into becoming Christians. They literally try to scare the hell out of children by promoting misinformation about the "gay lifestyle," premarital sex, satanic rituals, and demonic possession. This reminds me of H.L. Mencken's comment that "Puritanism is the haunting fear that someone, somewhere may be happy."

I celebrated Halloween this year on October 25 with a 5K Zombie Run in a local county park. Some of us were runners and others dressed as zombies who stalked runners and grabbed "flags" worn on runners' belts.

We all had fun and survived this race for the "undead." Because of my tradition, I shouldn't be surprised by holiday wars. Here's a description of Jewish holidays: "They tried to kill us. We survived. Let's eat!"

Happy Halloween to all whose worldview doesn't preclude a little harmless fun.

Holiday Peace

7 Tips for Atheists at Thanksgiving Dinner

1. **Don't come out as an atheist during the Thanksgiving meal.** The blessing may seem like an appropriate occasion, but family gatherings have enough potential friction.

2. **Be yourself.** For instance, you need not bow your head for the blessing. Whoever notices likely isn't bowing either, so you might connect with other atheists.

3. **Sit respectfully while others give thanks to God.** If asked why you are not praying, mention that you are thankful we have the freedom to worship or not worship. Families thrive when they respect different points of view, including religious diversity.

4. **If you're asked to say the blessing, do it.** You might give thanks to farmers who grew the food, migrant workers who harvested it, truck drivers who brought the food, grocery store employees who displayed it, and family and friends who helped prepare it. (When invited to say "grace" to atheists or liberal religionists, I've sometimes quoted Bart Simpson: "Dear God. We paid for this food ourselves, so thanks for nothing.")

5. **Turn the blessing into a family affair.** A friend once led the blessing by asking family members to share something for which they were thankful. It started with jokes and then became quite touching until the most religious person thanked God for everything, but did not thank his wife, children, or friends. My friend learned about participants based on whom they thanked, and why.

6. **Consider this Bible verse, 1 Corinthians 13:11:** "When I was a child, I talked like a child, I thought like a child, I reasoned like a child. But when I became a man (or woman), I put away childish things." You

need not mention, unless asked, that you put away childish biblical stories.

7. **If you're not ready to come out, don't.** I was outed to my family by accident in 1990, at age 48, when I became a candidate for governor of South Carolina to challenge the provision in the State Constitution prohibiting atheists from holding public office. The Associated Press picked up the story and I got a call from a very distressed woman in Philadelphia—my mother. I had to acknowledge that the *Philadelphia Inquirer* was not the best way for my mother to find out that her only child was a candidate for governor—and an atheist! As it turned out, my mother didn't much mind my being an atheist, but she worried about how this revelation would damage my reputation.

7 Things Not to Say to the Atheist in Your Family

1. **Why are you angry with God?** Only God-believers can be angry with God.

2. **You'll be a believer when you have a big problem**. This is an offshoot of the "no atheists in foxholes" cliché. Atheists look for practical solutions to problems, and sometimes turn to supportive friends, family, and medical doctors.

3. **Why are you rejecting our family?** Would you ask this question if she voted for a different political candidate or came out as gay?

4. **I feel sorry for you.** How would you feel if he said he feels sorry for you because you are basing your life on nonsense?

5. **You got into a bad crowd.** It might be a different crowd, but it's the right crowd for her. She might have been influenced by discussions with friends or by books.

6. **I know my beliefs are right**. You can discuss differences in beliefs, but show him the same respect you want him to show you.

7. **We just want to make sure you will be with us in heaven.** This makes her think your God is petty and arbitrary for condemning her to hell because of an incorrect belief.

7 Ways to Talk to Your Family Atheist

1. **Listen to the atheist**. Understand his point of view, even if you disagree. That's a prerequisite for most conversations, especially ones that can become touchy or emotional.

2. **Look for common ground.** You might differ on God beliefs, but you can talk about common interests. If you think behavior is more important than belief, say so.

3. **Explain how your religious beliefs have changed since childhood**. She might assume that her religious views have matured, but yours have not. (Skip this suggestion if you have the same religious beliefs as when you were five years old.)

4. **Invite the atheist to ask you questions**. He has frequently been asked why he became an atheist, and he will appreciate the opportunity to ask why you believe as you do.

5. **Ask for her favorite quotes about religion**. She might quote Robert Ingersoll: "The hands that help are better far than lips that pray." Or Abraham Lincoln: "When I do good, I feel good. When I do bad, I feel bad. That is my religion." She'll love it if you offer to discuss these quotes.

6. **Mention that being a minority within the family is not so bad.** Describe how you, too, are a minority in some ways, and each family member is a minority in some larger community. That's why you appreciate the importance of treating minorities with respect.

7. **Discuss the reason for the season.** The family has gathered for a reason: a holiday, anniversary, or another special event. You can end with an aphorism that can be a reason for every season, like a hope for peace on earth and goodwill toward men and women.

18

ISLAM

Problems with Islam

Laughter, the Best Islamic Medicine

As for how the Obama administration should respond to the current turmoil in Iran, I offer the advice doctors give some patients diagnosed with prostate cancer: watchful waiting. Trying to remove perceived evil can do more harm than good. Foreign interventions, overt or clandestine, have often given despots an excuse to further restrict the rights of citizens. Whether theocracy or democracy prevails in Iran or elsewhere, even more fundamental to me is respect for human rights. Such rights include equality and due process under the law, protection of minority rights, as well as freedom of speech, religion, and assembly. So far, Iran fails this human rights test.

While a democratic society accepts differences of opinion, a theocracy cannot. Few citizens would argue that a constitution is an infallible document, which is why there are mechanisms to change it. On the other hand, accepting any book as inerrant leaves no room for change or even disagreement. A good rule of thumb for me is whether a country allows its citizens to poke fun at its leaders and its "sacred cows," including sacred religions. Freedom of speech must include freedom to laugh.

Pluralism at Ground Zero

During my lifetime, our foreign policy has been defined by a cold war with Soviet-style communism and a hot war with Islamic-style terrorism. Cold is better. This is no way justifies the horrible dictatorships in the

Soviet Union. That regime had much in common with many Middle East countries: an ideology that suppressed dissent and brutalized its citizens; old men holding onto power and eliminating rivals at any cost; lack of human rights or freedom of conscience.

There are differences, too. Mutual Assured Destruction (MAD) was the doctrine that assumed neither the Soviet Union nor the United States would launch its nuclear weaponry on the other, for fear of retaliation in which millions of its own citizens would be destroyed. Leaders of both superpowers preferred life to death. Not so in theocracies, where some suicide bombers kill innocent civilians because they expect rewards in an afterlife. The 9/11 attack was a faith-based initiative, conceived and carried out by people radicalized in Saudi Arabia and further radicalized in Afghanistan.

I could support two types of remembrance ceremonies. The first would be a completely secular ceremony, unheard of in theocracies. The second would be for all groups to participate in a diverse ceremony that does not favor one religion over another, or religion over nonreligion. It would include Christians, Jews, Muslims, Hindus, Buddhists, pagans, humanists, atheists, and any other groups wishing to participate in unifying people of all faiths and none. In other words, *E pluribus unum.* This might help us turn the worst of times into the best of times.

A Very Brief History of Jews, Christians, and Muslims
First there were Jews with their holy book, then Christians with their holy book, and then Muslims with their holy book. These monotheistic religions have lots in common and lots not. Christianity, a cult of Judaism that eventually had enough members to rise to the status of sect, became a separate religion when they added their New Testament holy book. Muslims then added their Quran holy book, but also consider Jewish and Christian Bibles holy. Each religion added prophets. Jews included Noah, Abraham, and Moses, Christians added Jesus, and Muslims added Muhammad.

Here's what else these religions have in common: If you can find an interpretation in one holy book to justify an atrocity, then you can likely find a comparable interpretation and justification in the other holy books. These include genocide, holy wars, slavery, misogyny, and death for crimes like blasphemy, homosexuality, and worshipping the wrong god or even the right god in the wrong way.

I'm not interested in trying to decide the best and worst "holy" books because all contain both ridiculous and reasonable passages. As an atheist, I read portions of ancient books written by fallible humans and follow only what makes sense to me.

More Muslims today invoke their holy texts to justify violence than do adherents of other religions. Often these atrocities are inspired or justified by passages in the Quran that are similar to those from Judaism or Christianity. Recently, Islamic militants ransacked Mosul's central museum, destroying priceless artifacts because they represented idols. That reminded me of the mythical story of Abraham smashing his father's idols instead of worshipping the one "true" God. And when the Islamic State indiscriminately kills innocent people, I think of the Christian Crusades when Pope Urban II promised in 1095 that all who died in the holy war would go straight to paradise.

I'm not so concerned with people who have ludicrous religious beliefs as long as their beliefs don't interfere with those who don't share such beliefs. And I'm happy to live in a country where people can choose to be Jews, Christians, Muslims, atheists, and any other religion or nonreligion, without being persecuted as an infidel.

Theological Terrorism

There are many reasons why ISIS successfully recruits dedicated members for its cause, which includes what I call *Theological Terrorism*. ISIS bases its apocalyptic ideology on Muhammad's prophesies of a final battle against Western infidels, ending in victory for an established caliphate. The majority of Muslims in the Middle East believe we are living in the end times, and they want to be on the right side when the Day of Judgment comes. While relatively few Muslims support ISIS, there are many Islamic terrorists (yes, I'm a liberal who uses that phrase) willing to fight and die to establish a caliphate that will hasten the end times.

Many Muslims got the preposterous end-times idea from interpretations of their holy book, the Quran. But it's not just Muslims who hold that belief. Portions of the Quran are "inspired" by the Christian Bible, many of whose adherents also anticipate an imminent end of the world. Astoundingly, 41 percent of US adults, 54 percent of Protestants, and 77 percent of Evangelicals believe the world is now living in the biblical end times!

I sometimes think there are more Christians than Jews because Christianity promises a better afterlife. So watch out for Islam, which promises a paradise with sensual young women and unlimited wine. That sounds like an earthly paradise for heterosexual men and lesbians, and a lot more fun than an afterlife of sycophantic praises and hallelujahs.

If people follow a holy book, I want to know which passages and how they interpret them. ISIS seems to follow the worst passages of the Quran and interpret them in the worst possible way. I hope the world moves away from theocratic terrorism and toward loving our neighbors. We don't need holy books to justify loving our neighbor.

To Show Solidarity with Muslims, I Spent a Day at a Local Mosque
After Donald Trump's inflammatory speech on the aircraft carrier Yorktown near my home in Charleston, my wife Sharon and I wanted to counter some of the unfair anti-Muslim sentiment in our state and country. So we visited the local mosque to say how pleased we are to live in the same community with Muslims. The imam and three other leaders greeted us, and they appreciated our show of support. I mentioned that atheists are also sometimes demonized, and it's important for those of all faiths and none to find common ground and work together. They agreed, but the imam asked, "How can you not believe in God?" Sharon had wisely recommended that I not talk about religion during this visit, so I just said that I saw no evidence for any gods. I didn't respond when the imam told me there is evidence everywhere.

We accepted their invitation to a "Meet Your Muslim Neighbor" open house. The speaker was Imam Eessa Wood, who specializes in community outreach presentations. He said that Muhammad is the final prophet, but that anyone who believes in the one true God can still go to heaven.

Imam Wood gave the same answer to all questions about atrocities committed by Muslims: "They aren't true Muslims." And he gave the same answer to violent-sounding quotes in the Quran, like killing infidels: "That passage is taken out of context. We study and understand the whole Quran based on how Muhammad lived it." When an audience member asked about the Muslim position on gays, the local Imam said that being gay is wrong and there are no gay Muslims. I said to Imam Wood, "Almost no Jews believe literally in the Old Testament, and most Christians don't believe literally in the New Testament. How many Muslims don't believe literally in the Quran?" He said that not believing literally would be grounds for *excommunication*.

Recently, Dutch pranksters disguised a copy of the Bible as the Quran, and read provocative biblical quotes to passersby. The pranksters asked them if such beliefs were consistent with Western norms and values. The people queried thought the quotes from the Quran were ridiculous, unbelievable, and oppressive. And they developed even less respect for Muslims until learning how they had been pranked. I take it as a positive about Jews and Christians that they either don't know or don't care about ridiculous passages in their ancient scriptures. I hope one day to see Muslims openly disavow the kind of passages in the Quran that Jews and Christians reject in their holy books.

Israel and Saudi Arabia: America's Favorite Middle Eastern Countries
Republicans and Democrats rarely agree on anything, but they all claim to love America and Israel. We hear no such love pronouncements or unconditional support for actions of England, Canada, or other allies. Israel became America's favorite Middle East country in part because of common interests and shared democratic ideals, but I'm disturbed that Saudi Arabia is our second-favorite. In 1948, dozens of countries supported the Universal Declaration of Human Rights adopted by the United Nations General Assembly, including most Muslim countries. However, Saudi Arabia refused to sign because it claimed the provisions violated sharia law. A partial list of Saudi interpretations of sharia include: not allowing Muslims to change religion; no right to change the government peacefully; no access to legal counsel during interrogation and trial; denial of fair and public trials; legal domestic violence against women; legal torture and physical abuse.

We rarely hear about human rights violations by our Saudi ally, one notable exception being the 2002 fire in a girls' school in Mecca that claimed the lives of 15 girls. The "Committee for the Promotion of Virtue and the Prevention of Vice" (CPVPV) prevented these 13-year-olds from escaping to safety because they were not wearing hijabs. Nadin al-Badir, a brave Saudi journalist, exposed this tragedy. Saudi authorities then apologized for the overzealous reaction, and said they had plans to limit the power of their religious police. But only one person was threatened with arrest for the incident. A Saudi judge called for the arrest of Nadin al-Badir—for publicly criticizing the CPVPV.

It would be bad enough if Wahhabism, the strict brand of Islam practiced by Saudis, stayed within its borders. It shouldn't be surprising that 15 of the 19 hijackers on 9/11 were Saudi citizens. Not one was from Iraq, which our administration held largely responsible. Saudi Arabia funds Wahhabi mosques and ideology globally. Wahhabi publications in US mosques call for Muslims to oppose "infidels" in every way, claiming that democracy is responsible for all horrible wars. The Saudi government said it was trying to overhaul its education system, but it's a "massive undertaking."

We rightly view ISIS as our greatest threat at the moment, but we should recognize similarities between ISIS and Saudi Arabia, including Wahhabi theology. Both behead people, enslave women, kill people for apostasy and blasphemy, and consider their version of Sharia law as binding. However, America focuses almost exclusively on benefits from Saudis. We get their oil, they are of some help in promoting regional stability, and they provide air space for us.

James Carville, strategist for Bill Clinton in his 1992 presidential campaign, coined the phrase "It's the economy, stupid." I long to hear politicians employ a much-needed foreign policy phrase, "It's the human rights, stupid."

Islamophobia

Islamo- and Atheistophobia

All religious freedom is not created equal, as shown in a recent poll. Americans place the highest priority on religious freedom for Christians. Only about 60 percent thought protecting religious freedom for Muslims and atheists is important.

Given the high-profile atrocities committed by some Muslims in the name of their religion, I understand why a number of people are concerned about giving complete religious freedom to Muslims. However, we need to distinguish between peaceful believers and those inspired by their holy books to commit atrocities. It becomes *Islamophobia* when we lump all Muslims into the same category.

What about *Atheistophobia* (my made up word)? How can people justify denigrating or discriminating against atheists? We might advocate for separation of church and state in ways religious people disagree, but we do so peacefully. You might believe we are theologically incorrect, but everybody believes those of other religions are theologically incorrect. We have the free-speech right to make fun of religion, just as religious people have the free-speech right to make fun of atheists. Christians and Muslims in the past or present have sentenced people to death for blasphemy.

We shouldn't blame all people in a religion because of atrocities committed by some in the name of that religion. We shouldn't blame all atheists if some commit atrocities in the name of atheism. And just as an exercise, how many of them can you name?

Onward Secular Peacemakers

When President Bush referred to America's war on terror as a "crusade," I hoped the word was merely one of his many slips of the tongue. I became less hopeful after reading how Secretary of Defense Rumsfeld, around the time of the US invasion of Iraq, sent President Bush numerous inspirational Bible verses printed over military images. One showed US tanks roaring through the desert with a quote from Isaiah 26:2: "Open the gates that the righteous nation may enter, the nation that keeps faith." Over a picture of Saddam Hussein was this passage from 1 Peter 2:15: "It is God's will that by doing good you should silence the ignorant talk of foolish men."

I hope President Obama will point out that peace-loving people must work to marginalize those whose religious beliefs lead them to kill innocent people. We must not honor those who, in effect, say, "My God can beat up your God."

We're All Stereotypes

A lawyer friend once told me, "It's those 98 percent of lawyers who give the rest of us a bad name." We are all prone to stereotyping. Absent additional information, I'm more likely to trust a lawyer who works for a nonprofit than one who specializes in corporate takeovers; to believe math professors rather than religious leaders; to expect my students who sit near the front to do better than those in the back. However, I need to be especially careful not to let stereotypes cloud my judgment about individuals.

Each of us is a minority in some way. It might be race, religion, sexual orientation, nationality, or any other trait by which we may be regarded as different. Each of us is also part of some majority. It is when we wear our majority hats that we need to be most mindful of how we treat others. The worst tragedies in history were usually the result of dehumanizing humans because of a stereotypical category in which they were placed, whether it was Jews in Nazi Germany or enslaved blacks in this country.

William Boykin, a Pentagon general, publically said the United States is a Christian nation doing battle against Satan in Iraq. His views mirrored those of Osama bin Laden, who justified the 9/11 attack as an Islamic nation doing battle against Satan. Same imaginary Satan, different stereotype.

Fashion, Freedom, and Coercion

President Sarkozy made this puzzling comment: "The burqa is not a religious sign. It is a sign of subservience, a sign of debasement." Subservience and debasement are integral parts of many religions, with women usually featured as the subserved and debased. In my Jewish Orthodox days, I used to recite a traditional daily prayer in which I thanked God that I was not born a woman. There were no reciprocal prayers for women. Passages in the Christian Bible describe how women were made for the sake of man, and that women must keep silent and not have authority over men.

The essential issue regarding Muslim attire is one of coercion, not religious practice.

There's another risk posed by Sarkozy's proposal. If Muslim women are prohibited from wearing burqas outside, their husbands might prevent them from going outside. That would be a cure worse than the disease.

Hate Your Neighbor, but Don't Forget to Say Grace

The Barry McGuire song "Eve of Destruction" was my favorite protest song during the 1960s. Mostly it was about hypocrisy. Presidential candidate Mike Huckabee's comments about Islam reminded me of a line in the last stanza of that song, "Hate your next-door neighbor, but don't forget to say grace."

Huckabee said Muslims believe "Jesus Christ and all the people that follow him are a bunch of infidels who should be essentially obliterated." Such self-righteous certainty that his is the only "right" religion leads Huckabee to consider himself an authority on Muslim belief, though Muslims deny Huckabee's claim. Some Muslims consider Christians infidels and some Christians consider Muslims infidels. I'm an infidel to Muslims and Christians because I disbelieve the tenets of both (and all other) religions.

We need to distinguish between peaceful infidels and infidels whose love of a god trumps love for humans. We continue to have Middle East wars, where people are willing to die and kill in order to hasten the first coming of a Jewish messiah, the second coming of a Jesus messiah, or who knows what other comings necessary for an alleged messianic age.

Maybe we should all look, instead, for ways we can better love our neighbor, which all philosophies (religious or otherwise) claim to espouse. Instead of waiting for a messiah to solve our problems, maybe we should listen to the advice in John Lennon's song, "All we are saying is give peace a chance." And it isn't hard to imagine how much easier we could do this with no religion, too.

Neither Catholic nor Sharia Law
As far as I can tell, the Catholic Church is on the wrong side of all issues pertaining to sex. The church wants heterosexual couples to remain celibate until marriage and then to have as many children as nature (excuse me, "God") provides, whether they want to or can afford them. The exception is for priests and nuns who must remain celibate their entire lives because ....
(fill in the blank, since the reasons have changed over centuries.) It's bad for straight couples to cohabitate, but good if they commit to a monogamous marriage; it's bad for gay couples to cohabitate, and even worse if they commit to a monogamous marriage. Don't anyone even think of the sin of masturbation, which is safe sex for pleasure only. And I won't get into why the church concluded that the sexual permissiveness of the 1960s led to pedophilia by church officials.

Surprisingly, some Christians fear that unless we have laws opposing sharia law we will be forced to live under it. I'm more worried about Christian laws being imposed in this country. Republican candidates for president were asked about sharia law. Here are some of their answers, where I take the liberty to substitute "Christian" for "Sharia."

Herman Cain: There is this creeping attempt to gradually ease [Christian] law into our government. It does not belong in our government.

Newt Gingrich: We should have a federal law that says [Christian] law cannot be recognized by any court in the United States.

Sarah Palin: [Christian] law, if that were allowed to govern in our country, it will be the downfall of America."

Rick Santorum: [Christian] law is incompatible with American jurisprudence and our Constitution.

As long as we keep high the wall of separation between religion and government, neither Catholic bishops nor any other religious leaders will have a right to dictate public policy for those outside their faiths.

Theocratic State?

South Carolina legislators proposed a bill to counteract their perceived risk of sharia law being used by the state's legal system. While I don't want South Carolina to become a theocratic state, I'm not the least bit worried. I am concerned about South Carolina creeping toward a theocracy. Our state House of Representatives passed a resolution that refers to Israel's "God-given right" to its territory because "Israel has been granted her lands under and through the oldest recorded deed as reported in the Old Testament." The resolution added, "God has never rescinded his grant of said lands." The legislators bolstered their argument by quoting Leviticus 20:24: "Ye shall inherit their land, and I will give it unto you to possess it, a land that floweth with milk and honey."

The land now flows with too much blood and not enough milk and honey. The resolution implies that we are governed by a theocracy. Our politicians may conduct their private lives according to the Bible, the Quran, or any other holy book. But they were elected to govern according to our state and US constitutions, not biblical or sharia law.

A Conservative Christian Engaged in a Christian War

I have a loose connection to Anders Breivik, who killed 77 people in Norway. You see, he lifted words for his manifesto from the manifesto of "Unabomber" Ted Kaczynski. I never met Ted, but he and I were in the same research field of geometric function theory, and I published some joint papers with Kaczynski's dissertation advisor. When Kaczynski was caught, a slightly paranoid math colleague became unnecessarily concerned that there might be an anti-mathematician backlash. It helped that nobody could think of other mathematicians who were guilty of anything more than eccentric behavior. History shows that violence was more likely to be committed against, rather than by, mathematicians. Hypatia of Alexandria had an illustrious math career until she was burned alive in 415 by a mob of Christian monks. And St. Augustine said, "The good Christian should beware of mathematicians, and all those who make empty prophecies. The danger already exists that the mathematicians have made a covenant with the devil to darken the spirit and to confine man in the bonds of hell."

Kaczynski never made any connections between his mathematics and his violent acts, but Breivik indicated in his manifesto that he was a Christian engaged in a Christian war to defend Europe against the threat of Muslim domination. His acts are consistent with both Christian theology and Christian behavior. Some say that Breivik is not a "true" Christian because of his actions. Yes he is, just as Osama bin Laden was a true Muslim. The Crusaders were true Christians, as were those who murdered abortion doctors, as were most Nazis.

Despite Ted Kaczynski's terrorist acts, he is a true mathematician. I wish my math publications were as impressive. But math and morality don't always go together, and neither do religion and morality. Compared to the general population, there are smaller percentages of mathematicians (and atheists) than Christians in prison for violent crimes.

19

JUDAISM

Jewish Identity

Whose Jews?

A major problem in any survey of Jews is deciding who is Jewish and who decides. Orthodox Jews demand that the mother be Jewish, while liberal Jews accept those with a gentile mother if the father is Jewish. Jews stopped proselytizing in the fourth century C.E. for a practical reason. The Roman Empire, having adopted Christianity as the state religion, made conversion to Judaism a criminal offense punishable by death. Conversion is no longer a crime, but Orthodox rabbis discourage conversion and many reject would-be converts three times. Different branches of Judaism are more welcoming, but Orthodox Jews don't recognize converts to Judaism by other branches.

And then there are Jews with adjectives: Unitarian Jews, Buddhist Jews, Quaker Jews, atheist Jews, etc. Religious Jews are generally not much bothered by atheist Jews like me. They reserve their antagonism for Messianic Jews (Jews for Jesus), because many Jews believe them to be Christians with the ulterior motive of converting Jews to Christianity. So Jews are fine with Jews who don't believe in God, but are concerned and embarrassed by Jews who believe that God has a son.

Who Is a Jew? What Is a Christian?

While I'm often asked how I can be both a Jew and an atheist, this question hardly ever comes from Jews. According to all branches of Judaism, a person is Jewish if born to a Jewish mother. Since my mother was Jewish, so am I. End of story.

I think it's more difficult to define Christian than Jew. Christians believe that Jesus was/is a very special person, but they differ on significant issues like whether Jesus is the only begotten son of God, was born of a virgin, was resurrected bodily and died for your sins, whether everything in the New Testament is literally true, whether and when he will be returning, and whether such beliefs will be the difference between going to heaven or hell. What all Christians seem to have in common is a belief that many who claim to be Christian are not *real* Christians. I prefer to let people self-identify, though this appears not to be the "Christian" thing to do.

Now for the cross (pun intended) between Jews and Christians—Messianic Jews (Jews for Jesus). Interestingly, ultra-Orthodox Jews have more religious beliefs in common with Jews for Jesus than with atheist Jews. Both sects believe a Messiah is coming, though they differ on whether it will be his first or second trip to Earth. There have been dozens of Jewish Messiah claimants over the centuries. Some in the Hasidic sect expect the imminent return of Mendel Schneerson, who died in 1994. I'm as confident of Schneerson's return as of Jesus's return. Jesus purportedly said he would return before his own generation passed, and the clock is still ticking.

Godless Jews

I'm not accustomed to being part of a majority in anything, especially religion. One notable exception is a Harris survey that shows the majority (52 percent) of American Jews do *not* believe in God. I'm mildly surprised, but not totally shocked. Well-known Christians like Billy Graham, Pat Robertson, Jerry Falwell, Mother Teresa, and the pope are quite religious. But most well known Jews are atheists, including Albert Einstein, Sigmund Freud, Karl Marx, Groucho Marx, Mel Brooks, Woody Allen, Jon Stewart, and Sarah Silverman (no relation, unfortunately). I'm hard-pressed to name a pious Jew, dead or alive, who is a household name worldwide—except maybe Jesus. And I have my doubts about him.

When a rabbi from the Reform Synagogue in Charleston spoke to our local secular humanist group, one of our members asked him how many in his congregation were atheists. He said, "I don't know. We don't ask such embarrassing questions." The rabbi just laughed when another member asked, "Which answer would be more embarrassing?" The rabbi later told me that he was an atheist.

The Jew/Atheist Paradox

Following the Harris survey showing that most Jews are atheists, there comes a Pew Research Center survey on how Americans feel about different religious and nonreligious groups: Jews are viewed the *most* warmly and atheists the *least*. Go figure! Evangelical Christians give Jews the highest rating, a case of unrequited love because Jews rate evangelical Christians the lowest. Not surprisingly, Jews and atheists regard each other warmly, while both rank evangelical Christians at the bottom.

Christians may not know that most Jews are atheists, but they do know that Jews believe Jesus was just an ordinary Jew with extraordinary delusions of grandeur. And rejection of Jesus inspired Christian anti-Semitism since the time of Jesus. So what has turned anti-Semitism to philo-Semitism?

Many Christians began deemphasizing biblical passages that contributed to anti-Semitism and perhaps even to the Holocaust. Not so much emphasis on passages that say the blood of Jesus will be on Jews and on their children, and the Devil is father of the Jews. Post-Holocaust Christians concentrate more on Jews as "chosen" people, where God says about Abraham and his descendants in Genesis 12:3, "I will bless those who bless you and curse those who curse you." Of course, God and the Devil are both absentee fathers.

There's another reason many evangelical Christians strongly support the land of Israel, perhaps more than most Jews. In a word, it's "rapture." According to the strangest book in the New Testament, *Revelation*, there will be a final apocalyptic battle in Armageddon. Israel triumphs, Jesus returns, takes believers up to heaven, and incinerates everyone who doesn't believe in Jesus, including Jews. So much for God's chosen people! If I were to watch this event unfold, I'd have evidence to become a believer. But it would be too late because evidence-free beliefs are required.

Humoristic Judaism

The play *Two Thousand Years* is about a secular Jewish family with a shy son in his twenties who lives at home. He's a social misfit, but the family tolerates his behavior until he starts wearing a yarmulke. This sends his father into shock. He shouts, "It's like having a *Muslim* in the house!" His grandfather is a socialist who grew up on a kibbutz in Israel, and he continues to fulminate about how the Zionism he once supported was hijacked by religious extremists.

The son had been yearning for a sense of identity and hopes his "conversion" will bring him the satisfaction he craves. It doesn't. After family reactions, the son at first just wants to be left alone. He later becomes uncharacteristically defiant and asks his relatives what it means for them to be a Jew. Their answers are enlightening: "I was born a Jew." "I can't imagine not being a Jew." "I'm committed to social justice." "I like to argue."

The father says he's Jewish because he likes Jewish jokes, which he tells continually. Here's one of them: A reporter asks the following question of an American, a Russian, a North Korean, and an Israeli: "Excuse me, what is your opinion of the meat shortage?" The American says, "What's a shortage?" The Russian says, "What's meat?" The North Korean says, "What's an opinion?" And the Israeli says, "What's excuse me?"

None of these family rationales for being Jewish satisfies the son. Even family members don't seem particularly convinced by their answers. Yet they all view the religious son as somehow less Jewish than they are. Their Jewish equivalent of "real men don't eat quiche" is "real Jews don't wear yarmulkes."

The son grows comfortable standing up to strong and accomplished family members. The last scene shows him without a yarmulke, confidently playing chess with his father. This indicates the son's return to secular Judaism, becoming a *mensch* (an admirable person) in the eyes of his family.

Since Jewish humor is such an integral part of Judaism, I'll end with three Jewish jokes.

1. A journalist from the *Jerusalem Post* lived in an apartment overlooking the Western Wall. After several weeks, he realized that whenever he looked at the wall he saw the same old Jew praying vigorously. Sensing a story, the journalist said to the old man, "You pray at the wall every day. What are you praying for?" The man replied, "In the morning, I pray for world peace; in the afternoon, for the brotherhood of man; in the evening, for the eradication of illness and disease from the earth." The journalist asked, "And how long have you been doing this?" The old man said, "Every day, for twenty-seven years." Amazed, the journalist asked how it felt to pray every day for those things. The old Jew replied, "How does it feel? It feels like I'm talking to a wall!"

2. Some members of an Orthodox synagogue think they should stand for a particular prayer, but others think they should sit. They can't reach consensus, so they agree to send one member, Jacob, to the next town where there is a learned rabbi whose opinion they all respect. Jacob asks Rabbi Cohen if the tradition is to stand. Rabbi Cohen says, "No." So then Jonathan says, "Good. Then the tradition is to sit." Again, Rabbi Cohen says, "No." Frustrated, Jacob pleads with Rabbi Cohen, "Please help us find a solution. Members of our congregation do nothing but argue about whether to stand or sit." Rabbi Cohen smiles, and says, "Aha! THAT is the tradition.

3. Four rabbis are arguing about a Talmudic passage. Three give one interpretation, but Rabbi Levy gives another. After several hours of Rabbi Levy trying to convince the other three, he looks to the sky in desperation and says, "God, please give us a sign as to who is correct." Suddenly, it gets pitch dark, begins to thunder, and a booming voice shouts: "Levy is correct!" After a stunned silence one of the other rabbis says, "OK. That makes it three to two."

Five Reasons I Might Join the Ku Klux Klan

Groucho Marx famously said, "I don't want to belong to any club that will accept me as a member." I'm thinking about joining a club that I thought would *never* accept me as a member. A Ku Klux Klan chapter is now accepting Jews.

My only public comment about the KKK, in 1987, was supportive—sort of. When the Charleston City Council asked for citizen comments about whether to grant the KKK a parade permit to march, I said, "The Ku Klux Klan has done hundreds of horrible things, but I don't want to deny them the one appropriate thing they do—use their free speech right to demonstrate for a cause." The Klan was allowed to march, and it was especially ironic that the KKK Grand Dragon had to listen when our black, Jewish police chief, Reuben Greenberg, read him the permit rules and regulations.

So why would a liberal Jew like me consider joining a hate group like the Ku Klux Klan?

1. **I like diversity.**

   Only one KKK chapter thus far is opening its membership to Jews, but that's a start. I enjoy seeing hate groups argue among themselves. KKK Imperial Wizard Bradley Jenkins angrily said that the new chapter goes against everything the KKK stands for.

2. **My wife wants me to get new attire.**

   I'd wear the traditional KKK costume of a white robe and conical hood, but I could still wear an atheist T-shirt under my robe and a Jewish skullcap on top of my hood.

3. **I would learn my color.**

   I'm confused when Klansmen say their organization is for "whites only," not blacks or Jews. I get that black is black, but what color is Jew? I also want to know how a Christian organization like the KKK can hate Jews, yet worship one. And what color was Jesus?

4. **Lively dinner parties.**

   It would be fun trying to recruit my Jewish friends into the KKK. Since most of them are also atheists, I'd suggest forming a Humanistic Judaism Klan. I might threaten dissenting Jewish friends with burning a Mezuzah (Jewish symbol) on their front lawn.

5. **Springtime for Klansmen**

   The Producers, a dark comedy written and directed by Mel Brooks, features the song "Springtime for Hitler." There's a time to fear and a time to make fun. While still a threat, I hope we are approaching a time when we can best combat the KKK and neo-Nazis with humor. I also look forward to a day when we can sing "Springtime for ISIS."

Israel

God's Welfare Dilemma

In a study of 137 countries, atheism was more widespread in those with well-developed welfare programs. Countries that provide universal health care and education, along with adequate social safety nets, are likely to have citizens who feel more secure and in control of their own lives. Atheism flourishes with economic satisfaction, while religion thrives when people are undereducated and desperate.

Israel is one of the most secular countries in the world and it provides significant welfare benefits to its citizens. So why do I and probably all other atheists think there is a major flaw in the Israeli welfare system? The problem started in 1949, when the first chief rabbi of Israel persuaded Prime Minister David Ben-Gurion to exempt a limited number of ultra-Orthodox students from military service so they could study full time in yeshivas. The rationale was that tens of thousands of students in Europe had been wiped out during the Holocaust and the best surviving scholars should be released from military obligations and given financial assistance in order to continue their religious studies.

That temporary solution became permanent, and the original handful grew to 60,000. Even the Haredim (ultra-Orthodox) acknowledge that not all are fine scholars, but they insist on continued military exemptions and generous taxpayer subsidies for all who wish to devote their lives to Torah study. Graduates from these religious schools receive the equivalent of zero to four years of secular education, while secular work force participation among Haredi men is only about 40 percent. Haredim are about 9 percent of the population, but receive half the country's welfare payments. To make matters worse, the situation is rapidly becoming even more unsustainable because of astronomical fertility rates in these impoverished and ghettoized religious communities, while the more affluent Israeli secular Jews aren't bound by a "be fruitful and multiply" theology.

The American religious right seems to offer the most unequivocal support for Israel and its policies. What would they think about a group of able-bodied American citizens who refused to work and expected taxpayer support through welfare subsidies? Further, what if they wanted to have as many children as possible, and encourage them to live off life-long welfare subsidies? Conservatives are the loudest to complain about foreign aid, except when it comes to aid for Israel.

Why I No Longer Support Israel
My family shed tears of joy on May 14, 1948 when the Jewish State of Israel was established as a safe haven for Jews. I was five at the time and didn't understand its significance, but I had been taught that an integral part of Judaism was anti anti-Semitism. Jewish displaced persons (DPs) lived in my neighborhood, including some who had been in concentration camps. I also had relatives who had died in the Holocaust, and my family warned me never to trust the *goyim* (gentiles).

When I became a secular Jew, I still felt a nonreligious affinity to my Jewish "homeland." I had no desire to make Israel my home, but I viewed it as a prophylactic against future Holocausts. I later learned that the establishment of Israel was not a day of unadulterated joy for everyone—because Jews settled in a country inhabited by others and forced many of them to leave. In other words, Israel created Palestinian DPs. Nevertheless, I continued to support Israel, focusing mostly on the anti-Semitism of countries in the Middle East that denied Israel's right to exist. However, I had a more nuanced view, balancing security for Israelis with human rights for Palestinians.

Were it not for the Holocaust, there would not be a Jewish state to provide safe haven for Jews. I now think the Right of Return has outlived its usefulness. I'm fine with Israel taking Jews in danger elsewhere, but not for giving immediate citizenship to all Jews. Besides, you can't literally "return" to a place you've never been. Displaced Palestinians are more deserving of the right to return than I am.

Israel's Declaration of Independence in 1948 called for a Jewish state that "ensures complete equality of social and political rights to all its inhabitants, irrespective of religion, race, or sex." However, the Israeli cabinet approved a bill to define Israel as the nation-state of the Jewish people, reserving national rights for Jews. This antidemocratic bill would officially relegate the 20 percent of non-Jews living in Israel to second-class status. Such a law is an Orwellian modification of their Declaration of Independence saying, in effect, "All citizens are equal, but some citizens are more equal than others."

Israel is facing the same kind of struggle that many countries have encountered—between democracy and theocracy. Unfortunately, Israel is headed in the wrong direction. I can support Israel when it lives up to the ideals in its Declaration by putting human rights and social justice above sectarian concern, and treating its minorities as equal citizens.

Holidays

My Passover Evolution

Passover was my favorite holiday as a child because children were an integral part of the ceremony. After the Seder leader hid the *afikomen* (piece of matzo) during the meal, the child who found it received a small prize. I enjoyed sipping the ritual wine, while my mother voiced her concern that I would become an alcoholic. (I now think that Manischewitz wine is an effective one-step program to prevent alcoholism.)

I especially looked forward to the *Mah nishtanah . . .*, the question asked by a child, which translates to "Why is this night different from all the other nights?" The scripted answers from the leader represent the substance of the Seder. Though I no longer believe the answers, the question reminds me of my favorite Passover joke:

> Because of his charitable contributions in England, Morris was to become the first Jew knighted by the queen. Morris memorized what he would have to say in Latin for the ceremony. But when the queen approached, Morris panicked and forgot the Latin passage. So he blurted out a familiar phrase, "Mah nishtanah halaylah hazeh mikol halaylot?" Surprised, the puzzled queen whispered to a member of her entourage, "Why is this knight different from all the other knights?"

When invited to Seders, I tell the host I'm an atheist. As a new faculty member in 1969 at Clark University, I went to a Seder at the home of an ultra-Orthodox (Hasidic) colleague, Joseph. What I most remember that evening was a near-marital experience. Joseph's aunt asked if I was married, and I told her I wasn't. She asked if I'd like to meet her lovely niece in Toronto. After casually saying, "Okay," Joseph took me aside and explained, "If you like the niece, you'll be expected to marry her." Joseph and I agreed that I should find an excuse to cancel my "date." I had my opportunity when the aunt said, "I must tell you that my niece is kosher, but not glatt kosher." (Hasidim require special rabbis to inspect the food according to a more stringent "glatt" standard.) My response to the aunt was, "In that case, I'm not interested." Joseph could hardly contain his laughter.

I had neither arrived at nor left that Seder alone. Joseph had asked me to accompany a couple of female Orthodox students on a two-mile walk to the Seder. I agreed, knowing that Orthodox Jews don't ride on holy days. On the walk home, I asked them how long they had been Orthodox. They said they weren't, but their professor (Joseph) had told them I was, and he asked them to keep me company on the walk. Joseph sure told a lot of lies on one of his holiest days of the year.

A Godless Passover

It's only fitting for two religions (Judaism and Christianity) to celebrate Passover. For me, Passover represents twos. It's false and true, disgusting and uplifting, religious and secular, traditional and nontraditional. There is no historical or archaeological evidence that Moses existed, that Israelites were slaves in Egypt, or that they wandered in the desert for 40 years. And that's the good news, because the Passover story of the Exodus is inhumane: an insecure and sadistic God hardened Pharaoh's heart so God could respond by bringing 10 plagues to Egypt, which culminated in killing innocent first-born Egyptian sons. God also told the Israelites to kill a lamb and put its blood on their doors so God would *pass over* first-born Israeli sons. (You'd think an all-knowing God wouldn't need blood markers to find where Israelites lived.)

The traditional God of both Judaism and Christianity thrives on and even requires blood sacrifice of innocent animals and humans. The "Last Supper" of Jesus was a Passover Seder. Those aren't the kind of Passovers I celebrate. Humanistic Passover celebrations are more about the present and future than the past, emphasizing themes of human freedom and dignity. We recognize the struggles of people trying to overcome oppression and achieve freedom and equality. We also look for ways to do our small part.

High Holidays for Jewish Atheists

Since Rosh Hashanah and Yom Kippur are the most sacred days of the Jewish calendar, why would an atheist Jew like me note these high holidays? Regardless of belief, there is a one-word reason why most Jews remember Jewish holidays—God. Without that concept, there would be no Jews. So I'm happy to credit God for the holidays, even if he/she/it doesn't exist. I commemorate this time of year partly from Jewish tradition, but also because I want to help change that tradition into a more godless one.

There are two religious reasons for celebrating the Jewish New Year of Rosh Hashanah. One is bad, the other is worse. Rosh Hashanah commemorates the scientifically indefensible anniversary of the creation of the world, 5,774 years ago. Even worse, it's the anniversary of Abraham agreeing to kill his son Isaac as proof of his faith and obedience to God. This Torah portion in Genesis 22 is read every Rosh Hashanah.

Discussion of death is appropriate on Rosh Hashanah, when God supposedly decides who will die in the coming year. It's also a time to promote long, if not eternal, life. The tradition that Rosh Hashanah is the beginning of year 5774 also credits Methuselah with living 969 years. Most Jews can laugh at these made-up stories. So I'll commemorate the holidays in the Jewish Humoristic tradition, by closing with two jokes for the season.

A rabbi delivers a moving Rosh Hashanah sermon telling how we are nothing in this vast universe and that we must let God know we are appropriately humble. After the sermon, the assistant rabbi runs to the front and yells, "I am nothing!" followed by the president of the congregation who does the same. Then a newcomer runs up yelling, "I am nothing!" At this, an old congregant pokes the man sitting next to him and complains, "So look who thinks *he's* nothing."

On another occasion a Jew tries to enter the shul (synagogue) during the high holidays and is stopped by the shammas (caretaker) who asks for his ticket. The man hadn't paid for one, but says he just wants to come in for a minute so he can give an important message to a friend. The shammas agrees to let him pass, but warns, "Now, don't let me catch you praying in this shul!"

Jewish Atheists and Koufax Jews
In the 1950s, Jews played the celebrity game: "Jew, not a Jew?" Most of my favorite comedians, including Milton Berle, Sid Caesar, Groucho Marx, Jack Benny, George Burns, Jerry Lewis, Red Buttons, and Phil Silvers, passed the Jew test. Many gentiles didn't know they were Jews because they didn't mention it publicly. In contrast, some of my favorite comedians today, such as Woody Allen, Mel Brooks, Jon Stewart, Jerry Seinfeld, Larry David, and Sarah Silverman not only pass the Jew test but make Judaism part of their shtick. Now I play a variant of my '50s game: "atheist Jew, not an atheist Jew?" The '50s comedians were probably all closeted atheist Jews, while the modern ones are open about being atheist Jews. Our Jewish culture has changed for the better.

Anti-Semitism has inspired much Jewish humor (better to laugh than to cry). After a Danish newspaper published the Muhammad cartoons in 2005, an Iranian paper responded with a Holocaust cartoon contest. I was especially proud to be a Jew when a group of Israelis countered with their own anti-Semitic cartoon contest. An organizer said, "We'll show the world we can do the best, sharpest, most offensive Jew-hating cartoons ever published! No Iranian will beat us on our home turf!"

I can't draw cartoons, but here's one of my favorite anti-Semitic jokes: Two Jews see a sign in front of a church that says "$100 to convert." One of the Jews says, "Why not? It's an easy way to make a quick buck." The other Jew waits outside to see if it works. After 45 minutes the first Jew comes out and the second Jew asks, "Well, did you get the $100?" The first responds, "Is that all you Jews ever think about, money?"

Growing up, whenever a Jew did something publicly my family and many other Jewish families took it personally. As a baseball fan in 1951, I was listening to the radio as Bobby Thomson hit his dramatic, pennant-winning home run. When we started shouting, my Hungarian grandmother, who knew nothing about baseball, asked the natural question: "Is this good or bad for the Jews?" She was surprised when we answered, "Neither." Her question isn't asked much anymore, and I think that's because of what happened on October 6, 1965, which I consider the best day for American Jews in my lifetime, perhaps in the history of America.

The Jew who led American Jews to a promised land of inclusion was not the fictional Abraham or Moses, but the real Sandy Koufax. He was the best baseball pitcher in 1965, and the obvious choice to pitch the opening game of the World Series for the Dodgers. What transpired was the most important nonevent event imaginable for me and many other Jews. Sandy Koufax declined to play because it was Yom Kippur, considered the holiest day of the year by Jews. (Don Drysdale, the Dodgers pitcher who replaced Koufax, pitched poorly, and when the manager came to take him out Drysdale asked, "Don't you wish I was Jewish, too?")

Sandy Koufax, to me, was the Jewish Jackie Robinson. I don't mean in any way to equate the considerable racism against African Americans in this country with the relatively minor anti-Semitism, but in some ways Koufax did for Jewish Americans what Robinson did for African Americans. Nothing seemed as American as baseball, and nothing in baseball is as important as the World Series. Koufax showed that Jews could succeed in a non-Jewish world. No longer would we always look through the "good or bad for the Jews" lens. We became Americans who felt more comfortable being openly Jewish.

So what kind of Jew was Sandy Koufax? He was a secular Jew who stayed in his hotel room on October 6, 1965, belying the reports of thousands of Jews who said they saw Koufax at various synagogues. Jews observe Yom

Kippur in various ways, and some not at all. My nonobservant tradition is to think back to the game Sandy Koufax didn't pitch, and what it means to be open about who you are. Barney Frank acknowledged being a Jewish atheist after retiring from Congress, but he doesn't go out in public on Yom Kippur to show his respect for Judaism.

I've come up with another label to go along with Orthodox, Conservative, Reform, and Humanistic Jew. A *Koufax Jew* is a Jewish atheist who chooses not to work on Yom Kippur. Though I'm not one, I respect those who are. As far as I'm concerned, whatever you do on Yom Kippur is good for the Jews.

20

LGBT

Even Churches Need to Grow Up

Gays are perverts and child molesters, or so I believed as a high school student decades ago. This embarrasses me, but I never harmed gays through word or deed. I had never met one, which means that nobody I knew acknowledged being gay. Had some been out of the closet, I likely would have undergone an attitude adjustment. If the concept of human rights even existed thousands of years ago, it was different from today. Scripture doesn't change, but humans do. When reading a scriptural passage that seems hurtful, you can go in three directions: follow it to the letter because God's law trumps human rights; interpret it in a way that you can do what you know is right; ignore it because it was written by fallible humans. Atheists have an easy choice.

Gays Are Not an "Uppity Minority"

Kirkpatrick Sale's op-ed, "How did gay power get so much clout?" contains a number of unintentionally humorous comments. I'll mention just two. First, he accuses gays of being an uppity minority, compared with other minorities like Jews. As proof he says, "Are Jews boycotting stores that sell pork?" No, and gays don't boycott heterosexual weddings. Second, he decries "the bizarre idea of marriage between two people of the same sex, which for most of human history was not only not proposed but not even thought of." Interracial marriage was viewed as bizarre through most of South Carolina history, and illegal until the Supreme Court overturned miscegenation laws in 1967.

Those who prefer to live in the past may choose to do so as long as it doesn't interfere with equal rights for everyone else. Gays are a minority, but I agree with Dorothy Parker: "Heterosexuality is not normal, it's just common."

I'm Not Gay, but I Am Jealous

Since 1937, Gallup has been asking people if they would vote for a generally well-qualified presidential candidate nominated by their party should the nominee be Catholic, Mormon, black, woman, atheist, etc. Gays weren't even included in the survey until 1978, and they ranked last. Today atheists are at the bottom. The good news is that there is less discrimination against all minorities, and in 2012 for the first time a poll indicated that a slim majority (54 percent) would consider voting for an atheist. While I may be jealous of gays because they have advanced more rapidly than atheists, we are on the same team. Religious conservatives demonize gays and atheists, and an advance for either group helps the other. Gays may be winning the culture war more rapidly than atheists, but young people are helping both. In another generation, I expect people will ask what the gay marriage controversy was all about. Every new survey describes rapid movement away from Christianity and into the "none" or the humanist/atheist camp. If this trend continues, I look forward to an America where the influence of conservative religion is mainly limited to within the walls of churches, not the halls of Congress.

Interfaith and Faithless

I went to church on Sunday evening, August 7, 2016, something an atheist like me rarely does. However, I was eager to attend because Rev. Jeremy Rutledge of Circular Congregational Church in Charleston invited me to a special "interfaith and philosophy" service in honor of Pride Week in Charleston. He also asked me to promote the event to other members of my local humanist group. I was pleasantly surprised to see humanists explicitly included and publicly acknowledged in the ceremony. Rev. Rutledge began, "We gather here, as people of many different faiths and philosophies, to say clearly and unapologetically that our message is love, not hate." I normally wince when a preacher talks about the one "true" religion. However, I silently applauded when Rev. Rutledge said, "The true religion is love," adding, "religion has so often been used, and continues to be used, as an instrument of intolerance, division and outright hate."

The keynote speaker was Warren Redman-Gress, executive director of the Alliance for Full Acceptance. He talked about the importance of the LGBTQ community standing out, and his evolution from closeted gay, uncomfortable with flamboyant gays, to his acceptance of all. He reminded us that it is important for everyone to stand out in support of those who are persecuted for being members of the LGBTQ community.

After the service, over refreshments, I told Warren that everything in his address also applies to atheists, and he agreed that gays and atheists improve their standing in the community when they come out and stand out and that we should collaborate more frequently. I wore our humanist group's t-shirt to the event, and received smiles and praise for my favorite pun on the back: "A Non-Prophet Organization." Many attendees told me that they don't believe in prophets, either. I mentioned that I enjoyed the ceremony, except for the prayers and hymns praising God. Some people said that "God" is mostly a metaphor to them and we are free to substitute "Good" for "God." They sounded like secular humanists, and I invited them to join our local group.

One woman told me she believes God is queer, or at least queer-friendly. A few days later, I read a *New York Times* op-ed by Rabbi Mark Sameth titled, "Is God Transgender?" All this reminded me of the joke, "If God is a Unitarian, he probably spends all day questioning his existence." Or maybe it isn't meant to be a joke.

I attended the Pride parade on Saturday, and was envious of how much greater acceptance the gay community has achieved, compared with the atheist community. Charleston Mayor John Tecklenburg was Grand Marshall, with dozens of sponsors and thousands of supporters cheering the passing parade along the route. All kinds of organizations marched with banners, including our secular humanist group. I saw a few signs on the sidewalk warning about sinners going to hell, but I just smiled, wondering if they believe a special place in hell is reserved for gay-friendly atheists.

Earlier that week, my wife Sharon and I went to a Gay Bingo event. I hadn't played bingo since I was ten years old, but I don't think I've lost my bingo skills. I was curious about how the event would differ from the bingo of my youth. Unfortunately, all 500 tickets for the event had previously sold online. At the Saturday parade, I saw a friend who had attended the bingo event and I asked her how gay bingo was different. Her response: "No straight line on the bingo card could win."

Even at the parade, Donald Trump was channeled. Among the clever signs was "Make America Gay Again." Perhaps we now need atheist and humanist signs that say "Make America Secular Again." The world would be a better place if serious events would incorporate some friendly humor. The last time I played bingo, the word "gay" was a synonym for "happy." In that sense, I hope we *can* make America gay again.

The Bathroom War Between the States

North Carolina usually seems more reasonable than South Carolina, but a notable exception was North Carolina's approval of a law blocking local governments from passing antidiscrimination rules that grant protections to gay and transgender people. This is a solution searching for a problem. There are zero recorded instances of harassment by transgender people in bathrooms, though there are at least three recorded instances of Republican politicians being arrested for lewd behavior in public restrooms.

My favorite protest came from the porn site X-hamster, which blocked its website from North Carolinians and replaced it with a petition to repeal the law. A spokesperson for X-Hamster said, "Judging by the stats of what you North Carolinians watch, we feel this punishment is a severe one. We will not stand by and pump revenue into a system that promotes this type of garbage. We respect all sexualities and embrace them." (Note to my wife: I hadn't visited the site before reading about the issue.)

A Republican South Carolina senator ironically named Lee Bright proposed the same legislation in his state. He is on the Board of Visitors for the Southeastern Baptist Theological Seminary, whose core beliefs include "wives should forsake resistance to their husbands' authority and grow in willing, joyful submission to their husbands' leadership." While many South Carolinians agreed that it was finally time to remove the Confederate flag from state capitol grounds after the massacre of nine African Americans in a Charleston church, not so for a true confederate like Sen. Bright. Abusive husbands are problematic in South Carolina, but Bright had an interesting take as he summed up the Civil War: "The North was an abusive husband the South wanted to leave."

Even so, some South Carolina groups consider Sen. Lee Bright too moderate. It is no surprise that the South Carolina Secessionist Party plans to raise the Confederate flag during a rally at the state capitol on July 10, the first anniversary of the flag's controversial removal. However, the Secessionist Party just celebrated the 151st anniversary of Abraham Lincoln's assassination, calling April 14 "a true southern holiday" as it marked the date "the greatest American dictator was shot."

I know what you might be thinking, but I'm not making this up.

21

MARRIAGE

My Wife and Her Husbands

My wife is married to another man (in the eyes of the Catholic Church), even though she got a civil divorce over 25 years ago. She and her former husband, also happily remarried, are adulterers according to a church that does not recognize such second marriages when the church blessed the first one. A colleague of mine married a Catholic who got an annulment after 20 years of marriage and three children. He married for the first (church) or second (state) time. I enthusiastically endorse my wife's two divorces: one legally from her first husband, and one metaphorically from the Catholic Church.

Religions may decide what marriages to sanction, what the intended must believe or pretend to believe, what they must promise about child-rearing, who is to obey whom, and when a marriage is over or never existed. The government should only intervene in religious marriages when civil laws are violated. The right to freely practice religion does not include the right to impose religious beliefs on others.

Those who oppose same-sex marriage because marriage is "sacred" don't go far enough. To be consistent, they should prohibit judges, sea captains, and me from performing secular (godless) marriages, which I do regularly as a Humanist Celebrant. In fact, they should try to invalidate my own godless marriage. And don't tell me that a good reason to oppose same-sex marriage is that no children could come from such a union. My wife and I married in our 50s and are no more likely to produce a child than would a same-sex couple. Prohibiting gays from marrying does nothing to defend the institution of marriage. A better defense would be through programs on financial management, domestic violence, contraception, and basic parenting skills.

Interfaithless Marriage Works, Especially for the Secular

Some in my family were upset that I married a gentile. When I told an aunt that Sharon is an atheist like me, she asked, "Couldn't you marry a *Jewish* atheist?" Sharon and I have lived happily ever after in our interfaithless marriage.

I think interfaith marriage works best when neither party takes faith very seriously. To modify the old cliché, "The family that never prays usually stays." Love doesn't conquer all, and religious beliefs often pose serious obstacles that love fails to conquer. Shared values at the beginning of a relationship may become unshared as time passes. Since so many people are reluctant to be open and think through their true religious feelings, including whether to raise a child in one religion or another, is it any wonder that religious differences often cause marriages to fail?

Find Meaning in Marriage Without Religion

Marriage is religious in the same sense that eating dinner, scoring touchdowns, or listening to Bach is religious. It can be if you want it to be, but it doesn't have to be. For many people marriage is simply a ritual, with nearly half ending in a divorce ritual. Atheists and agnostics have significantly lower divorce rates than religious people, and states in the Bible Belt have higher divorce rates than other states. I'm hesitant to give advice about marriage because, unlike "experts" like Rush Limbaugh and Newt Gingrich, I've been married only once.

Making a legal or religious commitment to love each other is fine for those who want to do it. Not making it is fine, too, because the only essential words in the preceding sentence are love and commitment. After Sharon and I had been living together for ten years, she said we were getting too old to be boyfriend and girlfriend, and suggested we get married. I was uncomfortable with the idea, so it required discussion. We often base decisions on whether one of us wants something more than the other doesn't. Since Sharon wanted us to get married more than I didn't, we got married. My first-year anniversary present to Sharon was to tell her, "You know, being married isn't as bad as I thought it would be." She smiled and responded, "That's the most romantic thing you ever said to me." And it probably was.

An Atheist's Defense of Marriage Act

I've been married for many years, although not particularly enthusiastic about it—until now. Don't misunderstand. Sharon and I have had a loving, committed relationship for decades. But recent consciousness-raising arguments over same-sex marriage changed my overall opinion about marriage. You might even say that support for gay marriage became my personal DOMA (Defense of Marriage Act).

In 1999, after living happily together for 10 years, Sharon suggested we marry. I responded with a cliché, "If it ain't broke, don't fix it." I quipped that religious conservatives rant about the evils of "living in sin," so I wanted to promote the joys of sin. I also wanted to boycott heterosexual marriage until gays had the right to marry. Sharon and I married on January 1, 2000. We had a nice secular ceremony at midnight in our home, with friends sharing our delicious Ben & Jerry ice cream wedding cake.

So why did same-sex marriage change me from marriage detractor to marriage supporter? I learned that same-sex couples weren't simply advocating for marriage equality. While listening to arguments for same-sex marriage, I discovered there are about 400 state benefits and over 1,000 federal benefits to marriage. I don't see why married couples should have so many economic and legal rights unavailable to equally committed unmarried couples, but I take advantage of them, just as I take advantage of breaks in a tax system that I think should be more progressive.

Here's a final insight. My parents had a happy marriage, but the type in which I would have been miserable. My father went to work, as men were supposed to do; my mother took care of the home, as women were supposed to do. They seemed comfortable in their stereotypical roles. Perhaps these marital interactions during my formative years led to my "post-traumatic parental marriage syndrome." Since I can't imagine what gender roles would look like in a marriage between two men or two women, I'm finally able to free myself from PTPMS and appreciate fully my own wonderful marriage.

The L-word

My personal tradition has been to avoid the L-word. This has little to do with my secular humanism, other than valuing evidence. When I was a math professor in the 1970s at Clark University in Massachusetts, a woman I had been dating for several months told me she loved me. I was taken aback, thanked her, and reciprocated by saying that I liked her but didn't know what love was. She broke up with me shortly thereafter.

A few months later, I was invited to appear on a radio talk show to discuss, "The joys of bachelorhood." The host told me I'd be free to speak my mind, but I couldn't use certain words on the air. When I asked, "What words?" he said, "You know, like the four-letter word that rhymes with fire truck." I repeated his warning on air, adding, "As far as I'm concerned, the four-letter word that has caused the most harm, the word that has been the source of the most hypocrisy, is the word *love*." The host shouted, "That's the most disgusting thing I've ever heard. You should be ashamed, making fun of such a beautiful word. We better take a commercial break now and come back for phone calls."

During the break, he said matter-of-factly, "I agree with you. I think the show is going quite well, don't you?" My first radio interview taught me that you couldn't necessarily expect hosts to believe what they spout. I wasn't sure if my attitude about love was motivated more by honesty or fear of commitment. I eventually concluded that I was probably just being a jerk. In 1990, I finally felt comfortable using a word I couldn't define. Before I met Sharon, I could make the same claim as Woody Allen's character in *Manhattan*, that I hadn't had a relationship with a woman that lasted longer than the one between Adolph Hitler and Eva Braun. Though I don't believe in souls, I'm comfortable saying that Sharon has been my soul mate (and my first love) for the past 25+ years.

22

MORMONISM

Humor Is in the Eye of the Beholder
The Book of Mormon musical makes fun of the Mormon religion and its foundational story. I don't distinguish religious satire from political satire or other forms of social satire, and there was not much protest from Mormons or calls to ban the musical. People I like most don't take themselves too seriously. How religious people react to humor is often far more damning to the religion than the humor, itself. Muslims could have treated the Danish cartoons of Muhammad as a teachable moment about their faith, or protested peacefully. Claims that Islam is a peaceful religion were not hurt by the cartoons, but by the ensuing violent reaction to them.

A Presidential Candidate Good for the Atheists
Here is my surprise choice for a presidential candidate in 2008 who would be good for atheists: Mitt Romney, a Mormon. The only thing atheists and Mormons have in common is that a significant number of Americans wouldn't vote for either. But I'm hoping for at least three unintended consequences if Romney becomes the nominee.

1. Conservative Christians will denounce outlandish portions of Mormon dogma, and ask whether somebody who believes such nonsense is fit to hold the office of President. Then atheists will have an opportunity to "defend" Mormon beliefs by pointing out that they are no more unbelievable to an outsider than dogma in other holy books.

2. Some people will say that Mormon belief is exceptionally bizarre because you would expect more evidence for nineteenth century miracles than for first century miracles. Atheists can then point out that our twenty-first century minds lead us to withhold belief without evidence, regardless of the period in which there was no evidence.

3. Many Romney supporters will say that his religious beliefs are a private matter and that you should judge a candidate by what he has said and done, rather than by some of the tenets in his holy book. Fair enough. Whenever candidates promote their religious beliefs, we should ask them how their beliefs would impact public policy. Most likely Romney will try to have it both ways by speaking about his faith when it pleases conservative Christians, while neither denying nor admitting to other religious underpinnings (and undergarments) of the Mormon faith.

    An old commercial had different companies pitch a manager to buy their copier because "It's just as good as a Xerox." The manager says to the next pitchman, "I know. It's just as good as a Xerox." The response was, "No, it *is* a Xerox," followed by the manager's handshake. I'm willing to vote for candidates who claim they can compartmentalize their irrational, faith-based religious beliefs and govern rationally on evidence-based information. In other words, the unwritten campaign strategy of candidates would be to say they would govern as if they were atheists. So why not elect the real thing? Too bad there's not yet an acknowledged atheist candidate.

We Should Judge Their Politics, Not Their Religion

On my office wall is a cartoon showing a bearded guru with a sign-up sheet. A giant thermometer in the cartoon marks off increasingly larger categories of religion, starting at the bottom with "handful of wackos," and then up the thermometer with bunch of nuts, cult, sect, and at the top—mainstream religion. The poster next to the guru says, "Join us and help us reach our goal!"

In trying to explain how reasonable Mormonism is, Romney said, "The most unusual thing in my church is that we believe there was once a flood upon the earth, and that a man took a boat and put two of each animal inside the boat, and saved humanity by doing that." Romney essentially said that his holy book is no more preposterous than the holy books of the other candidates. He has a point.

Regardless of how "mainstream" a politician's religion, we should not stereotype. Mo Udall and Glenn Beck have nothing in common other than calling themselves Mormons. The same can be said about Christian Reverends Pat Robertson and Jesse Jackson or Jewish Senators Joe Lieberman and Bernie Sanders. And I can't think of another Quaker who supported Quaker President Richard Nixon's widening the war in Southeast Asia and secretly bombing Cambodia. Ideally, we should judge candidates on the content of their character and political positions, not on their professed religious beliefs.

Mixing Religion and Politics

It's odd that a Mormon (Mitt Romney) and two Catholics (Rick Santorum and Newt Gingrich) are the leading 2012 presidential candidates in a Republican party dominated by Protestant evangelicals. Unfortunately, this is not the kind of religious diversity espoused by presidential candidate John F. Kennedy in 1960, when he assured Protestant ministers in Houston that he believed in an America where separation of church and state is absolute. President Kennedy gave good secular arguments for decisions he made on behalf of the country. When Santorum was asked if he supported President Kennedy's statement, Santorum said he "almost threw up."

Since no Mormon has yet been president, Romney's religion will undoubtedly undergo close scrutiny, and its beliefs will seem strange. According to the Book of Mormon, in a story chiseled in Egyptian hieroglyphics on gold plates and buried in Palmyra, New York, after Jesus died, but before he went to heaven, he stopped in the United States. In 1827, the angel Moroni led Joseph Smith to the gold plates and a magic stone, which Smith placed in his hat so he could translate the gold plates into English. This story sounds as reasonable to me as the one about how Jesus rose from the dead, or that a person can drink his blood and eat his body every Sunday, or that a talking snake tricked Adam and Eve into eating a piece of fruit.

Another peculiar Mormon practice is baptizing dead people. Many Jews are upset that Mormons have posthumously baptized Holocaust victims, including Anne Frank and Simon Wiesenthal's parents. Perhaps they've also baptized a few of my relatives who died in the Holocaust. That's fine with me, because this ridiculous practice does no harm to my dead relatives or me. In fact, it seems like an expression of good will, much like, "I'll pray for you." I believe in its sentiment, if not its efficacy. I prefer the Mormon imaginary afterlife to the Christian one. Mormons would give me a posthumous chance to convert. I've always said I'd become a believer if presented with evidence. Christians, on the other hand, would simply have me burn in hell forever. I think the probability of either scenario is zero, but the Mormon one sounds more compassionate.

Mitt Romney: A Reasonable Man?
Here's a hypothetical scene in which four presidential candidates are asked about their religious views.

> **Candidate 1**: "It does me no injury for my neighbor to say there are twenty gods or no God. It neither picks my pocket nor breaks my leg," adding, "The day will come when the mystical generation of Jesus, by the supreme being as his father in the womb of a virgin will be classed with the fable of the generation of Minerva in the brain of Jupiter."

> **Candidate 2**: "As I understand the Christian religion, it was, and is, a revelation. But how has it happened that millions of fables, tales, legends, have been blended with both Jewish and Christian revelation that have made them the most bloody religion that ever existed?"

> **Candidate 3**: "During almost fifteen centuries has the legal establishment of Christianity been on trial. What have been its fruits? More or less, in all places, pride and indolence in the clergy; ignorance and servility in the laity; in both, superstition, bigotry and persecution."

> **Candidate 4**: "When I do good, I feel good; when I do bad, I feel bad. That is my religion."

Were this to take place at a public debate, Candidates 1 (Thomas Jefferson), 2 (John Adams), 3 (James Madison), and 4 (Abraham Lincoln) would be booed off the stage, their political careers ended.

I think the most reasonable 2012 Republican candidates are the two Mormons (John Huntsman and Mitt Romney). My bar is set pretty low: they never talk about their deity telling them to run or how to vote. The major truth-telling test for me is whether a candidate expresses a view that he or she knows will be politically detrimental. That's why I'll believe any candidate in this country who says he's an atheist, and I'll believe any candidate in Iran who says he's a Jew or Christian. The important question to ask all candidates is if and how their faith would impact public policy.

23

PRAYER

Prayer (Private)

Still Hoping for a Secular Miracle

I'm tempted to write the shortest answer by any *Washington Post* panelist to any question we've ever been asked. **Question**: Does God endorse candidates? **Answer**: No!

I wish more religious people would answer as I did, especially politicians. If a candidate says God endorses his or her run, I run the other way. Any candidate who believes God is responsible for his or her election is deluded, and deluded people don't make rational decisions. Psychologist Thomas Szasz said, "If you talk to God, you are praying. If God talks to you, you have schizophrenia."

Only Humans Can Solve Human Problems

Prayer, at best, can be an effective placebo. It helps believers feel they are doing something positive, and prayers might even "cure" some psychosomatic disorders. Several presidential candidates prayed to God asking whether they should run, and God answered "yes" to all of them. It's funny how God's plan always seems to be the same as that of the politician who asks for guidance.

A more effective way to solve problems would be to seek guidance from another book with talking animals, *Aesop's Fables*. In one fable, the wheels of a wagon get stuck in the mud and the driver gets on his knees to pray. Hercules appears and says, "Get up and put your shoulder to the wheel. The gods help them that help themselves." Ben Franklin also made this statement a number of centuries later, but with a singular God. In other words, only humans can solve human problems.

My Plan Is God's Plan

Last week my wife Sharon and I passed an ice cream store and I jokingly told her that God planned for me to buy a large scoop of pistachio ice cream. (God's plan for me seems always to be the same as mine.) Sharon found my comment mildly amusing and added that a small scoop of chocolate was God's plan for her. Not so amusing are people who delude themselves or others into believing the equivalent of my ice cream parable.

The Power of Positive Praying—Even for Atheists

George Washington likely would have lived longer had he requested prayer for his throat inflammation instead of bloodletting. Usually performed by barbers, bloodletting was the most common medical practice until the late nineteenth century. The traditional red and white striped poles outside barbershops represented red for blood and white for bandages to soak up the blood. Mary Baker Eddy, who founded the Christian Science religion in 1879, taught that the sick should be treated by a special form of prayer rather than by the medicine of the day. Eddy may have attracted followers because she inadvertently adhered to the advice Hippocrates gave 2,400 years ago: "First do no harm," as valid today as it was then. For theist and atheist alike, prayer is better than harmful medicine.

Here's a harmless (and humorous) form of prayer. The Vatican declared that a person who follows prayer tweets from Pope Francis would get time off from purgatory. I don't believe in heaven or hell, but I'm especially puzzled by purgatory—which God forgot to mention in the Bible. Apparently, it's a halfway house for punishment until you've suffered enough to go to heaven.

Here are some of my tweet questions for Pope Francis. Would, say, a reduction of a thousand purgatory years be based on earth time? And how does the pope (or God) calculate "time" in eternity? Unlike former indulgences, at least the tweeting is free for those with a smart phone. But is God's "get out of purgatory" pass really fair to those who can't afford a tweeting device?

Prayer (Public)

National Day of Nonprayer?

Imagine this hypothetical headline: "President Obama will sign a proclamation recognizing National Day of Nonprayer." Of course, I would not expect the president to set aside a special day for what I happily choose to do every day—not pray.

Hindus would be delighted if President Obama were to call for a national day to recognize the god Vishnu, and Christians would object. Vishnu is as real to me as Yahweh, Zeus, or any other gods. But National Vishnu Day would give Americans something to think about, and thinking is more effective than praying.

A president who wants to base decisions more on evidence than on faith might consider issuing a proclamation recognizing a "National Day of Reason." After all, who could object to a president promoting reason?

A National Day of Reason?

There would be no need for a National Day of Reason in 2012 if there were not a government-endorsed National Day of Prayer. Our government should never tell its citizens when, how, or whether to pray. Christian Coalition spokesperson Billy McCormack claimed that the National Day of Reason is "a blatant assault on Christianity." Would those who object to reason also object to a National Day of Science? There was a time when Americans would feel embarrassed by their ignorance of science or their disdain of reason. Not so much, anymore.

I hope that some religious people can support the proclamation sponsored by Rep. Pete Stark (D-Cal), which begins: "The National Day of Reason celebrates the application of reason and the positive impact it has had on humanity. It is also an opportunity to reaffirm the Constitutional separation of religion and government." Many secular groups observe the day by performing community service projects and other good works. That's consistent with the philosophy of Robert Ingersoll, a nineteenth-century atheist (and Republican): "The hands that help are better far than the lips that pray."

An Atheist's Favorite National Day of Prayer

In 1952, Congress established the National Day of Prayer, observed the first

Thursday in May since 1988. The Thursday, May 1, 2014 Day of Prayer was my favorite—by default. It was the first I attended, quite by accident. A film crew from Holland's Humanist Broadcasting Foundation came to Charleston to interview me about atheism in the Bible Belt. They would be filming me at a Reason Fest event sponsored by our local humanist group, but when they learned that the National Day of Prayer rally would be nearby, they thought it would also be fun to film me there.

The event was more divisive than I had anticipated. The theme came from Romans 15:6: "So that with one mind and one voice you may glorify the God and Father of our Lord Jesus Christ." The Charleston paper did not write the usual puff piece about such prayer events. Instead, the story began with the Dutch film crew and my presence. Reporters probably get bored writing the same annual story, and we provided a new perspective.

An Orthodox rabbi, the token non-Christian, was scheduled to offer a prayer at the rally. I asked him if his congregation might be uncomfortable seeing a photo of him with a large cross in the background. He hadn't noticed the cross, and looked chagrined. I then invited him to our more inclusive Reason Fest event that was about to begin.

Some at our event described their paths to reason, telling why and how they left religion. The rabbi did skip the prayer rally and came, instead, to our Reason Fest. He later told me that he enjoyed being with our group. He thanked me for pointing out the large cross under which he would have spoken, and called my kindness to him a real mitzvah (a good deed). My reasonable nonprayer for America is that we treat every day as a National Day of Mitzvah.

Why the Supreme Court's Conservative and Liberal Judges Are All Greek to Me
In the 2014 US Supreme Court case *Greece v. Galloway,* the five conservative justices ruled that sectarian content is permissible in public invocations and official prayer, while the four liberal dissenting justices felt that religious leaders should give nonsectarian prayers at government functions. I disagree with all nine justices. Their opinions reminded me of the quip from former Justice Potter Stewart that while he couldn't define pornography, "I know it when I see it."

I can neither define nor have I seen a nonsectarian prayer, but I know a sectarian prayer when I see it. Justice Anthony Kennedy, arguing for the majority, said that the government should not "act as supervisors and censors of religious speech," yet went on to describe when they should. Kennedy said that clerics should not "denigrate nonbelievers or religious minorities, threaten damnation, or preach conversion."

I'd rather hear an honest fire-and-brimstone prayer than a watered-down hypocritical prayer. I feel more excluded by prayers to a nondenominational Almighty meant to be inclusive of all faiths because this dismisses those of us with no faith in deities. Religion is inherently divisive. Prayer at government functions promotes the idea that decisions are guided by a higher power rather than by thoughtful deliberations. Further, such government endorsements create theological insiders (almost always Christian) and outsiders. Government bodies will have to decide which faith (or secular?) groups they deem acceptable to speak at public meetings. Does anybody see conflicts ahead?

I wish government bodies would simply begin with government business. But if prayer is part of government business, let's treat it as such. Since there is often time at public meetings for questions and comments, would it not be appropriate to question the content of the opening prayer? If so, given religious sensitivities, there might not be time for any other business—another reason to keep religion out of government.

Nonspecific Deity
Invocation guidelines recently passed by the Charleston County School Board allow for a reference to one divine being but no reference to a specific deity. The board chairman was satisfied with the guidelines because they showed that "the board was religious and believed in a supreme being." Excuse me? I thought people were religious, not boards.

Another board member said he was happy with the guidelines because members "were invoking the same deity that every religion worships." Were he to take a course in world religions at one of the schools he represents, he would learn that not all religions worship the same deity. Some worship different deities, some worship many deities, and some worship no deity at all. Instead of publicly worshipping a nonspecific deity as a board, members who wish to seek guidance from a deity of their choice should do so in private. Perhaps if school board members didn't devote so much public time and energy on how to pray at public meetings and how to avoid lawsuits for so doing, they would spend more time on the difficult task of improving the quality of education for our children in public schools.

24

PRESIDENTIAL PRIMARIES

2012

How Would Jesus Vote?

Christianity is sometimes described by category, rather than denomination, as conservative, liberal or cultural. To that, I would add a fourth category: **political Christian**, a candidate who feels the need to profess deeply held Christian beliefs.

In my home state of South Carolina, Governor Nikki Haley was raised as a Sikh and converted to Christian before running for public office. When she first became a gubernatorial candidate, her website said, "I believe in the power and grace of Almighty God." She later felt the need to change to "My faith in Christ has a profound impact on my daily life. Being a Christian is not about words, but about living for Christ every day."

A cynic might say, "Maybe it's also about winning elections."

Politicians who continually proclaim their faith are likely to be more hypocritical than those who don't. If Charlestonian Stephen Colbert agrees to run, I'll definitely vote for him in the Republican primary. He's a Christian with a sense of humor, and he doesn't use his faith to pander for votes. I wish Romney, Paul, Gingrich, Santorum, and Perry would learn that marketing their faith for political gain might just be sending some voters running to support the "none of the above" candidate, Stephen Colbert.

Martin Luther King and the Republican Race for Righteousness

If I believed in a god, and one with a sense of humor, I would think she had a big chuckle over timing the South Carolina Republican primary for the same week the nation celebrates Martin Luther King Day. On May 2, 2000, South Carolina became the last state to make King's birthday an official state holiday. But South Carolina also created another official state holiday on May 10—Confederate Memorial Day. Prior to this legislation, state employees had the choice of celebrating the birthday of Robert E. Lee, Jefferson Davis, or Martin Luther King.

Some South Carolina politicians think nothing of falsifying history, even when they can easily be caught. For instance, Congressman Joe Wilson claimed that he spearheaded the effort to have King's birthday recognized. Wilson's colleague said he must have been confused about which holiday he supported, which was really Confederate Memorial Day. When confronted with evidence, Wilson said his memory must have failed him. (This is the same Joe Wilson who famously yelled "You lie!" at the country's first African-American president during his State of the Union speech.)

Candidate Ron Paul voted against Martin Luther King Day both in 1979 and 1983, when the bill passed. In one of his newsletters, Paul referred to the holiday as "Hate Whitey Day." Candidates are being asked about whether the Confederate battle flag should remain atop the State Capitol. The safest, if not the most courageous, answer for Republican national candidates is to call it a state issue. Newt Gingrich said, "I have a very strong opinion: it's up to the people of South Carolina." He added that he is opposed to segregation and slavery. Well, that's a relief! I'm quite sure that Martin Luther King would disagree with Newt about what he told a Charleston audience was the biggest domestic threat to America: "Removing God from the public arena."

South Carolina Primary Humor, Intentional and Unintentional
For me, the highlight of the South Carolina primary campaign was hearing Stephen Colbert speak to an overflow crowd on my College of Charleston campus. He's the most honest "politician" of the primary season, and he spoke eloquently and humorously about a critical campaign issue— the "Citizens United" Supreme Court decision that paved the way for Super PACs as long as there is no coordination between the PAC and the candidate. Colbert's coordination with Jon Stewart on the "Definitely Not Coordinating with Stephen Colbert Super PAC" shows how coordinated such uncoordinated Super PACs can legally be.

Sometimes the most effective way to change a corrupt system is to make fun of it. I almost always vote against rather than for a candidate. My primary vote was an exception. I voted FOR Herman Cain because Colbert introduced and endorsed Cain at the rally. I'm not sure if Cain understood that Colbert really endorsed himself, but no matter. The following day, I walked out of my polling place with a smile on my face.

Newt Gingrich, a Catholic, won the South Carolina primary with strong evangelical support. Newt would never say that he believes in an America where the separation of church and state is absolute, which is what our only Catholic president said. All Gingrich seems to have in common with JFK is well-publicized, adulterous relationships. Newt sounded funnier than Colbert when he indicated that his passion for our country led him to adulterous affairs. Perhaps Newt won because of his attack on the media for asking about his second ex-wife. I guess evangelicals are more opposed to so-called liberal media bias than to adultery, especially if you claim that God forgave you for it.

Newt also received key endorsements from two beauty queens, Miss Teen Powdersville and Miss Powdersville. Miss Teen would vote for Newt because he's a great guy, but she is only 15. Miss Powdersville liked him because he supports Christianity and he would take us back to the Bible. She couldn't think of any other issues.

Stephen Colbert is intentionally funny, but not the funniest person I heard during the South Carolina primary spectacle.

Hypocritical Values

During the 2008 primaries, I awarded my "hypocrisy" prize to Mitt Romney. He supported gay rights and abortion rights as governor of Massachusetts, but his positions "evolved" as a Republican candidate for president. He was *for* equal rights before he was *against* them.

In this primary, my "hypocrisy" prize goes to Newt Gingrich. I agree with his comment about politics to Christian pastors: "If you don't start with values, the rest of it doesn't matter." Gingrich's values seem to center on political pandering and hypocrisy.

South Carolina is home to Susan Smith, who in 1994 tragically drowned her two children and blamed it on a fictitious black carjacker. Three days after the drowning, Gingrich took the opportunity to say that such violence somehow arose from a Democratic-controlled political system. However, Susan Smith's stepfather, Beverly Russell, hadn't been campaigning for depraved Democrats, but for Newt Gingrich. Russell had been a Republican leader in South Carolina and local organizer of Pat Robertson's Christian Coalition, championing "family values" and "school prayer" as partisan Republican issues. Gingrich, however, remained silent during Smith's trial, when it was revealed that Russell had molested her since she was fifteen, and she had attempted suicide twice by age eighteen. That's a hard one to blame on Democrats.

While it's scary to have hypocrites like Romney and Gingrich as viable candidates, I'm even more worried about potential candidates like Bachman, Palin, or Huckabee, who might actually believe what they say God is telling them to do. My values are secular based on evidence, not theocratic based on imaginary voices.

2016

Who Is God's Candidate?

Republican presidential candidate Ben Carson said he would not support a Muslim for president because the Islamic faith is inconsistent with the US Constitution. He later added that whoever takes the White House should be "sworn in on a stack of Bibles, not a Koran." Here is my *very* qualified agreement with Ben Carson: strict adherence to the Koran is inconsistent with the Constitution, but so is strict adherence to the Bible. Lawmakers take an oath to follow the Constitution, and I don't see why they should swear on the Koran, stacks of Bibles, or any other so-called holy books. President John Quincy Adams was sworn in with his hand on a book of US laws to demonstrate that he recognized a barrier between church and state and his loyalty was to our nation's laws above all else. Teddy Roosevelt also did not use a Bible at his first swearing in ceremony.

So would I vote for a Muslim for president? It would depend on the positions the Muslim were to take on issues important to me, just as it would for Christian, Jewish, Hindu, or atheist candidates. I would not vote for a candidate who claims that a god told him or her to run. That eliminates Ben Carson, Mike Huckabee, Bobby Jindal, John Kasich, Rick Perry, Rick Santorum, and Scott Walker. Given the number of candidates God supports, he/she/it must have a commitment problem or is hedging bets like a wealthy contributor. God used the same strategy in 2012, when he backed Herman Cain, Michelle Bachmann, Rick Santorum, and perhaps others. God's track record hasn't been so good.

Sharia, Christian, or Constitutional Law?

Newt Gingrich said, "We should test every person here who is of a Muslim background, and if they believe in sharia, they should be deported." Aside from violating the US Constitution, how impractical would it be to round up all Muslims in the country and give them such a religious test? Many patriotic Americans who practice the Muslim faith would undoubtedly become anti-American if required to take that test. Ironically, conservative Christians who seem most worried about sharia agree with more tenets of sharia law than do atheists like me. From what I understand, sharia is opposed to abortion, contraceptives, and sex education, considers being gay a sin, has little tolerance for other religions, and treats women as subservient to men while claiming women are privileged within the religion. Sharia also wants a religion-based government. Hmm, seems to me I've heard that song before.

The 2016 Republican Party's platform demands that lawmakers use religion as a guide, stipulating "that man-made law must be consistent with God-given rights." So what about man-made laws in our Constitution that members of Congress have sworn to uphold? Here is a legitimate question to ask all who seek public office: "Will you support and enforce the laws of the land even if you believe your religion or your god tells you to do otherwise?" Neither sharia nor Christian law should take priority over our secular Constitutional law. Theocracies rule by "God's law," but we are not now and must never become a theocracy.

My Brief Support for Marco Rubio

I came close to supporting Marco Rubio for president when he reportedly had the courage to say that there are not many answers in the Bible. I say "reportedly" because this was one of many Ted Cruz fabrications. Rubio really said, "All the answers are in the Bible."

He added, "This nation was founded on the principle that our rights come from our Creator," and "If there is no creator, then where did your rights come from?"

Good question. Rubio's rights-granting creator, the God of the Bible, condemns many rights guaranteed by our Constitution and Bill of Rights.

For instance, the First Commandment (thou shalt have no other gods) conflicts with our First Amendment, which guarantees the right to worship one, many, or no gods. You won't find democracy in the Bible, but you will find the divine right of kings. You won't find treating women as equals or condemnation of slavery, but you will find punishment for blasphemy.

Rights have evolved over millennia, thanks to evidence, rational thought, empathy, and moving away from bronze-age theology. No creator endowed us with the right to life, liberty, and the pursuit of happiness. These rights are specified in our founding documents, written by some of the best thinkers in the Enlightenment era. All cultures have promoted variations of the "Golden Rule," the major difference being who was included within the scope of moral norms. For much of human existence, only members of a person's tribe, clan, ethnic group, or religion were entitled to moral respect, but that changed when we became more enlightened. Religions endorsed tribal morality when that was the prevailing ethic, and now most religions are inclined to support the prevailing ethic of universal human rights.

Those who find all their answers in the Bible presumably ignore the Constitution when it conflicts with the Bible. But those who would rather be governed according to biblical rights (and wrongs) might prefer living under a theocracy—as long as it is *their* theocracy and not some theocracy of infidels.

Politically Incorrect, Literally
In Orwellian fashion, some political candidates proclaim they are *not* "politically correct" because it's a politically correct ploy to gain political support. Ben Carson received a boost for his presidential campaign when he denounced political correctness at the 2013 National Prayer Breakfast. However, he failed to note that attending the prayer breakfast *is* politically correct. How many candidates would have the courage to decline such an appearance because they don't believe in the power of prayer?Not to be outdone, ever, Donald Trump told a crowd of South Carolina business leaders, "I'm so tired of this politically correct crap," and then surged in political polls.

Some candidates employ "politically incorrect" to justify any bad behavior, which includes bigotry, offensive comments, scientific ignorance, and refusal to answer difficult questions. Since when did rejecting the overwhelming consensus of scientists about evolution and climate change become a proud politically incorrect position?

Are Secular Progressives Murderers?

With the exception of Sen. Bernie Sanders, all presidential candidates in both parties bring their Christian beliefs into the campaign. Some even base their campaign positions on what they believe God wants for America. Many conservative Christians claim their religious freedom is under attack whenever they must obey the same nondiscrimination laws as all Americans. We can tell how much discrimination there is against Christians by how many politicians are in the closet about being Christian and how many proclaim during their campaigns how proud they are to be atheists. Perhaps instead of an Openly Secular campaign, whose goal is to favorably change the public's perspective of atheists, someone should start an "Openly Christian" campaign.

Ben Carson has said many puzzling things, but I was astonished by his pronouncement that he thinks he is in great danger and needs Secret Service protection because he challenges the Secular Progressive movement to its very core. Presidential candidates need protection from the many lunatics in this country, yet I'm taken aback by Carson's stated reason for his request. Whether you agree or disagree with secular progressives, this is the first time I've heard them accused of being violent. Sure, they challenge Carson on most of the political and religious positions he takes.

But … killing people we disagree with? Sadly, this has all the trappings of carefully crafted propaganda, starring Carson as a brave patriot willing to put his life on the line for his beliefs and caricaturing his political opponents as extremists so dangerous and unscrupulous that they would kill their opponents.

Did WikiLeaks Reveal I Was a Shill For Hillary Clinton?

No, but it might look that way. In a Wiki-leaked email, Democratic National Committee CFO Brad Marshall appeared to want someone to ask Bernie Sanders if he believed in God, as a way to hurt Bernie's campaign. However, that email was written in May and I asked the question in February, before the South Carolina primary. During the Q&A in a Sanders forum in Charleston, I commented, "I don't think you are the only Jewish socialist in the country who believes in God, so I'm hoping you will do for atheists what Barney Frank did for LGBTs and be the first senator to acknowledge being an atheist." Sanders paused for a moment, looking uncomfortable because of the audience's applause, and answered, "Not gonna happen." Sanders stressed that he was a Jew. (This is not an atheist disavowal. In fact, 52 percent of American Jews do not believe in God.)

I did not ask my question to help Hillary. In fact, I supported and voted for Bernie in the South Carolina primary. I asked because one of the best ways to change atheist stereotypes is to have respected leaders come out of the closet. What many of us like about Bernie Sanders is that he is an honest politician with consistent core values. Sanders became properly outraged when he learned that Marshall tried to hurt his campaign by branding him an atheist, and said, "I am not an atheist."

However, I was disappointed when Bernie didn't acknowledge that atheists are also fine and decent Americans. He most certainly would have done so had he been "accused" of being a Hindu, Buddhist, Muslim, or any other religious or ethnic minority. The theme of the Democratic Party Convention seemed to be inclusion. The platform made a commitment to "protect religious minorities and the fundamental right of freedom of religion." Notably absent at the convention was the word "atheist," an important constituency that the Democratic Party consistently ignores.

One of the most interesting comments among the speeches at the convention was Hillary Clinton's, "I believe in science." What made it interesting was that it needed to be said in 2016 and that it drew significant applause. Perhaps that indirectly was a nod to atheists and others who live in a reality-based universe. A noteworthy post-convention comment came from Sarah Silverman, a Bernie Sanders supporter. When asked if there was anything she had wanted to say in her speech that the DNC wouldn't allow, I expected it to be a phrase from her "colorful" vocabulary. Not so. She said she was not allowed to say, "I've been with this possibly agnostic Jew." Sarah is open about not believing in God, but she did not mention that in her convention speech.

Atheists, agnostics, humanists, and others who get their ethics and values from non-religious sources have been silent for too long, but times are changing. On the opening day of the Democratic National Convention, the Secular Coalition for America hosted a Secular Democratic Reception for nonreligious delegates and attendees. It was an opportunity for nonreligious Democrats to learn about ways they can advocate for church/state separation, science-based policy, and increase the visibility of nontheists in their local Democratic parties. State secular caucuses have formed, and more are expected to take part in future state party platforms. I hope that all political parties will become less inclined to demonize or ignore our growing and increasingly organized communities.

Post-Election Healing: An Atheist's Perspective

This presidential campaign has been the most divisive and hate-filled in my lifetime, and I acknowledge being both shocked and disappointed by the outcome. However, here are a few thoughts on turning some campaign lemons into lemonade as we move forward.

1. **Sexual Assault**: I'm encouraged by the song of Nobel-prize winning Bob Dylan, "The Times, They Are a-Changin." But for women who think the times have not changed enough to allow them to go public, I recommend an even older song, "I'm Gonna Sit Right Down and Write Myself a Letter." Write down all relevant details in a letter to yourself. Mail it and when you receive your postmarked letter, place it unopened in a safe deposit box to be unsealed at an appropriate time. Undoubtedly, several women associated with Donald Trump now wish they had followed this procedure.

2. **Evangelical Divide**: Here I'm cautiously optimistic, with emphasis on "cautiously." Do the many white evangelical Protestants who endorsed Donald Trump now suggest that a candidate's religious beliefs might not matter so much? Many Christians recognize the danger of ignoring social justice issues to focus exclusively on an anti-abortion agenda. Some might worry that religious leaders are selling their souls for personal power and political influence instead of pursuing their more traditional mission of saving souls.

3. **Political Correctness**: If political correctness means you can't speak openly and honestly about controversial topics or act in ways that might offend some people, then count me out. I was a politically incorrect liberal before it became cool (thanks, Bill Maher). For instance, I refused to open car doors for my dates or pull chairs out for them as a teen in the 1950s, which might explain why I didn't lose my virginity until graduate school. Today that behavior would go unnoticed, so

I sympathize with Trump supporters who don't appreciate political correctness. I hope this election has taught people that we not only have the free-speech right to be politically incorrect, but also the right and responsibility to call out bigotry. And violence and assault are not just politically incorrect—they're criminal.

4. **Outsiders**: The two surprise vote getters during this campaign were Bernie Sanders and Donald Trump, both populists outside the political mainstream who would like to end business as usual. I do, too, which is why I voted for Sanders in the primary. Although Trump and Sanders differ on almost all issues, they have one thing in common: They are probably both atheists, though neither is "politically incorrect" enough to acknowledge it.

5. **Atheists in Public Office**: Although religious tests are unconstitutional, the electorate seems to apply an unwritten religious test that candidates express some sort of religious belief. Only when closeted atheists in Congress come out, and when more open atheists run for and win public office, will the atheist taboo finally be broken. A secular US Constitution helped make America great. When religion mingled with politics is no longer business as usual, we together can make America even greater. With less importance placed on religion in this presidential election, I'm hoping future candidates will be judged on their political positions and their character, rather than on their professed religious beliefs. That's the politically correct and morally correct thing to do.

25

REVIEWS

Books

How to Read (and Think) Like an Atheist

There were two types of people in the 1950s: those who could name one book by an atheist and those who could not. I joined the small first category in 1958 at age sixteen, after fortuitously discovering Bertrand Russell's *Why I am Not a Christian.* That book was the atheist wing in my local library. For the first time, I heard articulate arguments that confirmed and gave voice to my own skepticism and doubts. Russell probably led some true believers on a thoughtful journey toward altered religious states.

Today there are countless "nonspiritual" heirs to Bertrand Russell, including best-selling books by Richard Dawkins, Christopher Hitchens, Sam Harris, Carl Sagan, Daniel Dennett, and others. These authors give persuasive arguments for why God is both a delusion and not great, and why our lives would improve if we could bring an end to faith by breaking the spell of a demon-haunted world. Conservative religionists might believe that Satan inspired these authors, but godless views are gaining traction in our culture.

Aside from books about God's nonexistence, there are companion books about why and how secular Americans should organize, how to be good without gods, how to raise children without gods, and even how to have better sex without gods. There are scores of atheist blogs in flavors from plain vanilla to hot pepper. Long story short, atheists are here to stay and, in fact, their numbers are growing. The Internet has probably been the single most important factor in empowering young people with inquiring minds to learn about many choices for religious belief or nonbelief. The figurative genie is out of the bottle. No matter how hard religious and social conservatives strain to put the genie back in the bottle, they will not succeed in attempts to pray the atheist away.

Religious Fiction: Isn't That Redundant?
Authors can often choose whether to call their books fiction or nonfiction. But we don't always know the author's identity, as with the Bible. Some biblical writers made up stories to motivate people to believe or act in certain ways, some composed poetry, some described events that likely occurred, and some wrote "just so" stories to explain what they didn't understand. I would classify all God stories as fiction, but bookstores won't risk community outrage by filing the Bible under "religious fiction."

This brings me to *Heaven Is for Real: A Little Boy's Astounding Story of His Trip to Heaven and Back*, a book that climbed to the top of the *New York Times* nonfiction bestseller list in 2010. The book gives four-year-old Colton Burpo's account of his visit to heaven as he almost died on an operating table. His pastor father wrote the book, with help from Sarah Palin's ghostwriter. The most compelling "evidence" for Colton's heavenly experience is that he met a sister (from his mother's miscarriage) who his parents had never told him about. Do all fetuses go to heaven? Colton's sister in heaven looked a lot like his sister on earth.

Colton also met God, Jesus, and John the Baptist in heaven. God is a really big man. How big is he? Big enough to hold the whole world in his hands, confirming the Sunday school song. Colton sat on Jesus's lap and observed his stigmata and sparkling blue eyes. Colton met his great-grandfather, who had wings. Colton had many more adventures in heaven during the brief time he was under anesthesia on earth. It must be a coincidence that Colton's stories about heaven mimic stories told to children by Christian adults.

I'm not surprised by Colton's beliefs, ingrained from infancy, though I don't know how much of the pastor's faith in Colton's visit to heaven might be inspired by fame and fortune. What most disturbs me about the success of the book are the countless people who feel such a need for knowledge of an afterlife that they are willing to believe almost anything—even when it comes from a four-year-old who also believes in Santa Claus.

5 Books Atheists and Other Outsiders Should Read

Each book changed my worldview and my way of thinking to varying degrees. They are listed in the order I read them. Most of us are more open to new ideas when we are young, and I read all but the last before the age of twenty.

1. ***The Bible*** by authors unknown

   I "knew" as a child that the Bible was God's word, and consequently the most important book in the world. My best Hebrew teachers encouraged us to question what we read. Unlike Ken Ham, I found no answers in Genesis. Long before Judy Collins had any hit songs, I could say: "I've looked at Torah (Hebrew Bible) from both sides now, from Orthodox Jew and atheist, too. But it's Torah's illusion I recall. I really don't know Torah at all." The Bible and the monotheistic religions it spawned have deeply influenced our culture and the world. For that reason alone, the Bible is worth reading.

2. ***The Scarlet Letter*** by Nathanial Hawthorne

   Hester Prynne was required to wear a Scarlet A on her chest for her "sin" of adultery. She refused to reveal that the baby's father was the respected Reverend Dimmesdale. Though shunned by her community, Hester lived an exemplary life and raised her daughter to be a fine young woman, while the hypocrite Dimmesdale died a broken man. The Scarlet A has evolved into a red A that some atheists wear proudly in pin form as part of an "Out Campaign." From *The Scarlet Letter* I learned that to be comfortable in your own skin (or letter) is better than hiding who you are to please those you don't respect.

3. ***Why I am Not a Christian*** by Bertrand Russell

   After reading Hawthorne's classic, I wondered about scarlet letters I might be hiding. I hadn't told anyone that I no longer believed in God, thinking everybody else was a believer until I read Russell's book. I felt better about myself after learning that he was more than just not a Christian. He was as many "nots" as I was. I wanted to emulate Russell. Learning he was a mathematician at least partially inspired me to become one.

4. *A Collection of Essays* by George Orwell

Orwell was thoughtful, insightful, wrote clearly, and was honest about himself. I read these essays before I had even heard of *1984* or *Animal Farm*. Three stood out for me.

"Shooting an Elephant" begins with "In Moulmein, in Lower Burma, I was hated by large numbers of people—the only time in my life that I have been important enough for this to happen to me." I wondered if I'd ever be important enough to be hated by any group of people. That day came when I ran for governor of South Carolina (see book #5 below).

"Politics and the English Language" clarified for me the importance of honest and clear language, and that misleading and vague language can be a tool for political manipulation. I learned not to use a long word when a short one will do. Orwell pointed out that those who simplify their language would be freed from the worst forms of orthodoxy, and that when you make a stupid remark its stupidity should be obvious, even to yourself. Orwell worried that political language was designed to make lies sound truthful, which must have been on his mind when he later wrote *1984*.

"Why I Write" explains motives that inspired Orwell: sheer egoism, aesthetic enthusiasm, historical impulse, and political purpose. Those motives spoke to me then, and do so even more now.

I didn't know Orwell was an atheist when I first read him. "Big Brother" appears to be an omnipotent, omniscient, eternal, authoritarian figure who demands absolute obedience. Here is Orwell's explanation: "In *1984*, the concept of Big Brother is a parody of God. You never see him, but the fact of him is drilled into people's minds so that they become robots, almost. Plus . . . If you speak bad against Big Brother, it's a Thoughtcrime."

5. *Candidate Without a Prayer: An Autobiography of a Jewish Atheist in the Bible Belt* by Herb Silverman

This is not meant to be a shameless plug for my own book, but maybe a little. (Note that I didn't choose the five best books, just the five that influenced *me* the most.) I discovered that one of the best ways to learn about yourself is to write about yourself. We should write about what we know well, and we are all likely world experts on ourselves.

How Can a Made-up Bible Still Be God's Word?

Perhaps I was inspired to read *The Bible Tells Me So*, by Peter Enns, because of childhood memories of a song with the same simplistic title. I agree with much of what Enns says about the Bible, but we come to opposite conclusions.

Points of Agreement

Enns says the Bible largely consists of made-up stories by unknown authors attempting to explain their views of the world and its origins. They sometimes modified stories from earlier cultures to shape their present needs and goals. The Bible has countless contradictions, as well as historical and scientific falsities. We should not accept the Bible as literal truth or attempt to make sense out of nonsense. The God of the Bible is no role model. He can be a tyrant who orders enslaving or killing innocent people (including children) because they worship the wrong gods or live in lands that God wants his chosen people to occupy. God commands the Israelites to kill everything that breathes in Canaan.

Enns' Conclusion

We need to trust the Bible to say what it says and allow God's word to challenge us. The Bible is God's word, but not God's *final* word or the center of Christian faith. Access to God comes through faith in Christ and obedience to him. Jesus was crucified by the Romans and became a resurrected messiah. The reality of a risen Jesus *necessarily* transforms Israel's story, as he is savior of the world, not just of Jews.

My Conclusion

How can any thoughtful person acknowledge so many made-up biblical stories, yet unquestioningly refer to the "reality" of a risen Jesus? Many people want to remain part of a religious family tradition, but it's especially difficult to maintain as a core belief that someone rose from the dead and will grant everlasting life to faithful believers of such a story. We should accept only the parts of the Bible that make sense to us, as with any other book, and not give unwarranted credibility to so-called "holy" books.

Churches

Church Invitation: An Atheist on American Anglicans and Amazing Grace
I visited St. Andrews Anglican Church, whose vision is to re-evangelize our society and transform our culture. It was established in 1827, and now has more than 3,000 members. The homily was "TODAY: How Should I Read the Bible?" I translated it in my mind to "How Should I Read the Bible TODAY?" However, the homily was about reading the Bible without concessions to modernity.

The minister told us to read the Bible "humbly, prayerfully, thoughtfully, expectantly, and obediently." No mention of "skeptically." He warned of scorners (like me, I guess) who use difficult passages to undermine the Bible's authority. He alerted us about cultural biases that might lead us to follow only parts of the Bible, saying that if any parts offend us, it's because we don't understand them. He made one reference to atheism, claiming that inaccuracies in the film *Noah* were expected because the film's director is an atheist. He added that we must trust only Jesus rather than those who appear to be good and moral. (Hmm . . . should congregants not trust the minister?)

Congregants were supportive of one another, but I didn't hear much interest in the outside community. I tried to think of what they might have been inspired to do after leaving the service. They heard about church support groups and volunteer opportunities for church activities, but congregants were mostly told to love Jesus, read the Bible, put money in the collection plate, and return to church next week.

As I left, I saw a police officer standing by my car in the parking lot. While I was inside, someone called the police after he saw a woman sideswipe my car and then park elsewhere. When the woman returned to her car, the officer confronted her with the evidence. She said she was planning to leave a note on my car, and that her insurance company would pay for the damage. The officer told me I could press charges, but I declined because nobody was hurt and I didn't want to bother going to court. The last words the woman who hit my car said to me were, "God bless you!" Her car had an "In God We Trust" license tag, while mine had an "In Reason We Trust" tag.

I recognized only one song at the service, "Amazing Grace," which always moves me. I associate that song and "We Shall Overcome" with

1960s marches for civil rights and against the Vietnam War. In church, however, I had an urge to tell congregants, "I am not a wretch" (as the song implies). Driving home, and for the next several days, I occasionally found myself quietly singing "Amazing Grace." But don't read anything into it—there's nothing supernatural about earworms.

One of America's Best Kept Religious Secrets
Unsurprisingly, Christianity is the largest religion in all 50 states. Surprisingly, Bahá'í is the second largest religion in my home state of South Carolina, with more Bahá'í than Jews, Muslims, and Hindus combined. The Bahá'í faith became popular in South Carolina because of Louis Gregory, born in 1874, raised in Charleston, and one of the Bahá'í founders in America. After this grandson of a slave became a Bahá'í in 1909, he travelled the country promoting racial equality. Gregory married a white Bahá'í woman in 1912, when interracial marriage was a crime in parts of the country.

I attended a Bahá'í meeting at a local home in Charleston, with 15 adherents. I assumed that the host, Dave, was the leader, but he said there are no Bahá'í leaders. Members periodically open their homes for meetings like the one I attended. We sat in a circle and the service began with Dave playing a plaintive melody on a recorder. Attendees then read aloud from a pamphlet called "Reflections on the Spirit of Unity." Dave told us to think about how the writings might apply to ourselves, not about what others should do.

Diversity of race and culture were praised; racism, nationalism, social class, and gender-based hierarchy were seen as artificial impediments to unity. And, indeed, the participants were white and black, male and female, young and old, rich and poor. I agreed with just about all the messages, except for the God parts.

Over a healthful dinner, I discussed Bahá'í theology with Dave and others. I asked about their belief that God has revealed himself through a series of divine messengers, including Abraham, Krishna, Zoroaster, Moses, Buddha, Jesus, and Muhammad. Dave gave an evolutionary justification: God sends different messages as cultures evolve and are more capable of understanding and accepting them. This fits with the Bahá'í belief in the importance of unity and the goal of achieving world peace when there is unity among world religions. My favorite religions are human centered without any gods, like Humanist Unitarians, Humanistic Judaism, and

Ethical Culture. Since the Bahá'í Faith seems to be a human-centered religion with God, it might be my favorite theistic religion.

Bahá'ís abstain from partisan politics. They can't endorse or run for political office. Thought experiment: How would our country change if Christians declared a 10-year moratorium on running for public office?

God Must Be Proud of Atheists

I was intrigued by that title of a sermon at our local Unitarian Church in Charleston, given by visiting minister Dr. J. William Harris (Doctor of Divinity), so I attended. The church is atheist-friendly, but often too new-age spiritual for me. Dr. Harris had been the minister at First Baptist Church in conservative Greenwood, South Carolina. As his beliefs gradually changed, so did his sermons, sometimes to the chagrin of parishioners. Ten years after becoming a Universalist, he began preaching about it in his church. A hell-free afterlife for *everyone* was more than some in his flock could bear, so he is no longer minister at First Baptist Church, and he is now closer theologically to Unitarian Universalism than to South Carolina Baptist.

Though I appreciated his sermon, I found lots with which to disagree. Part of his theology is consistent with a T-shirt of mine that says, "Smile, there is no hell," but I wouldn't wear a T-shirt with another part of his theology, "Smile, everybody goes to heaven." He believes that in death we will all be one with God, whatever that means. The scriptural passage most meaningful to him is "God is love" (I John 4:8). So Dr. Harris seems to be saying that God is proud of atheists because God is proud of and loves everyone.

At the coffee hour, I asked Dr. Harris if an accurate elevator summary of his sermon would be, "God is love, I love God, so I love *love*?" He said, "That sounds about right." I then told him I couldn't help humming to myself the Rodgers and Hammerstein song, "Falling in love with love is falling for make believe." He laughed and said he understood how people could come to that conclusion. When I asked if his Universalist beliefs meant that Adolph Hitler was being treated well in heaven, he acknowledged that he hadn't worked out the problem of evil yet. But he likes to think that Jews are at a banquet table with Hitler having some laughs and good conversation. (I've never known any Jews who conceived of that kind of heaven.)

Dr. Harris admits he is closer to atheism than to theism, but still maintains belief in a mystical God who does not exercise any control over our lives. I told him of one advantage he had over me. "If you're right about a universal heavenly afterlife, you'll be able to say, 'I told you so.' But if I'm right about no afterlife, I won't be able to say, 'I told you so.'" He liked my take, and said he'll use it in future discussions with atheists.

Movies

What's God Got to Do with It?
The Invention of Lying is a movie about a culture in which nobody can lie until one person develops the ability. With the best of intentions, our liar-hero (Mark) tries to comfort his dying mother by telling her that she will be going to a wonderful afterlife. Of course she and others believe him. Soon everyone wants information about this afterlife. Every word Mark makes up is taken as, well, gospel. In the biggest lie of all, he tells the world there is a Man in the Sky responsible for everything, and they will be happy up there with him after death. When asked if the Man in the Sky is also responsible for cancer, Mark has to grapple with theodicy, a problem in all monotheistic religions: Why is there evil in a world created by an all-powerful and benevolent god? Incidentally, the Ten Rules for the World that Mark writes on Pizza Hut boxes is better than the Ten Commandments. The movie's message for me is that Man in the Sky religion is possible only in a world where people can lie.

Atheists Bad, Christians Good
That's my four-word summary of *God's Not Dead*. This anti-atheist movie would be more effective if it didn't portray every atheist as smug, angry, selfish, obnoxious, and unhappy. In contrast, nearly every Christian is kind, happy, generous . . . well, you get the idea. The movie's two protagonists are atheist philosophy Professor Jeffrey Radisson and Christian student Josh Wheaton at fictional Hadleigh University.

Professor Radisson is a bully who uses his bully pulpit to require each student to sign a "God is dead" statement or else convince him that God's not dead—and, failing that, receive an F in the course. Radisson has been doing this for years, presumably without a complaint from students, other faculty, or administrators. In fact, he is about to become head of the Philosophy Department. He has a live-in girlfriend whom he started dating when she was his student, and he continually berates and belittles her in front of his academic colleagues. She turns to Christianity and finds the strength to get out of this abusive relationship after talking to Pastor Dave (more about him later).

Freshman Josh Wheaton is the only student who refuses to sign the "God is dead" statement. Everyone encourages him to sign for the sake of his career—except for Pastor Dave, who gives Josh the strength to enter Radisson's lion's den, armed with Matthew 10:32–33: "Whoever acknowledges me before others, I will also acknowledge before my Father in heaven. But whoever disowns me before others, I will disown."

Radisson allows Josh three class sessions to make his case for God. Josh requests that the class act as jury, and Radisson agrees. After Josh wins the debate with a unanimous jury verdict, vindictive Professor Radisson confronts Josh for having had the audacity to embarrass him in class, and threatens to fail him. Josh asks Radisson why he's an atheist, and Radisson says his mother died when he was 12, despite his prayers. So Radisson hates God for killing his mother. (It's not explained how an atheist can hate God.)

God's Not Dead is probably intended for those who believe the myth that Christians in this country are being persecuted. Christians and atheists alike would be appalled if an institution of higher learning would expect students to sign a "God is dead" statement. As dogmatic as the fictional Professor Radisson is, he at least gives ample class time to a student with a different opinion. Not so at some Christian universities. Perhaps Josh "Wheaton" represents Wheaton College, a Christian institution where students and faculty must affirm a statement of faith and educational purpose that includes "God created Adam and Eve, distinct from all other living creatures." So much for any pretense of critical thinking at Wheaton.

The movie has a happy ending, at least for some Christians, because a car runs over Professor Radisson. Pastor Dave just happens to be nearby and encourages Radisson to become a Christian mere seconds before he dies. So the most effective way to convert atheists is not by reason or evidence, but by personal tragedy. Perhaps this will inspire some Christians to pray that atheists get run over or undergo some other misfortune, because the film reinforces the "no atheists in foxholes" cliché.

26

SCIENCE

The Gould Standard

In his appreciation of Stephen Jay Gould [Style, May 21], Joel Achenbach said, "[Mr.] Gould's politics were solidly left of center. He forcefully argued against the teaching of creationism in schools, a position that drew a great deal of fire." However true both sentences may be, Mr. Gould opposed the teaching of creationism in a science class not because he was a leftist but because he was a scientist.

Science Is Not Democratic

Republican presidential candidate Rick Perry is being compared to George W. Bush, our most recent president from Texas. Here is one place the comparison breaks down: Perry is not campaigning to be the "Education President," as Bush did. Whatever its merits, Bush was president when the "No Child Left Behind" act became law. Perry seems more interested in leaving every child behind.

When a little boy in New Hampshire was prompted by his mother to ask Perry about evolution, Perry replied that it's just a "theory" with "gaps," and added, "In Texas, we teach both creationism and evolution. I figure you're smart enough to figure out which one is right." Here are other questions Perry might ask small children: Does the earth look flat or round? Does it look like the sun is moving around the earth or the earth is moving around the sun at approximately 67,000 mph? Never mind the scientific consensus, you're smart enough to just know.

Some religions are threatened by evolution not just because it contradicts a biblical worldview, but also because we now understand that the first creatures who can be called human inherited their DNA from creatures who could not be called human. The first mammals got their DNA from their reptilian ancestors, and so it goes back to the first single-celled organism. Religious people can decide where a "soul" enters this picture.

Creationism should no more be taught as an alternative to the theory of evolution by natural selection than should the "stork theory" be taught as an alternative to reproduction. Creationism is an alternative to Zeus or Krishna, not to Darwin.

The "Stupid Party"

Louisiana Governor Bobby Jindal urged his Republican Party to "stop being the stupid party" and advised them to reject anti-intellectualism. While this sounds like an excellent step forward, it depends on the interpretation of "stupid" and "anti-intellectualism." This is the same Jindal who, in 2008, signed the Louisiana Science Education Act, which allows local school boards to approve supplemental materials for public school science classes as they discuss evolution, cloning, and global warming. Though marketed as support for critical thinking, the law was designed to open the door to teach creationism and scientifically unwarranted critiques of evolution in Louisiana science classes.

The Louisiana governor apparently doesn't understand that neither he nor the Republican Party can avoid being stupid and anti-intellectual when they oppose scientific discoveries established for more than a century. It's demonstrably unintelligent to weaken scientific standards for public schools just because those standards conflict with a literal interpretation of a "holy" book written in a pre-scientific era.

Perhaps Jindal was only telling his Republican colleagues not to be *politically* stupid.

Natural, Not Supernatural, Disasters

I'm not particularly concerned about flat earthers and Holocaust deniers because they have no influence. I can't even name one, and that's a good thing. Unfortunately, the same can't be said about Pat Robertson, a household name to Americans. Even worse, he is influential and respected by millions. According to the book of Robertson, the reason for every disaster is sin, and the solution usually involves sending him money. That was Robertson's explanation on why God brought the earthquake in Haiti that killed thousands. Here's an alternative view: the "fault" lies under the Atlantic Ocean, not in the sins of Haitians. The earth's tectonic plates are neither good nor evil. The more we learn about their shifting, the better we will be able to predict future earthquakes.

Hawking and the Pope

New theories make a creator of the universe unnecessary, says Stephen Hawking in his latest book, *The Grand Design*, co-authored with Leonard Mlodinow. Even if the theory is proved beyond reasonable doubt, most believers will either ignore the evidence or create arguments to make the findings consistent with their god beliefs. M-theory predicts that the universe in which we live is just one of countless universes and that a universe can and will create itself from nothing.

The more we learn scientifically, the less significant humans seem in our natural world. Darwin showed that humans are animals and Copernicus displaced humanity from the center of the universe. If M-theory is correct, we are an unremarkable species living in an unremarkable part of an unremarkable universe. While there is some evidence for M-theory, it still sounds incredible to me. But here's a more incredible hypothesis, devoid of any evidence, that many believe: "A benevolent deity always existed in nothingness, and then created a universe. Billions of years later, he decided he was lonely and created human beings. His only interest in humans is in how much they love him and how they worship him. When humans die, they will either be rewarded or punished for eternity based solely on whether they believed this story to be true."

Stephen Hawking once met Pope John Paul II at a cosmology conference at the Vatican, and quoted the pope as saying, "It's OK to study the universe and where it began. But we should not inquire into the beginning itself because that was the moment of creation and the work of God." Pope Benedict, who also briefly met with Hawking at an event hosted by the Pontifical Academy of Sciences, described science as the pursuit of knowledge about God's creation. Such popes fail to grasp the rudiments of scientific inquiry. Science is about asking and trying to solve problems, not limiting or discouraging questions. When St. Augustine was asked what God did before making the world, Augustine replied, "He was creating a Hell for people who ask questions like that."

Yes, Mr. Hawking, Evidence Should Determine Belief

Famed physicist Stephen Hawking rejects the idea of heaven, calling it a "fairy story" for people afraid to die. As accomplished a cosmologist as Stephen Hawking is, no scientist would ever declare, "Hawking said it, I believe it, that settles it." Scientists require evidence, not an appeal to authority.

That science can't disprove a god's existence does not constitute evidence for a god's existence, anymore than not disproving unicorns is evidence that unicorns exist. But the more science advances, the less we need attribute to a god. Unlike Stephen Hawking, I wouldn't compare supernatural religious beliefs to fairy stories. At age ten, I didn't believe in demons, devils, and talking animals in fairy tales, but I learned valuable lessons from the stories. Unfortunately, some believe literally in their holy books and base their lives on these stories. Even worse, the beliefs affect us all. Religious interest groups have influenced politicians to favor faith-based legislation over science-based legislation to the detriment of our education system. If only we would treat the Bible and other holy books as fairy tales. The faith of a child in a good story is better than the faith of an adult who believes a made-up story.

A Godless Apocalypse

My tradition is reality based. It says that the earth is a medium-sized planet revolving around an average star (our sun), one of billions in our Milky Way galaxy, which is one of billions of galaxies. Earth is a relatively tiny object in a massive universe, of interest to us only because we happen to live here. According to modern astrophysics, the world will end when our sun runs out of hydrogen, its primary solar fuel. A superheated atmosphere will expand across space, embrace nearby planets, and incinerate everything on earth in perhaps five billion years.

It will be a godless apocalypse.

Faith-based communities argue over when their scriptures predict the world will come to an end. My best scriptural guess is that the world ended about 1,900 years ago. Mark 13:30, Matthew 16:28, Luke 9:27, and other passages indicate heaven and earth would pass away and Jesus would return in that generation. In the last 2,000 years, Christians in every new generation believed their times would be the end times. To all such past and present prognosticators, I have but one question: How's that working out for you?

Perpetuating Ignorance

Florida Senator Marco Rubio said he couldn't tell how old the earth is, whether created in seven days, or seven actual eras, or whatever science claims. He added, dismissively, "I'm not a scientist man." You don't have to be a scientist to accept the noncontroversial findings among scientists that the Earth is 4.54 billion years old, plus or minus 50 million years. These personal (or pandering?) views are bad enough, but for Rubio the crux of the disagreement is "whether what a parent teaches their children at home should be mocked and derided and undone at the public school level." He added, "I don't want a school system that teaches kids that what they're learning at home is wrong." Because some parents teach their children that blacks are inferior to whites and women should be subservient to men, does Rubio also think that schools should shrink from offering more modern points of view? If so, why not just keep children away from schools so they won't be exposed to scientific and social views that conflict with what their parents believe? Oh, wait! We do allow home schooling.

Science Solution

A recent letter said we should not have wasted $10 billion of government money to replicate the Big Bang in order to determine how the earth was formed, because we could find that out by just picking up a Bible. Let's take it further. We can save much more money by using the Bible as our only scientific source and eliminate expensive research. Biblical science was completed some two to three thousand years ago, so look at all the money we would save by removing science from the school curriculum.

But wait, there's more. Rising health care costs would end. James tells us that prayer should be the only allowable healing method. Expensive surgery would be unnecessary, according to Matthew. If your right eye offends you, pluck it out; if your right hand offends you, cut it off. And I saved the best for last. We would no longer worry about the solvency of Social Security. By strictly following biblical science, very few people would live long enough to collect from the resulting Social Security surplus.

How God Led Me to Mathematics and Then Turned Me into an Atheist

When I was a child, an infinite God with infinite power who had lived an infinite time fascinated me. Yet a God who created everything perplexed me. Did God create himself? And if not, then who created God? When

I asked my rabbi, he told me to concentrate on the study of Torah (the Hebrew Bible).

After getting nowhere, I began to feel that studying "infinity" rather than Torah was a better means to understand God. I became enthralled with Zeno's Paradox (300 BCE), an updated version of the tortoise and hare fable of Aesop (600 BCE). A descendant of the rabbit asked a descendant of the turtle for a rematch. The turtle agreed, with the provision that he be given a 100-yard head start in the mile run. The turtle reasoned, "When the rabbit gets to where I just was, I will have gone farther. If I keep doing this, the rabbit will never catch me and I will surely win." Of course, the rabbit easily avenged the humiliation of his ancestor, leaving the turtle and lots of Greeks befuddled.

When I heard that this paradox as well as other puzzles of the infinite could be resolved mathematically, I became a devotee of mathematics. I continued to equate the mysteries of "infinity" and "God." I learned that infinity was not sensible (known through the senses) and that there are many infinities. Are there also many gods?

I learned that infinity was a useful construct created by humans and does not exist in reality. "Infinity" could just as well replace "God" in a remark of Voltaire that "God does a lot of good in the world, even if He doesn't exist." My students sometimes falsely think they can treat infinity as if it actually existed as a real number, and such misuse gets them into a lot of trouble. And so it is with many God believers.

There is a wide range of religious belief among mathematicians, though the value placed on reason makes for far fewer religious believers among mathematicians than among the general public. I'm just happy that I can freely discuss my views without meeting the same fate as Giordano Bruno in 1600. He taught that the universe was infinite with an infinite number of worlds like ours. It was considered heretical for finite man to discover the nature of the infinite, which was so clearly allied with the nature of God. Bruno was burned at the stake, one of the last victims of the Inquisition.

God *IS* Great

I have a fantasy that I participate in a debate against Christopher Hitchens, author of *God Is Not Great: How Religion Poisons Everything*. The debate topic is identical to the one Hitchens took up with Rev. Al Sharpton on May 9, 2007 at the New York Public Library: "Is God Great?" And I take the affirmative position! Here is my argument, which world-class debater Hitchens would have to concede is valid:

> If I say that everyone in this room is a billionaire, you can disprove this claim by pointing out that you are not a billionaire. But you can't disprove my claim that everyone in this room who is ten feet tall is a billionaire. To falsify this claim, you would have to provide someone who is both ten feet tall and not a billionaire. Similarly, if I say all gods are great, there is only one way to falsify this claim. You would have to produce a god who is not great. Since we agree that no such god exists, the debate is over. I win!

Here's a similar argument I heard as a child, which I didn't recognize as faulty logic by creationists to discount what they thought evolutionists believed: "If the moon is made of green cheese, then I'm a monkey's uncle." This is a true statement, because it could only be false if the moon were made of green cheese. However, this statement is false: "If the moon contains iron and silicon (it does), then I'm a monkey's uncle."

While we're talking about the moon, here is a popular story I later discovered was too good to be true, but it illustrates an important point. When Neil Armstrong walked on the moon, his first words were, "That's one small step for man, one giant leap for mankind." As he was leaving the moon, he also uttered words into an open microphone that few people heard. "Good luck, Mr. Gorsky." When Armstrong returned to earth, the press asked him who Mr. Gorsky was. Armstrong just smiled and said it was a personal moment. Recently, a reporter asked him again and Armstrong agreed to explain, saying that everyone involved had died and there was no chance of anyone's being embarrassed.

As a child, Armstrong's next-door neighbors were named Gorsky. One afternoon when he and his brother were playing baseball, his brother hit a ball over the fence into the Gorsky yard. Neil went to retrieve the ball that had landed under their open bedroom window. As he picked up the ball, he heard Mrs. Gorsky say, "Sex! You want sex? I'll give you sex when the kid next door walks on the moon!"

Mrs. Gorsky constructed what she thought would be a valid argument to avoid sex (at least with her husband) for the rest of her life. On July 20, 1969, the day her unlikely premise (and promise) came true, Mrs. Gorsky was obligated to fulfill her husband's request. It would have been more prudent for Mrs. Gorsky to have promised sexual favors to her husband only when the Messiah makes an appearance.

Three Equals One

This is an equation that Catholics claim to "understand:" three gods equal one god. Though the real number of gods is probably zero, I'm concerned that many atheists sometimes seem as comfortable appealing to authority as do Catholics. I occasionally ask my beginning college mathematics students why we don't allow division by zero. The most frequent reply is, "My teacher told me it can't be done!"

Does critical thinking about theological claims qualify us to be called "critical thinkers?" What about my Mormon colleague who applies critical thinking in his mathematical research? We must not oversimplify by partitioning humanity into critical and noncritical thinkers. None of us can or even wants to analyze all of our assumptions, or how and why everything works. But critical thinking requires us to at least know what we don't know. My major concern is that so many people are proud to be noncritical thinkers (or, more accurately, nonthinkers).

Now back to zero. If division by zero were permitted, then from the axioms of our number system we would be able to show that all numbers are the same. To see this, note that $3 \times 0 = 1 \times 0$. Dividing both sides by zero we have $3 = 1$, which would make Catholics right after all.

27

SEPARATION OF CHURCH AND STATE

Inaugural Prayerfest No Godsend

Americans may disagree about whether God was at President Obama's inauguration, but His name was omnipresent in remarks by a variety of religious leaders. Like every incoming US president before him, Barack Obama repeated the constitutionally prescribed one sentence oath to "preserve, protect, and defend the Constitution of the United States." Chief Justice John Roberts then prompted President Obama to recite the nonprescribed words, "So help me, God." To understand how some atheists might feel, just substitute "Zeus" for "God" in public ceremonies.

Like most Americans, I felt a wonderful and profound chill watching Barack Obama become the first African-American president. I'm delighted that the new president offered a token mention of atheists during his eloquent address ("We are a nation of Christians and Muslims, Jews and Hindus—and nonbelievers"), something our secular community isn't used to hearing from politicians, but he ended with the more traditional plea of politicians for God to bless the USA.

A United States for Nonbelievers?

Inauguration festivities send symbolic messages, and I'm pleased that President Obama talked about treating people equally regardless of race, creed, gender, national origin, or sexual orientation. I liked his message, but not the justification for it—God. What would we think if our president had said "Freedom is a gift from Odin" or we must preserve our planet because it is "commanded by Gaia, the goddess of the Earth?"

Despite Obama's inclusiveness he took a step back from his first inaugural address when he gave a token nod to atheists. At this inaugural, nonbelievers were as invisible as deities. Although Obama tried to deliver a bi-partisan message for Democrats and Republicans, I wish he had also included a bi-theological message for theists and atheists.

Why Atheists Should Embrace America's Godless Constitution

Despite discrimination against atheists, our secular Constitution makes no mention of any gods and guarantees freedom of religion. Atheists here can count their "blessings" that they don't live in countries like Afghanistan, Iran, Maldives, Mauritania, Pakistan, Saudi Arabia, and Sudan where open atheists can face the death penalty. Other Islamic countries, including Bangladesh, Bahrain, Egypt, Indonesia, Kuwait, Tunisia and Turkey have stepped up prosecution for "blasphemy" and for any criticism of religion.

Freedom from Religion

I was appalled by the incorrect and insulting statement of Joseph Lieberman: "The Constitution guarantees freedom of religion, not freedom from religion." It is incorrect because Article VI of the Constitution says "no religious test shall ever be required as a qualification to any office or public trust." Article VI allowed me to successfully challenge in the state Supreme Court of South Carolina the unconstitutional provision that atheists cannot be allowed to hold public office. After a seven-year battle, I earned the right to become a notary public in South Carolina.

Mr. Lieberman's comments were also insulting when he implied that the solution to a stagnating moral life would be "as a people to reaffirm our faith." Were we to follow his lead to discuss our faith in public, Mr. Lieberman would discover that there are more secular Jews like me in this country than there are Orthodox Jews like him. We cannot have freedom of religion without also guaranteeing freedom from religion.

Taxation for Religious Discrimination

I'm an eighteenth century tea bagger, not a twenty-first century one. The Boston Tea Party was a protest against taxation without representation. Residents of Boston believed that a British tea tax violated their right to be taxed only by elected representatives. Today's vocal tea baggers have representation, but feel they have the right to shout down government representatives with whom they disagree. Taxation for religious discrimination is *my* tea party issue, involuntarily contributing to a religion without representation. I'm uncomfortable with tax breaks for individuals who donate to a religion, or huge property tax advantages for wealthy churches, and I'm appalled that the government allocates my tax dollars to support religious discrimination.

All Taxpayers Are Created Equal

If you get a federal grant, you can't use that grant money to discriminate on the basis of your religion. These are not my words, but the words of a well-known former constitutional law professor from the University of Chicago. Barack Obama delivered them in a speech about faith-based initiatives in 2008. Despite his admirable words, he still lets stand this Bush-era violation of separation of church and state. I oppose taxpayer money going to religious institutions, but especially money that condones discrimination. Religious freedom allows religions to discriminate, but not on the taxpayer's dime.

If the government stops funding religious discrimination, some religions will modify their discriminatory policies. This happened gradually with one religion, which some call an academic institution, in my home state of South Carolina. Fundamentalist Christian Bob Jones University, in danger of losing its tax-exempt status, changed in steps from not admitting blacks, to admitting married blacks (1971), to admitting unmarried blacks (1975), and finally (gasp) to ending its ban on interracial dating (2000).

A Few Kind Words for Satan

As an atheist, I'm often asked if I believe in Satan because "I have to believe in something." I point out that I don't believe in any supernatural forces, including Yahweh, Satan, angels, or devils. But I can make theological and strategic cases for embracing the mythical Satan, who comes out looking pretty good in Genesis.

After God tells Adam he will die on the day he eats a particular piece of fruit, Satan (in a snake costume) tells Eve that the snack will give them knowledge. So they eat and enjoy their newly acquired knowledge. Though many Christians view this disobedience as the "original sin," God's claim that they would die on that day was the "original lie." Here's how the biblical Satan can motivate people to live decent, rational lives: be curious and seek knowledge; question the sacred; reject authorities that expect blind obedience; encourage free inquiry; welcome diversity of opinion; respect the freedom of others; and acknowledge the worth and dignity of the "out" group.

The word "Satan" in Hebrew means adversary. The Catholic Church recognized this adversarial role in 1587 when it established the position "Promoter of the Faith," more commonly known as "devil's advocate." A canon lawyer played this role to argue against declaring a particular dead person a saint, and to be skeptical of the miracles attributed to that person. I think the devil's advocates were incompetent (the number of miracles I accept is zero), but Pope John Paul II must have thought that these advocates were too evidence-based because he abolished the position in 1983, and then named to sainthood more than five times as many as had all his twentieth-century predecessors combined.

Although devil's advocates were Catholic, members of the Satanic Temple are atheists. It's a religion that rejects tax-exempt status because of its principled position against government support for religion. These Satanists might be having a little fun with the name (Satan), but their primary purpose is to promote secularism. The Satanic Temple gained international attention for its forays into the church-state debate by asserting equal rights for Satanists when religious privileges have been granted. The most notable example is in Oklahoma, where a Ten Commandments monument was placed on Capitol grounds. The Satanic Temple applied for a place on the Capitol grounds for a statue that would "complement and contrast" with the Ten Commandments monument, knowing that government may not privilege one religion over another, or religion over nonreligion.

Is America a Christian Nation?
(Part of my debate with Pastor Ray Moore, President of Exodus Mandate) America is a Christian nation in the same way it is a white nation. The majority are white and Christian, but we are not now nor have we ever officially been a white or Christian nation. Those who believe otherwise might be harkening back to the first Europeans who settled here. Unlike our eighteenth-century founders, the Pilgrims and Puritans were religious dissenters from Europe who sought freedom of worship for their own versions of Christianity, but not religious freedom for others.

In forming a federal government, a minority faction in the

Constitutional Convention of 1787 sought recognition of Christianity, but more enlightened founders carried the day. They wisely established a secular nation whose authority rests with "We the People" (the first three words of the US Constitution) and not with "Thou the Deity." We the people are free to worship one, many, or no gods.

Unambiguous language from our founders should settle the debate over whether America is a Christian nation. The Treaty of Tripoli was negotiated by George Washington, signed by John Adams, and ratified unanimously by the Senate. It stated in part: "The government of the United States is not in any sense founded on the Christian religion." I wonder what part of "not" the Christian-nation advocates don't understand. There have always been people who erroneously believe that the founders intended to establish a Christian nation, but the founders were careful and thoughtful writers. Had they wanted a Christian republic, it seems highly unlikely that they would somehow have forgotten to include their Christian intentions in the supreme law of the land. And I defy anyone to find the words "God" or "Jesus" in the Constitution.

Do Christian Conservatives Believe in the First Amendment?
Most Americans agree on the importance of religious freedom as enshrined in the First Amendment, though they disagree about specifics. Should the government promote religion? Give special tax breaks to religion? Favor one religion over another? Favor religion over nonreligion? My answers are no, no, no, and no.

Talk about strange bedfellows. I find myself in bed with Louisiana Rep. Valarie Hodges, who no longer backs Gov. Jindal's school voucher program after hearing that public money would go to Muslim schools, not just to Christian schools. She said, "I actually support funding for teaching the fundamentals of America's founding fathers' religion, which is Christianity, in public schools or private schools. I liked the idea of giving parents the option of sending their children to a public school or a Christian school." I can't think of a better argument for the separation of religion and government than the unintentional one provided by Rep. Hodges.

"In God We Trust," When Politically Convenient
The House of Representatives voted overwhelmingly in favor of a Congressional resolution reaffirming "In God We Trust" as the national

motto and supporting its placement on public buildings, public schools, and other government institutions. It was sponsored by Randy Forbes (R-Va.), who added, "As our nation faces challenging times, it is appropriate for Members of Congress and our nation, like our predecessors, to firmly declare our trust in God, believing that it will sustain us for generations to come."

What many Americans fail to recognize or acknowledge is that "In God We Trust" only became our official motto in 1956 at the height of the Cold War as a means to separate us from godless communism. The de facto motto established by our founders had been *E pluribus unum*, Latin for "out of many, one." This phrase affirms American diversity as our source of strength, a country made up of people of many faiths and none. Our secular government must remain neutral with respect to religion. A government that feels entitled to tell you to trust in God can also feel entitled to tell you there is no God.

The Problem of Religious Privilege for Prisoners

Religious prisoners should not be privileged over nonreligious, but I think most prisoners should receive more privileges and help than they now have. A substantial number are in prison because of our cruel and ineffective War on Drugs. More than 60 percent of inmates are functionally illiterate, and people who learn to read are more likely to become productive citizens and less likely to end up in jail. Those who learn a trade and coping skills while in prison are less likely to return once they are free. Help in finding a job upon release cuts recidivism significantly, and reducing recidivism through rehabilitation is less costly, more humane, and safer for the community.

Here are three recent court cases about religious privileging in prison: a Muslim sues to grow a beard, a Jew sues to have kosher food, and an inmate sues to dress like a pirate.

The prisoner whose religious beliefs are closest to mine is a member of the Church of the Flying Spaghetti Monster. Adherents claim there is no more evidence for intelligent design than for a Flying Spaghetti Monster, so if intelligent design is to be given equal time with evolution in public schools, the Flying Spaghetti Monster also deserves equal time. He says that the "religious clothing" he needs is full pirate regalia. A parody, perhaps, but it raises an interesting point. I don't think religion should be privileged over conscience. I'm uncomfortable with the prerequisite of a religious designation in order to receive rights. I would much rather promote conscience than flying spaghetti monsters.

Matter of Prayer

Sen. Larry Grooms, R-Charleston, wants school board members to continue reciting the Lord's Prayer at public meetings. One board member referred to a suggested alternative moment of silence as "a moment of censorship." Not so. Our First Amendment guarantees the right of individuals to pray to whomever whenever they please, but our government must not endorse or favor one religion or religion over nonreligion. Sen. Grooms is also chair of the state Legislative Prayer Caucus, whose goal is to stress "the importance of prayer for our state." Speaking as a resident of the state, that's not my goal, nor should it be the goal of our state. History shows that required prayer is divisive.

The Lord's Prayer, which Grooms believes unites us, is even controversial among Christians. I was raised in Philadelphia, home of the 1844 "Bible riots" where both Catholics and Protestants were clubbed to death over which version of the Lord's Prayer should be recited in public school. Protestants won the political battle, which led to the formation of Catholic schools in 1860.

Politicians, as with all citizens, are free to pray alone or with one another before meetings. While I am not a Christian, I wish that those who are would heed the words of Jesus in Matthew 6:5–6: "When you pray, do not be like the hypocrites who love to pray where they can be seen by others. Instead, go into your room, close the door, and your Father will see what you have done in secret and reward you."

Three Wrongs Don't Make a Right

There may be conflicts between academic requirements and family religious celebrations. Balancing personal needs and work is part of life. What is not part of life is to expect everyone to accommodate and be inconvenienced by your beliefs. A deadly combination for public schools is the unholy alliance of religion and politics. Imam Talib, a leader of the campaign to add Muslim holidays to the New York City school calendar, said: "We really have confidence in the mayor's intelligence. It's an election year." Perhaps Imam Talib doesn't recognize the difference between intelligence and political pandering.

Vice President of Religion

I thought the most interesting question in the vice presidential debate was whether the candidates had ever struggled to balance their personal faith with a public policy decision. Tim Kaine mentioned he had struggled as governor of Virginia to uphold capital punishment, which his Roman Catholic faith opposes. He said that he doesn't believe the doctrines of any religion should be legislatively mandated for everyone. In short, Tim Kaine believes in separation of church and state.

Mike Pence brought up abortion, while not acknowledging any struggles between his personal faith and his public policy decisions. Pence quoted Jeremiah 1:5 to support his anti-abortion views: "Before you were formed in the womb, I knew you." He also wants to overturn Roe v. Wade, end funding for Planned Parenthood because it offers abortions, and even ban valuable fetal tissue research.

As long as we're quoting the Bible to make secular law, we can counter Pence's view that abortion is murder with other biblical passages. For instance, Exodus 21:22 says that if a man strikes a woman and she has a miscarriage, then he must pay a fine to her husband (for destroying his property). However, if his wife dies, then he is given the death penalty for committing murder. And according to Numbers 3:15, neither fetuses nor infants under one month are counted as people.

The Bible is full of contradictory and ambiguous statements, and politicians can pick and choose their biblical reasons for "moral" positions. Like Pence, I don't struggle with how to balance personal faith and public policy decisions—this is never a problem for atheists. I make decisions based on evidence, rather than anachronistic pronouncements from ancient texts. Religious or not, we deserve politicians who give good secular arguments for their decisions.

From Jefferson to Trump

Here in a nutshell is America's regression from Thomas Jefferson to Donald Trump.

Thomas Jefferson: "It does me no injury for my neighbor to say there are twenty gods or no God. It neither picks my pocket nor breaks my leg."

Donald Trump: "Imagine what our country could accomplish if we started working together as one people, under one God, saluting one American flag."

Donald Trump's vision excludes all who don't believe we are a nation under one God (presumably the Christian one). He takes pride in being politically incorrect. Trump's statements about religion and other American freedoms show him also to be constitutionally incorrect. He says the Bible is his favorite book, though I expect he has not read many passages other than those handed to him for speeches. He couldn't name his favorite verse, or which testament he prefers. His funniest flub occurred at Liberty University where he referred to Second Corinthians as "Two Corinthians." So Donald Trump is also "biblically incorrect."

This atheist, who still finds some wisdom in the Bible, suggests that Donald Trump spend a little time reading his favorite book. He can start with Luke 14:11: "He who exalts himself will be humbled, and he who humbles himself will be exalted." Or perhaps Proverbs 12:15: "The way of a fool is right in his own eyes, but a wise man listens to advice."

28
SEX

Doing What Comes Naturally

"When Adam ate the apple in the Garden and learned how to multiply and replenish, the other animals learned the Art, too, by watching Adam. It was cunning of them, it was neat; for they got all that was worth having out of the apple without tasting it and afflicting themselves with the disastrous Moral Sense, the parent of all the immoralities." Thus observed Mark Twain in *Letters from the Earth*.

So is this moral sense, which distinguishes human animals from other animals, beneficial or harmful when it comes to sex? The answer is not as black and white as Mark Twain and most religionists would have us believe. Perhaps "black and white" is an appropriate morality metaphor. When my white cat was in heat, she cared not at all if her partner were white, black, or orange. And she resided in South Carolina, which once prohibited coupling of black and white human animals on moral and religious grounds.

Sex is fun, which is why our pets and we are here today. Morality enters the picture for humans when we decide what kinds of constraints we should place on doing what comes naturally. Not all of us have the same criteria for constraints, and that's where religion often screws things up.

Here are my atheist and humanist constraints: Sex should be by mutual consent, without pressure, threats, or exploitation. It matters not whether partners are of the same or different sex. Adults who exploit children for sexual pleasure should feel the full weight of the law, whether they wear white, blue, or black collars. And masturbation is safe sex.

Ancient moral standards like "be fruitful and multiply" made more sense in an under-populated world. Some religions claim that sex should be for procreation, and Paul (1 Corinthians 7:9) doesn't even approve of sex for procreation. He says it's better that men not even touch women, but grudgingly permits marriage to prevent the sin of fornication. No wonder countless believers suffer so much guilt. To quote songwriter Butch Hancock, "We grew up believing that sex is dirty and nasty and awful, and you should save it for marriage with the one you love."

Finally, we often equate morality with sexual behavior. Ethical behavior and morality are about treating others with respect, dignity, and compassion. We should not exploit people, whether through sex or any other means. Morality should not be viewed through the narrow prism of sexual behavior. Sex is an important part of life, but there is more to life than sex, and more to morality than sex.

Changing an Unchanging Church

If Catholics choose to be counseled about marital or sexual difficulties by celibate priests, why should I care? As a humanist, I worry not only about a church whose leadership requirements are more likely to lead to abuses of the innocent faithful, but also about a politically engaged church trying to impose its religious prohibitions (contraception, gay marriage, stem cell research, etc.) on the rest of the world.

Celibacy didn't become church law until 1139, when every priest's marriage was declared invalid and priests were ordered to separate from their wives. This had more to do with capitalism than spiritualism, since property that used to pass to the priest's heirs became windfall church profits. Then to seal the deal against sexual outlets, the church prohibited masturbation, condemned as the sin of "onanism," by misunderstanding the biblical story. Onan was required to follow the levirate tradition of having sex with his dead brother's wife to produce a child for his brother's line, but Onan was punished for premature withdrawal because he wanted to become heir to his brother's property. So church law on both celibacy and masturbation involved the trading of sexual pleasure for real estate.

An "abstinence only" priestly requirement is by no means the church's most misguided sexual policy. It later decided that Onan's sin covers all forms of reliable birth control. And if church leaders can argue that putting yourself at risk for AIDS is more godly than using condoms, I can argue that the Catholic Church is helping to spread a virus that infects the entire world, not just its faithful sheep.

The Elephant in the Notre Dame Auditorium

President Obama gave a commencement speech at Notre Dame, despite protests for inviting someone who is allegedly pro-abortion. I've never met anyone who is "pro-abortion." We all agree that an abortion signifies a mistake, though we may disagree on what the mistake was and what to do about it.

Obama found common ground with, "Let us work together to reduce the number of women seeking abortions. Let's reduce unintended pregnancies." As means to these ends, he urged improving adoption and pre-natal support policies. Bowing to the Catholic Church prohibition against birth control, President Obama failed to point out the most realistic ways to reduce abortions and unintended pregnancies. Based on mounds of evidence, we must promote comprehensive sex education for young people, and readily available contraceptives for everyone. If I were seeking common ground with those who believe abortion to be a "mortal sin," I would at least suggest that they lighten up on the "venial sin" of condom use. Most Catholics disagree with the message of the Monty Python song, "Every Sperm is Sacred."

When Catholic Bishops Control Health Care for All of Us

I wouldn't want to be on a plane with a pilot who had never flown, nor would I seek sexual guidance from a Catholic bishop who, presumably, had never "flown." The Catholic faithful may choose to live their lives based on pronouncements by priests, bishops, and the pope, but they have no right to impose their sectarian beliefs on the rest of us. Catholic bishops have injected themselves into Congressional deliberations over health-care reform largely over abortion. Most people, religious and secular, advocate quality health care for the poor. Unfortunately, if the bishops don't get their way on abortion, they will try to scuttle health care reform for millions of Americans. The irony is that some women have abortions because they could not afford contraception and cannot afford to provide for a baby because of our inadequate health care system. As far as I can tell, the biblical Jesus said nothing about abortion, but had a lot to say about the poor. Perhaps some Catholic bishops should ask themselves, "What would Jesus do?"

Messy Path to Gay Progress

To me, same-sex marriage is a no-brainer and long overdue. Equal treatment under the law is not a radical idea. Same-sex couples should have the same rights, benefits, and protections as opposite-sex couples. Some give biblical justification that marriage should be between a man and a woman, just as a couple of generations ago they gave biblical justification that marriage should be between members of the same race. I could just as easily give biblical justification for marriage being between a man and no more than 700 women (I Kings 11:3). Solomon had 700 wives and 300 concubines, which means that his brain wasn't his most remarkable organ.

While I'm disappointed that we are arguing about the legality of same-sex marriage, I'm also pleased, because this wasn't even an issue a generation ago. I think public opinion is moving rapidly toward equality for all, and I predict a future generation will wonder why anyone ever opposed same-sex marriage, just as this generation wonders why anyone ever supported miscegenation laws.

29

SOUND BITES

God

What did God know, and when did he know it?

God: I'm all knowing, but where did I come from?

If everything is part of God's plan, why does he get angry and punish us when we do something he doesn't like?

Does God ever wonder if he has a higher purpose than how he relates to human beings?

God is 100% malevolent but only 70% effective, which explains our world today.

An all-knowing, all-powerful, all-loving god would know how to prove its existence to all, have the power to do so, and love us enough to do what it takes for us to avoid hell.

If your holy book can be misunderstood with murderous consequences, you should reconsider if it's really a message from a loving god.

Why would a supreme being make petty demands on his faithful, such as special diets, hats, clothing, and silly rituals?

Judaism began with a story about smashing idols, and many Jews today have smashed the biggest idol—belief in God.

Humans have to justify themselves to God but God doesn't have to justify himself to anybody, which is how it works with all dictators.

God is a divider, not a uniter.

Name one reason not to believe in other gods that does not apply to yours.

With thousands of gods, how do you know you've chosen the "right" vengeful god?

God expecting people to choose the one true religion by faith is no way to run a universe.

God likes atheists better because we never bother him for anything.

I believe in you, the creator, because you created god.

Atheists don't need reasons not to believe, but we do require reasons to believe.

Nobody dies young because God needs another angel.

In the beginning was the Word, and the word was Aardvark.

If Truth + God = Life, then Truth = Life – God.

Morality

How would you behave differently if you stopped believing in God?

As an atheist, I rape and murder as many people as I want: zero.

If fear of a deity stops you from raping and killing, then you are a sociopath.

Those who reject preached dogmas are left with the need to think about their actions.

Conservative religions define ethics primarily in terms of belief, rather than behavior.

God belief creates a separation between ethics and morality.

Is saving souls more important that saving lives?

When someone believes they act on God's behalf, they can justify anything they do.

Once we accept "Thou shall have no other gods," the arbitrary rules of each sect come into conflict with "Do unto others."

It's not what you believe that counts, but what you do.

Since we don't know what lies beyond, we need to lead the best lives we can here.

No religion has ever offered anything positive and unique in matters of morality.

Eternal torture is overkill.

Religions recycle values universally regarded as good, and then claim that without faith a person can't know right from wrong.

Gods don't kill people; people with gods kill people.

Religion

Religious liberty does not give you the right to discriminate.

If an argument for a policy is that it's your doctrine, why should it apply to everyone?

Believers look for interpretations of their holy books that speak to them, which is why these books have to be ambiguous and try to avoid obviously falsifiable claims.

Most people identify more with a religion than with a theology.

If the Bible is mistaken in telling us where we came from, why should we trust it to tell us where we are going?

Everything in the Bible is literally true, except what I say is metaphorical.

I believe in the Bible because I've seen one.

Religions promote dissatisfaction with this life so people can look forward to an imagined afterlife.

No religion should hinder or discourage asking questions about the world around us.

Unlike religion, glasses help you see the world more clearly.

If it was good enough for Bronze Age goat herders, then it should be good enough for us.

People don't make websites, books, and videos against belief in unicorns because people aren't basing real world decisions on belief in unicorns.

To ignore the facts does not change the facts.

You can believe that a bicycle is a boat, but don't expect me to peddle across the lake with you on your bicycle.

Christianity

How many times has Jesus come into the hearts of those who have never heard of Jesus?

The resurrection is something that should have been demonstrated to all of Jerusalem, not just to a handful of faithful followers.

I view the Christian god the same way Christians view the Greek gods.

The New Testament is a book of failed prophecy that first heralds the imminent return of Jesus and then a final apocalypse—neither of which has happened.

Being born again doesn't give you twice the rights of others.

Christians who say, "Love your neighbor" often disagree on what love entails and who your neighbor is.

The Old Testament God contented himself with mass murder; the New Testament God pursues his victims beyond the grave to torture them for all eternity.

Old Testament: "Obey the Lord or die" and New Testament: "Believe in Jesus or fry."

Faith

Faith-based knowledge is like regular knowledge, but without the knowledge.

Faith is intellectual laziness.

Faith does no better than random chance on every test of predictive capabilities.

Faith is making yourself believe (make believe).

Doubts based on evidence that contradict or prove doctrine wrong can only be countered by faith that helps you ignore the doubt and continue to believe without evidence.

Reality is that which, when you stop believing in it, doesn't go away.

Reality has a well-known secular bias.

What to say at a funeral: "We are gathered here today because your prayers didn't work."

Science

Science works whether you believe in it or not.

Science uses measurement and verifiability, while religion uses stories (myth) and threats (believe or else).

Scientists accept new discoveries whether they like them or not.

No one has ever been killed for failing to pledge allegiance to the Big Bang or Darwinian evolution.

If the universe was created with a purpose, that purpose must be to create stars.

Stars, not Jesus, died so you could live.

Religions claim credit for the efforts of scientists and doctors, asserting that a saved life is a "miracle."

Religion uses scientific advances and knowledge all the time, but science doesn't use any of religion's "advances."

Humans are just fish plus time.

Random Thoughts

Life is a sexually transmitted disease with a 100 percent mortality rate.

Light travels faster than sound, which is why some people appear bright until they speak.

What is the speed of dark?

Living on Earth is expensive, but it includes a free trip around the sun every year.

Birthdays are good for you; the more you have the longer you live.

We are all one year closer to death, but are we one year wiser?

The question isn't what to do with the rest of your life, but what to do next.

When tempted to fight fire with fire, notice that the fire department usually uses water.

It is only when you see a mosquito landing on your testicles that you realize there is always a way to solve problems without using violence.

Some days you're the dog and some days you're the hydrant.

If you find a stone in your shoe, you don't throw away the shoe.

Some cause happiness wherever they go, while others cause happiness whenever they go.

When you're dead you don't know you're dead and it's difficult only for others, which is also how it works when you're stupid.

Don't argue with a jerk; he'll drag you down to his level and beat you with experience.

I went to a bookstore and asked the salesperson where the self-help section was, and she said it would defeat the purpose if she told me.

What if there were no hypothetical questions?

If you try to fail, and succeed, which have you done?

Is there another word for synonym?

We never really grow up; we only learn how to act in public.

A clear conscience is usually the sign of a bad memory.

The early bird may get the worm, but the second mouse gets the cheese.

He who laughs last thinks slowest.

One good thing about Alzheimer's is you get to meet new people every day.

Forgetting to zip up isn't Alzheimer's, but forgetting to zip down is.

It is well known that 87.3 percent of statistics are made up.

There are 3 types of people: Those who can count and those who can't.

There are 10 types of people: Those who understand binary and those who don't.

30

SOUTH CAROLINA

A Christian Response: To What?

When I heard that a Christian Renewal prayer rally called "The Response" would be coming to Charleston, I said, "Here we go again with another unproductive prayer fest." But my interest piqued when I learned that Governor Nikki Haley endorsed and heavily promoted the event. She was the only celebrity on stage as she welcomed attendees and began the prayer. While Governor Haley invited people of all faiths, its stated purpose was to exalt the name of Jesus.

David Lane, president and founder of the American Renewal Project, was the leading backer. Though billed as apolitical, Lane organized similar "apolitical" rallies in Texas, where Governor Rick Perry spoke, and in Louisiana, where Governor Bobby Jindal spoke. Both became presidential candidates. Lane wants a religious right army to pick the next president. He believes homosexuality will lead to the destruction of America, and he thinks Christianity should be the official religion of the United States.

As a private citizen, Nikki Haley may attend any event. But it became legally problematic when she issued an invitation to The Response on letterhead with the Governor's Seal. Our local secular humanist group organized inclusive events on that day. While some evangelicals were clasping their hands in prayer, many of us used our hands in projects that included helping a Charleston Food Bank and building a wheelchair ramp as part of Operation Home. Similarly, Myrtle Beach Humanists and Freethinkers organized a Humanist Day of Service. Relying on a god to save us is no substitute for fixing things ourselves. Leadership involves getting things done, not leading a mass appeal for a god to do it for us.

Religious Beliefs

Rep. Mark Sanford often talks about his Christian beliefs, so I was surprised by this Sept. 11 quote from him, "I'm not a Buddhist." I doubt that many people thought he was, but he felt the need to respond to the rumor. Sanford added that he meant no offense to Buddhism and has "an appreciation for every faith around the world." Had someone called Sanford an atheist, I wonder if his denial would have included his appreciation for atheists. We are a country of all faiths and none. Atheists do not ask for special rights, but we are a growing minority who deserve no less respect than do people of faith.

Talking to "the Other"

Despite what Psalm 37 and Jesus say, I see little evidence of the meek inheriting the earth. However, I see much evidence for the belligerent and loud-mouthed inheriting talk shows, and the aggressive and cantankerous inheriting political careers. This topic became noteworthy at the recent State of the Union address, after the "You lie!" shout out by South Carolina Congressman Joe Wilson, who replaced my former governor Mark Sanford as the latest state buffoon of the week. Wilson is an undistinguished lightweight who made an impulsive and emotional outburst, but at least he later apologized.

However, Wilson never apologized for a more serious racist comment. After the death of South Carolina Senator Strom Thurmond, Essie Mae Washington-Williams finally revealed what many South Carolinians had known for a long time—that Strom was her biological father, having impregnated Essie Mae's mother when she was the sixteen-year-old Thurmond family maid. Wilson called the story untrue, and criticized Essie May for the "unseemly" revelation, saying that even if she were telling the truth, she should have kept the inconvenient facts to herself. Wilson certainly has a distorted view of civility.

As for the relationship between private faith and civil discourse, many among the faithful find justification in their holy books for not treating "the other" with civility. There is no hint of civil discourse in 2 Corinthians 6:14, where believers are warned about associating with unbelievers: "What fellowship hath righteousness and wickedness, and what communion has light with darkness?"

If the meek are to inherit something of value, we must seek ways to understand and respect those with whom we disagree. Instead of bashing each other, I suggest organizing the kind of BaSH (Baptists and Secular Humanists) group we formed in Charleston. We met periodically for conversation and refreshments, simply to get to know one another and learn about different perspectives and worldviews. Priority was given to finding common ground, without attempting conversion. We measured success by the number of new friendships, not conversions.

Rebel Flag Debate

In a letter on Martin Luther King Day, Robert Donegan said he and many other white Southerners will consider removing the Confederate flag from the state Capitol when "blacks stop calling themselves African Americans and stop wearing all those African clothes." He closed with, "We are just as proud of our heritage as the blacks are of theirs." Mr. Donegan is correct that the Confederate flag is a symbol of pride only to a portion of white Southerners, but government endorsement of the flag to represent all South Carolina can't be equated with what people wear or call themselves. The reluctance of white Southerners to stop wallowing in their secessionist, slave-owning past continually amazes.

Experiences with South Carolina Law

When South Carolina leads a national story, it's usually because of a horrible hurricane or racial incident. There hasn't been a major hurricane lately, but North Charleston became the focus of national and international attention when a white police officer named Michael Slager shot an unarmed black man, Walter Scott, five times in the back as he fled after being stopped for a broken tail light. Since police investigations in South Carolina and many other states almost always exonerate the officer in a questionable situation, it was nearly unprecedented for Slager to be arrested and charged with murder shortly after the shooting. However, because of the now-famous video taken by a passerby, I don't credit South Carolina law enforcement for their prompt action. The video shows Slager taking target practice on a black man's back, turning the "smoking gun" cliché into something literal. Were it not for the video, an internal police investigation might have exonerated Slager because he had claimed to fear for his life.

Local civil rights leaders periodically call for independent citizen review boards. Sometimes the South Carolina Law Enforcement Division (SLED) is brought in to investigate. SLED is an independent state law enforcement agency, kind of like a state FBI, but many who don't trust police officers also don't trust SLED.

I once had my own unpleasant experience with SLED, but let me emphasize that it was nothing like the ordeals countless blacks have had with law enforcement officials. I received the nomination of the United Citizens Party when I ran for governor in 1990 to challenge the unconstitutional state provision that prohibits atheists from holding public office. It's a black-led civil rights group formed in the 1960s, and relatively inactive in 1990. After the party nominated me, the South Carolina Election Commission suggested there might be "irregularities" in the way I had obtained the nomination, and voted 3-2 to recommend that SLED investigate.

I informed SLED of my willingness to cooperate and provide appropriate documentation. After hearing nothing for eight weeks, I called SLED. They said their inquiry was nearly complete and my input would not be needed. A few days later, the election commission announced that SLED had found irregularities and I wouldn't be allowed on the ballot.

I called the head of the United Citizens Party, Rev. Dawson, and asked what had happened. He told me that SLED investigators had badgered him about supporting an atheist, and he didn't want any trouble. Feeling pressured by SLED, Dawson said he hadn't understood the document he signed that gave me the party nomination, though I had witnesses who could have proved otherwise. My lawyer said I had a legitimate grievance, but advised me to move on because my legal case would not be jeopardized if I campaigned as a write-in candidate.

I lost the election for governor, of course, but I eventually won a unanimous South Carolina Supreme Court decision in 1997, allowing atheists in South Carolina to hold public office. Perhaps some South Carolina officials congratulated themselves in 1990 for finding a way to harass two disliked minorities (African Americans and atheists) at the same time. Then again, I don't know because nobody in power was talking.

Tragedy in South Carolina
I was stunned when a white gunman murdered nine innocent black people gathered at the historic Emanuel AME Church, three blocks from where I live. This church was once a secret meeting place for African-Americans who wanted to end slavery at a time when laws in Charleston banned all-

black church gatherings. The following day, I attended a vigil at nearby Morris Brown AME Church, also a traditionally black church, where the entire community was invited to pray for peace, understanding, and healing. I don't pray, but I support those goals. I thought of the antiwar song "Lay Down" by Melanie, and the line "Some came to sing, some came to pray, some came to keep the dark away." I was there to keep the dark away by showing support for beleaguered African-Americans.

About a third of the attendees were white. Many leaders of the AME Church commented appreciatively about the diversity of the audience, but never once used the word "white." They referred to the audience as a "colorful gathering" and looking like "patches of a South Carolina quilt." I applauded heartily when one minister told the crowd, "Pray, but also get off your knees and work to improve our community."

We held hands with our neighbors at the end and sang, "We Shall Overcome." It reminded me of singing it in the 1960s during civil rights marches and Vietnam War protests. We were asked to continue holding hands as we prayed to Jesus. I didn't want to withdraw my hand from the black man on my right, so we held hands as the minister prayed for Jesus to get rid of any hate in our heart and replace it with love. So it turned out that I did come to sing, pray, and keep the dark away.

Spiritual Shift

I appreciated the column by Rabbi Weiss about his visit to Emanuel AME Church. He was warmly welcomed to join their weekly Bible class in the same space where Rev. Pinckney and eight others were brutally massacred less than a month earlier. Though Jewish and Christian participants had different theologies and traditions, they came together as equal participants to comfort one another and show their common humanity during this time of sorrow.

After the service, Rabbi Weiss needed a ride to a location where he could say Kaddish (Jewish memorial prayer) for his father, who had recently died. A woman at the Bible study offered him a ride, which Rabbi Weiss accepted. Here is where the story takes an ironic twist. This woman would not have been allowed to become an active participant in the Kaddish service for Rabbi Weiss's father. A minyan of 10 adult Jewish males is required for an Orthodox Jewish service. A Jewish man drove 100 miles to be the tenth. As a Jewish atheist, I can be counted as part of a minyan.

However, I presently feel more of a kinship to Emanuel AME church than to Orthodox Judaism.

Heritage *and* Hate
My first week in Charleston, in 1976, I played duplicate bridge at the Christian Family Y. Afterward, I asked how this Y differed from the YMCA, and learned that this former YMCA had been kicked out of the national organization because it refused to integrate. That ended my duplicate bridge career in Charleston. Ironically, the Christian Family Y was eventually torn down and replaced by condominiums, and I now live in one of them.

A few weeks later, I learned that the Confederate flag flew atop the State Capitol. When I questioned Southerners about the flag, I often heard the h-word (heritage). But some heritage is hateful or worse, including what the Confederate flag and swastika represent to most of the world. The Confederate battle flag was moved in 2000 from the dome to the front of the Statehouse as a legislative "compromise."

There was more cultural sensitivity in 2015 after a white racist murdered nine blacks in a Charleston church. One of the most moving moments in Charleston occurred shortly thereafter when an estimated 20,000 people met on a local bridge in a show of solidarity with those affected by the church murders. Blacks and whites clasped hands and hugged. Despite and because of recent tragedies in Charleston, I've never been prouder of my city. In a city where blacks were once expected to get off the sidewalk to let a white person pass, I now see blacks and whites smiling at one another and carrying on conversations. We know that this is a historic moment for all of us in Charleston, and I hope that out of tragedy will come lasting good will.

The Confederate Flag and the Ten Commandments
There is nothing in the South Carolina or US Constitutions that prohibits flying the Confederate flag on public property, but the court of public opinion changed after a Confederate flag-promoting racist murdered nine African Americans in a church. I applaud many politicians who finally called for the removal of the Confederate flag from Statehouse grounds in an attempt to unify citizens who have diverse views on the flag.

On the other hand, many of these politicians in South Carolina and elsewhere endorse the Ten Commandments and want them placed on public buildings. Most people believe them to be the finest guidelines for a virtuous life, though hardly anyone can name them all. Even fewer have thought through the implications of how our pluralistic, democratic, and freedom-loving society would change were the Ten Commandments to become law.

The first commandment, "Thou shalt have no other gods," conflicts with the first amendment to the US Constitution that guarantees freedom of religion—the right to worship one, several, or no gods. The next three (no graven images, not taking God's name in vain, keeping the Sabbath holy) refer to specific kinds of worship. These religious edicts describe how to worship and pay homage to a jealous and vindictive God, and have nothing to do with ethical behavior.

The fifth commandment, about honoring parents, should not be so unconditional as to condone child abuse. There is no commandment about parents honoring their children or treating them humanely. The next four (proscriptions against murder, adultery, stealing, and lying) existed in cultures long before Moses.

The tenth commandment, "Thou shalt not covet thy neighbor's house, wife, slaves, ox, donkey, or any other property," condones slavery and treating women as property.

These commandments are notable for what they omit. Instead of condemning covetousness, why not condemn slavery, racism, sexual assault, child and spouse abuse, and torture? Most of us could come up with a better set of rules to live by.

The NAACP and Me

Dot Scott, longtime President of the Charleston Branch of the NAACP, has remained steadfast and outspoken despite receiving abuse over the economic boycott she helped organize over the Confederate flag. She persistently raised other uncomfortable issues, including police discrimination against black citizens, inferior education in de facto segregated public schools, and bias in employment and housing. Dot Scott is a deeply committed Christian and I am an atheist, but we have more in common than sets us apart. She supported me in 2003 after a disturbing incident at a Charleston City Council meeting at which I had been invited to give an invocation. As I approached the podium, half the council members walked out because I'm an atheist. When news of the walkout appeared in the *Post and Courier*, Dot wrote this letter to the editor:

I read with disbelief the actions of our councilmen who walked out of an official meeting during the invocation by Herb Silverman simply because of his religious views. It is most difficult for me, a Christian African-American female, who has probably experienced every kind of prejudice and intolerance imaginable, to understand an act that was not only disrespectful, but also unquestionably rude by folks elected to represent all of the citizens, regardless of race, creed, color, religion or sexual orientation. It is most regrettable that during a time when the fight is so fierce to have all citizens' rights protected and respected, some of us would neglect to do the same for others. When any elected official demonstrates such lack of tolerance, especially while performing his official duties, those of us of conscience must speak out and voice our outrage.

Some time later, Dot Scott was a dinner guest at my home. She told a shocking story about a fund for families of nine Charleston firefighters who had recently died in a furniture store fire in 2007. Some people wanted to contribute to the fund, but only if they could earmark donations to the *white* firefighters. When bad things happened in South Carolina, Dot said people consoled themselves with, "Thank you, Mississippi," but added that South Carolina is sometimes worse. I responded, "Dot, I've lived here long enough to know the real expression, so please feel free to say it correctly." She thanked me for not objecting to the phrase "Thank *God* for Mississippi," and I thanked her for recognizing that not all people are religious.

Only after a Confederate flag-promoting racist killed nine African Americans in a Charleston church did Gov. Nikki Haley, in her fifth year as governor, announce her belated conclusion that it was time for the flag to come down. Shortly thereafter, Rep. Jenny Horne made an emotional appeal in the state House of Representatives to remove the flag. When the flag finally came down a few days later, neither Dot Scott nor other local NAACP leaders were invited to participate in any of the public ceremonies.

Republicans Haley and Horne were praised for their shift in positions, and said to be suddenly qualified for higher office Vice President and Congress, respectively. While I appreciate the recent change of heart by Haley, Horne, and other legislators, clearly they did the right thing only when they realized it was politically safe to do so. Real courage, the Dot Scott kind, is demonstrated when something is difficult and unpopular.

31

WOMEN

Male Problem or Millennial Problem

Jimmy Carter is a good man who came to a humanistic conclusion that discrimination against women and girls is unacceptable. However, I disagree with his rationale that male religious leaders who think otherwise are basing their conclusions on faulty interpretations of their holy books. I find countless interpretations to justify treating women as second-class citizens or worse, but hardly any for treating women as equals. As a humanist, I don't have to do cartwheels (Carter wheels?) to find passages in holy books that justify equal treatment of women. We know through common sense and experience, rather than through ancient religious traditions, that treating women as equals is the right thing to do.

Religion's Outdated Notion of Gender

There are many variations of "Lead, follow, or get out of the way." When it comes to treating women as prescribed in ancient holy books, I would shorten it to "Get out of the way." According to Jewish tradition, a woman is unclean for one week after giving birth to a male and two weeks after giving birth to a female (Leviticus 12). A male is unclean for a day if he touches a menstruating woman. In the Christian tradition, women were made for the sake of man (1 Corinthians 11:9), should keep silent and have no authority over man (1 Timothy 2:12), and the head of every woman is a man (1 Corinthians 11:3). Passages in the Quran say or imply that women must obey men, that a man can beat a woman if she causes him trouble, and that women must be covered in public and never go out alone.

Claims that women are "separate but equal" lead more to separation than equality—whether in race, sex, or religion. We don't need justification from holy books to treat women equally. As the Book of Nike says, "Just do it!"

Palin: A Pat Robertson Feminist

I accept labels people give themselves, and Sarah Palin calls herself a feminist. In my experience, feminists who have worked for social, political, and economic equality have often been called aggressive, arrogant, intolerant, militant, and mean-spirited. Such accusations are usually false, but I think they ring true for Palin feminism. Palin calls herself a "frontier feminist," but she sounds more like a "Pat Robertson feminist." They are both guided by an unshakeable certainty about what God wants, and want to outlaw any actions that would displease God. The good news is an equality of the sexes; the bad news is that both sexes can be dangerously mistaken.

Speaking to members of the Susan B. Anthony List, Palin described her doubts about whether she'd be able to handle a baby with Down syndrome, but "chose" to have the baby because of her certainty that "God will never give us something we can't handle." Similarly, she said of her unwed and pregnant teenage daughter, "For Bristol, choosing life was not an easy decision." Note that both members of this advantaged family had the choice on whether to have an abortion, and chose not to. Sarah Palin claims that her God made sure these choices worked out well for her family, but she would like to prevent others from making a different choice. However, "one choice" is an oxymoron.

I don't know if Sister Margaret McBride considers herself a feminist, but she is closer to my brand of feminism than Sarah Palin. McBride had the courage to agree with the ethics committee at her hospital to allow an abortion that would save a mother's life. For this heroic act, McBride was excommunicated from her church. This nun would have remained a Catholic in good standing had she, instead, molested a child and confessed her "sin." The bishop's reaction to an abortion that saved a mother's life is just one more example of why thinking people should ignore some of the immoral and heartless teachings of the Catholic Church.

Opposite Games by Politicians

"Opposite Day" is a game played by children, when speech is modified so that statements mean the opposite of what they usually mean. We are now witnessing Opposite Day played by politicians. Here are two examples:

> A politician says, "This country was founded on individual freedom, and I want to keep our citizens free without government interference by a nanny state." He then tries to prevent women from exercising their legal options regarding their bodies, or allowing them to make informed choices after consultation with their doctor.

> A politician says, "I will do all in my power to reduce the number of abortions." He then opposes effective ways to do so: comprehensive evidence-based sex education in schools; contraception available for sexually active teens and others who want to avoid pregnancy; prenatal health care, day care programs, and other support systems for women wishing to give birth. Perhaps punishing sexually active women is a higher priority.

Opposite-minded politicians hate Planned Parenthood. Here are facts from its most recent annual report. Ninety percent of the health care provided is to prevent unintended pregnancies through contraception, reduce the spread of sexually transmitted diseases, and prevent cancer deaths through screenings. Pregnant women are offered prenatal care and referrals for adoption. Only three percent of its services are for abortion, a procedure increasingly harder to find at other clinics. Politicians who claim that Planned Parenthood is nothing but an abortion factory must prefer to live in Opposite Day Land.

Finally, an Anticontraception Ruling I (Sort of) Support
I support a woman's right to an abortion at any time for any reason. I think government healthcare should cover abortions and free contraception for women, no exceptions. I think Peter Singer, Professor of Bioethics at Princeton University, makes a reasonable case for infanticide under certain circumstances. So why am I cautiously optimistic about the recent ruling by Federal Judge Richard J. Leon in favor of the antichoice organization, March for Life, saying that it does not have to abide by Obamacare's birth control mandate?

Here's an analogy. When years ago some considered it "unladylike" for a woman to smoke, I had conversations with female smoking friends that went something like this:

Me: I don't think women should smoke.

She: That's ridiculous! Why is it OK for men to smoke, but not women?

Me: I don't think men should smoke, either.

Just as men shouldn't be privileged over women, religion shouldn't be privileged over conscience. That was the essence of the ruling. If employer health insurance plans covering contraceptives could be exempt for religious beliefs, then a secular organization like March for Life could also be exempt for "moral" beliefs. But here's my conflict: I also think everyone should be afforded the right to contraceptives regardless of the views of their employer. I hope we are moving closer to not privileging religion over conscience, as Judge Leon ruled in the March for Life case. If the government agrees to an exemption from a law because of religious belief, that same exemption should be available for conscientious belief, as in the 1965 case where the Supreme Court ruled in favor of an atheist conscientious objector to war.

Mark Oppenheimer recently offered a thoughtful suggestion in *Time Magazine*, proposing that we end tax exemptions for *all* nonprofit organizations, including religious institutions. Though politically difficult to overcome special interest opposition, such legislation would go a long way toward not privileging religion over conscience.

My Complaint About Oprah

Never having watched Oprah, I turned to the person whose opinion I most trust, my wife Sharon, and asked her about Oprah's status as a religious leader. Sharon told me, "Oprah believes in God and being spiritual, but has never to my knowledge pushed any particular religion or dogma. This keeps her grounded amid her enormous personal popularity and wealth, the kind of success that has led others to become arrogant and self-indulgent. I think women love Oprah because she is what they would hope to find in a best friend."

While I trusted Sharon, I still needed to verify. I learned that Oprah believes there are a variety of paths to God, for which many Christians criticize her because they believe there is only one path. As an atheist, I think there are no paths to any gods. Oprah is uncharacteristically humble compared to religious leaders with large followings. At least Oprah doesn't try to impose her religious beliefs on others or support legislation to do so.

While I give Oprah a good grade for a religious leader (I'm grading on a steep curve, here), I give her a failing grade for a reality-based worldview. She has promoted an assortment of quack cures. However well meaning and sincere, Oprah seems more convinced by testimonials from celebrity friends than from scientific evidence. This is especially irresponsible because Oprah has such a large base of supporters who follow her views "religiously." Encouraging women and others to think positively and to help themselves is certainly worthwhile, but I wish Oprah would also tell her audience to be skeptical about taking the advice of untrained professionals—including herself.

Pro-choice and Pro-life

I consider myself both pro-choice and pro-life because I support a woman's right to choose and I oppose capital punishment. I've heard reasoned and nuanced arguments from both sides on these issues, and I appreciate people who listen to those with whom they disagree. What I don't appreciate are pandering politicians who take simple positions with Bible-based answers, while ignoring any evidence-based, opposing points of view.

Were we living under biblical law, and praise be to the US Constitution we are not, I could still advocate for my positions. The Bible says that if two men are fighting and knock down a pregnant woman, then the death penalty is imposed on the perpetrator if the woman dies, but only a fine if the fetus is aborted (Exodus 21:22–25). And an abortion is even required if the woman is impregnated by a man who is not her husband (Numbers 5:11–31). So abortion is not a big deal, biblically speaking.

As for capital punishment, "Let he who is without sin cast the first stone" (John 8:7) and "Vengeance is mine saith the Lord" (Romans 12:19).

So what have I proved? Absolutely nothing! We could just as easily quote scripture for the opposite point of view. Here's a question: What do the countries in each of the two following groups have in common, and in which one does the United States belong?

1. Afghanistan, Ethiopia, Iran, Iraq, Pakistan, Saudi Arabia, Somalia, Uganda.

2. Australia, Canada, Denmark Finland, France, Germany, Greece, Iceland, Netherlands, New Zealand, Norway, Spain, Sweden, Switzerland, United Kingdom.

The United States is part of the first list, countries with the death penalty. Now guess which group most favors applying ancient scriptures when writing laws. It's the same group that is more likely to oppose abortions and find cause to go to war.

CREDITS

Articles in *On Faith*
www.faithstreet.com/onfaith/author/herb-silverman

Articles in *Huffington Post*
www.huffingtonpost.com/herb-silverman/

Articles in *The Humanist*
thehumanist.com/contributor/herb-silverman/

Debates and talks
lowcountryhumanists.org/default.php?page=videolibrary

Chapter 1

"Ten Things I Wish Everyone Knew About Atheism," *On Faith,* March 18, 2014, www.faithstreet.com/onfaith/2014/03/18/10-things-i-wish-everyone-knew-about-atheism/31345.

"Varieties of Atheist Experience," *On Faith,* July 31, 2013, www.faithstreet.com/onfaith/2013/07/31/varieties-of-atheist-experience/10966.

"Atheist or Agnostic—and Does It Matter?" *On Faith,* January 14, 2015. www.faithstreet.com/onfaith/2015/01/14/atheist-or-agnostic-and-does-it-matter/35823.

"The First Thing We Do, Let's Kill All the Agnostics," *Secular Nation.*

"God Talk for Atheists," *Free Inquiry*, vol. 33, Issue 5, July 25, 2013, www.secularhumanism.org/index.php/articles/3203.

"Positive Atheism," *The Humanist,* July-August 2016, thehumanist.com/magazine/july-august-2016/features/positive-atheism.

"God, an Addiction," *On Faith,* October 27, 2009, www.faithstreet.com/onfaith/2009/10/27/god-an-addiction/8018.

"Courting the 'Values Voters," *Washington Post,* November 16, 2004, www.washingtonpost.com/wp-dyn/articles/A55676-2004Nov16.html.

"Atheist's Afterlife," *Post and Courier* (Charleston), May 27, 2011, www.postandcourier.com/news/2011/may/27/letters-to-the-editor/.

"All Humans' Rights," *Post and Courier* (Charleston), January 5, 2000.

"Peace with Tolerance," *Post and Courier* (Charleston).

"To Whom Much Is Given, Much Is Expected," *On Faith,* May 24, 2010, www.faithstreet.com/onfaith/2010/05/24/to-whom-much-is-given-much-is-expected/1807.

"Institutional Apologies Fall Short," *On Faith,* June 23, 2009, www.faithstreet.com/onfaith/2009/06/23/wwgd-what-would-grandchildren-do/6183.

"Execution as Entertainment," *On Faith,* June 21, 2010, www.faithstreet.com/onfaith/2010/06/21/execution-as-entertainment/8363.

"Dark Ages," *Charleston Mercury.*

"Are Atheists Smarter and Humbler?" *On Faith,* September 3, 2013, www.faithstreet.com/onfaith/2013/09/03/are-atheists-smarter-and-humbler/15423.

"How Atheists Can Overcome a Reputation of Arrogance," *On Faith,* August 8, 2014, www.faithstreet.com/onfaith/2014/08/08/atheists-reputation-arrogance/33579.

"A New Atheist/Humanist Alliance," *Humanistic Judaism*, Summer/Autumn 2007.

"Zealotry: Good or Bad?" *Secular Nation.*

"Eight Examples of How I Agree with Religious Fundamentalists," *Friendly Atheist*, January 19, 2014, www.patheos.com/blogs/friendlyatheist/2014/01/19/eight-examples-of-how-i-agree-with-religious-fundamentalists/.

"On Religious Atheists," *On Faith,* July 3, 2013, www.faithstreet.com/onfaith/2013/07/03/on-religious-atheists/11015.

"Is Atheism Winning the Culture War?" *On Faith,* October 23, 2013, www.faithstreet.com/onfaith/2013/10/23/is-atheism-winning-the-culture-war/25174.

"Honesty Is the Best Policy," *On Faith,* March 15, 2015, www.faithstreet.com/onfaith/2010/03/15/honesty-is-the-best-policy/1209.

"Rest Is a Human Need," *On Faith,* August 18, 2011, www.faithstreet.com/onfaith/2011/08/18/rest-is-a-human-need/31446.

"A Case for Nothing," *On Faith*, October 8, 2009, www.faithstreet.com/onfaith/2009/10/08/a-case-for-nothing/2355.

"Faith in the Light of Science," *On Faith*, July 6, 2010, www.faithstreet.com/onfaith/2010/07/06/faith-in-the-light-of-science/3043.

"A Ghost Story Even I Can Believe," *On Faith*, September 12, 2009, www.faithstreet.com/onfaith/2014/09/12/a-ghost-story-even-i-can-believe/34043.

"For Secular Americans, Lip Service Beats No Service," *On Faith*, November 6, 2008, www.faithstreet.com/onfaith/2008/11/06/for-secular-americans-lip-serv/242.

"An Atheist Invocation and Its Aftermath," *Freethought Today*, May, 2003, ffrf.org/legacy/fttoday/2003/may/index.php?ft=silverman.

"Value Judgment," *Post and Courier* (Charleston).

"Bias Against Pomposity," *On Faith*, January 12, 2010, www.faithstreet.com/onfaith/2010/01/12/bias-against-pomposity/7896.

"Atheists Do Good Anyway," *On Faith*, November 13, 2013, www.faithstreet.com/onfaith/2013/11/13/atheists-do-good-anyway/30001.

Chapter 2

"No Two Christians Are Alike," *On Faith*, August 2, 1010, www.faithstreet.com/onfaith/2010/08/02/christians-and-snowflakes/864.

"I Have a Dream, Too," *On Faith*, August 30, 2010, www.faithstreet.com/onfaith/2010/08/30/i-have-a-dream-too/5582.

"Belief Versus Behavior," *On Faith*, March 3, 2011,www.faithstreet.com/onfaith/2011/03/16/belief-versus-behavior/33097.

"God in Papua New Guinea," *On Faith*, November 5, 2013, www.faithstreet.com/onfaith/2013/11/05/god-in-papua-new-guinea/25152.

"Boy Scouts, Unitarians, and Atheists," *Huffington Post*, May 31, 2015, www.huffingtonpost.com/herb-silverman/boy-scouts-unitarians-and_b_10211808.html.

"Jimmy Carter, Oliver Sacks, and Me," *Huffington Post*, August 31, 2015, www.huffingtonpost.com/herb-silverman/jimmy-carter-oliver-sacks_b_8062114.html.

Chapter 3

"For Atheists, All Religion Is Superstition," *On Faith*, May 29, 2013, www.faithstreet.com/onfaith/2013/05/29/for-atheists-all-religion-is-superstition/16649.

"Who's Afraid of a (Mostly) Fictional Bible?" *On Faith*, September 3, 2014, www.faithstreet.com/onfaith/2014/09/03/whos-afraid-of-a-mostly-fictional-bible/33914.

"An Atheist's Three Favorite Bible Stories," *On Faith*, January 26, 2013, www.faithstreet.com/onfaith/2013/01/26/why-this-atheist-likes-the-bible/11741.

"One Nation, Undereducated," *On Faith*, September 1, 2009, www.faithstreet.com/onfaith/2009/09/01/one-nation-under-educated/5413.

"The Constitution and the Bible," *Secular Nation*.

"Let's Give the Bible a Second Chance…By Changing It," *On Faith*, April 1, 2014, www.faithstreet.com/onfaith/2014/04/01/lets-give-the-bible-a-second-chance-by-making-a-new-bible/31539.

"To Talk or Not to Talk (About Religion)," *Huffington Post*, April 27, 2016, www.huffingtonpost.com/herb-silverman/to-talk-or-not-to-talk-ab_b_9785632.html.

"Slavery and Bible," *Post and Courier* (Charleston), May 9, 2000.

"God Is Opposed to Food Stamps? Let's Try an Evidence-Based Approach Instead," *On Faith*, June 12, 2013, www.faithstreet.com/onfaith/2013/06/12/god-is-opposed-to-food-stamps-lets-try-an-evidence-based-approach-to-hunger-instead/10729.

"Godless Faith in Social Justice," *On Faith*, April 12, 2010, www.faithstreet.com/onfaith/2010/04/12/godless-faith-in-social-justice/7392.

"Education or Indoctrination?" *Post and Courier* (Charleston), 1995.

"Lord of the Snickers: My Mt. Sinai Revelation," *Secular Nation*, Third Quarter, 2006.

"Do Atheists Go to Heaven?" *On Faith*, June 4, 2014, www.faithstreet.com/onfaith/2013/06/04/do-atheists-go-to-heaven/10852.

"Non-Human Animal Rights and Souls," *On Faith*, June 14, 2010, www.faithstreet.com/onfaith/2010/06/14/non-human-animal-rights-and-souls/5889.

"10 Questions About Hell from an Atheist," *On Faith*, July 8, 2015, www.faithstreet.com/onfaith/2015/07/08/10-questions-about-hell-from-an-atheist/37271.

Chapter 4

"Does This Candidate Have a Prayer?" *On Faith*, May 31, 2012, www.faithstreet.com/onfaith/2012/05/31/does-this-candidate-have-a-prayer/15564.

"Atheists in Office: Déjà Vu All Over Again," *On Faith*, December 14, 2009.

"Last Leper in the Colony," *The Humanist*, September-October, 2016, thehumanist.com/magazine/september-october-2016/arts_entertainment/last-leper-colony-atheist-runs-congress-bible-belt.

"Belief in the Almighty Dollar: Why We Need an Atheist PAC," *The Humanist*, January-February, 2014, thehumanist.com/magazine/january-february-2014/up-front/belief-in-the-almighty-dollar-why-we-need-an-atheist-pac.

"Political Atheism: The Last Taboo," *Huffington Post*, May 11, 2016, www.huffingtonpost.com/herb-silverman/political-atheism-the-las_b_9892864.html.

Chapter 5

"Pope Herb I," *Secular Nation*, 2008.

"How to Elect a Pope and Get Higher Ratings," *Friendly Atheist*, March 13, 2013, www.patheos.com/blogs/friendlyatheist/2013/03/13/how-to-elect-a-pope-and-get-higher-ratings/.

"To Life, Not Martyrdom," *On Faith*, May 17, 2013, www.faithstreet.com/onfaith/2013/05/17/to-life-not-martyrdom/16800.

"Sin: Making Sense Out of Nonsense," *On Faith*, March 5, 2014, www.faithstreet.com/onfaith/2014/03/05/making-sense-out-of-nonsense/31173.

"What Did He Know and When Did He Know It?" *On Faith*, March 27, 2010, www.faithstreet.com/onfaith/2010/03/27/what-did-he-know-and-when-did-he-know-it/6944.

"Political Popery a Bad Idea," *On Faith*, November 1, 2010, www.faithstreet.com/onfaith/2010/11/01/political-popery-a-bad-idea/2053.

"Papal Exoneration of Jews," *Post and Courier* (Charleston), March 29, 2011, www.postandcourier.com/news/2011/mar/29/letters-to-the-editor/.

"No Track to Sainthood," *On Faith*, July 9, 2013, www.faithstreet.com/onfaith/2013/07/09/no-track-to-sainthood/11476.

"Pope Francis Divides Atheists," *On Faith*, September 23, 2013, www.faithstreet.com/onfaith/2013/09/23/pope-francis-divides-atheists/10569.

"That's an Atheist Thing to Do," *On Faith*, October 7, 2013, www.faithstreet.com/onfaith/2013/10/07/thats-an-atheist-thing-to-do-pope-francis/25217.

"Dangerously Incurious Pope," *Friendly Atheist*, January 8, 2014, www.patheos.com/blogs/friendlyatheist/2014/01/08/a-dangerously-incurious-pope/.

"7 Family Issues Pope Francis Should—But Won't—Discuss," *On Faith*, October 10, 2014, www.onfaith.co/onfaith/2014/10/10/family-pope-francis-catholic-synod-women/34495.

"Why I Wish Pope Francis Was Joking About the Devil," *On Faith*, June 6, 2014, www.faithstreet.com/onfaith/2014/06/06/why-i-wish-pope-francis-was-joking-about-the-devil-and-other-beliefs/32336.

"Exorcist Training," *Post and Courier* (Charleston).

"An Invitation to Exorcise an Atheist," *On Faith*, July 17, 2014, www.faithstreet.com/onfaith/2014/07/17/an-invitation-to-exorcise-an-atheist/33128.

Chapter 6

"Atheists. Humanists. Freethinkers. Americans**,**" *Secular Nation*, Fourth Quarter 2006.

"Our Secular Coalition Visit to the White House," *On Faith*, February 28, 2010, www.faithstreet.com/onfaith/2010/02/28/our-secular-coalition-visit-to-the-white-house/7239.

"Secular Coalition for America and Clinton Foundation," *Huffington Post*, August 24, 2016, www.huffingtonpost.com/entry/secular-coalition-for-america-and-clinton-foundation_us_57b0cf0be4b03d06fe852c8b?

"Compete or Cooperate? Endorse, Ignore, or Oppose?" *The Humanist*, September-October, 2007, thehumanist.com/magazine/september-october-2007/up-front/compete-or-cooperate-endorse-ignore-or-oppose.

"Trailblazers Wanted: Perfection Not Required," *The Humanist*, March-April, 2010, thehumanist.com/magazine/march-april-2010/commentary/trailblazers-wanted-perfection-not-required.

"What Atheist Groups Learned from the Christian Coalition," *On Faith*, March 22, 2012, www.faithstreet.com/onfaith/2012/03/22/what-atheist-groups-learned-from-the-christian-coalition/16141.

"What Atheists Can Learn from the Gay Rights Movement," *On Faith*, April 3, 2013, www.faithstreet.com/onfaith/2013/04/03/what-atheists-can-learn-from-the-gay-rights-movement/21379.

"Faith in Reason," *On Faith*, October 25, 2010, www.faithstreet.com/onfaith/2010/10/25/faith-in-reason/181.

"Interfaith(less) Dialogue," *On Faith*, February 13, 2013, www.faithstreet.com/onfaith/2013/02/13/interfaithless-dialogue/16369.

"Us Versus Them," *Secular Nation*, Second Quarter 2003.

Chapter 7

"Militant Atheism vs. Militant Christianity," *On Faith,* August 3, 2011, www.faithstreet.com/onfaith/2011/08/03/militant-atheism-vs-militant-christianity/31275.

"Charity Doesn't Require Religion," *On Faith*, December 1, 2010, www.faithstreet.com/onfaith/2010/12/14/god-talk-unconvincing/2041.

"A Religious and Secular Studies Major," *On Faith*, August 31, 2011, www.faithstreet.com/onfaith/2011/08/31/a-religious-and-secular-studies-major/31452.

"College of Charleston Times, They Are a-Changin,'" *Huffington Post*, May 2, 2014, www.huffingtonpost.com/herb-silverman/college-of-charleston-tim_b_5233434.html.

Chapter 8

"Should Darwin Get His Day?" *On Faith*, February 5, 2013, www.faithstreet.com/onfaith/2013/02/05/on-feb-12-should-darwin-get-his-day/15567.

"Groundhog Day and Darwin Day: My Favorite Holidays," *Huffington Post*, February 17, 2014, www.huffingtonpost.com/herb-silverman/groundhog-day-and-darwin-_b_4804918.html.

"Hey Biblical Literalists, Stop Disparaging Darwin," *On Faith*, February 12, 2015, www.faithstreet.com/onfaith/2015/02/12/hey-biblical-literalists-stop-disparaging-darwin/36154.

"Theistic Evolution," *On Faith*, February 5, 2013, www.faithstreet.com/onfaith/2013/02/05/on-feb-12-should-darwin-get-his-day/15567.

Chapter 9

"Richard Dawkins Visits the Bible Belt," *On Faith*, March 15, 2013, www.faithstreet.com/onfaith/2013/03/15/richard-dawkins-goes-to-the-bible-belt/21007.

"Herb Silverman for U.S. Senate," By Richard Dawkins, *On Faith*, December 16, 2012, www.faithstreet.com/onfaith/2012/12/16/richard-dawkins-herb-silverman-for-us-senate/15540.

"Silverman Concedes U.S. Senate Race," *On Faith*, December 18, 2012, www.faithstreet.com/onfaith/2012/12/18/herb-silverman-concedes-us-senate-race/10757.

Chapter 10

"How to Debate Christians: Five Ways to Behave and Ten Questions to Answer," *On Faith*, April 16, 2014, www.faithstreet.com/onfaith/2014/04/16/how-to-debate-christians-five-ways-to-behave-and-ten-questions-to-answer/31714.

"Science Versus Bible: To Debate or Not to Debate?" *Huffington Post*, February 5, 2014, www.huffingtonpost.com/herb-silverman/science-versus-bible-to-d_b_4731285.html.

"Silverman's Wager," *Free Inquiry*, Spring 2001.

"Evangelizing: The Good, the Bad, & the Ugly," *The Humanist*, March–April, 2009, thehumanist.com/magazine/march-april-2009/first-person/evangelizing-the-good-the-bad-the-ugly.

"A Rose by any Other Name," *Secular Nation*.

"Winning by Losing," *Secular Nation*.

Chapter 11

"Neglect in the Name of Love," *On Faith*, May 23, 2009, www.faithstreet.com/onfaith/2009/05/23/neglect-in-the-name-of-love/5675.

"In Defense of Snake Handlers," *Huffington Post*, April 26, 2014, www.huffingtonpost.com/herb-silverman/in-defense-of-snake-handl_b_4847183.html.

"Ignorance and Faith," *On Faith*, September 28, 2010, www.faithstreet.com/onfaith/2010/09/28/ignorance-and-faith/5914.

"Obama, Prayer, and Reason," *Huffington Post*, February 9, 2016, www.huffingtonpost.com/herb-silverman/obama-prayer-and-reason_b_9185980.html.

Chapter 12

"Avoiding Armageddon," *On Faith*, September 28, 2009, www.faithstreet.com/onfaith/2009/09/28/avoiding-armageddon/3621.

"Theocracy: Always a Problem, Never a Solution," *On Faith*, October 5, 2009, www.faithstreet.com/onfaith/2009/10/05/theocracy-always-a-problem-never-a-solution/8928.

"Secular Nation, Secular Military," *On Faith*, November 9, 2009, www.faithstreet.com/onfaith/2009/11/09/secular-nation-secular-military/5206.

"Honor Tillman, Not McChrystal," *On Faith*, June 29, 2010, www.faithstreet.com/onfaith/2010/06/29/honor-tillman-not-mcchrystal/4893.

"Welcome to Holy War Land," *On Faith*, December 21, 2009, www.faithstreet.com/onfaith/2009/12/21/welcome-to-holy-war-land/1130.

"Foreign Policy + Religion = Recipe for Disaster," *The Humanist*, March 3, 2010, thehumanist.com/news/international/foreign-policy-religion-recipe-for-disaster.

"Land for Peace," *On Faith*, June 8, 2010, www.faithstreet.com/onfaith/2010/06/08/land-for-peace/4445.

"War's Peace," *On Faith*, September 13, 2010, www.faithstreet.com/onfaith/2010/09/13/wars-peace/4428.

"Consistent Values for an Inconsistent World," *On Faith*, February 15, 2011, www.faithstreet.com/onfaith/2011/02/15/consistent-values-for-an-inconsistent-world/4331.

"War is a Last Resort, Not an Olympic Sport," *On Faith*, February 3, 2015, www.faithstreet.com/onfaith/2011/05/03/war-is-a-last-resort-not-an-olympisport/33080.

Chapter 13

"The War on Christmas: A Holiday Tradition for All," *On Faith*, February 11, 2012, www.faithstreet.com/onfaith/2012/12/11/the-war-on-christmas-a-holiday-tradition-for-all/11935.

"Rezla Aslan Meets Experts on God," *On Faith*, August 13, 2013, www.faithstreet.com/onfaith/2013/08/13/reza-aslan-meets-experts-on-god/11777.

"Honest and Dishonest Bias," *On Faith*, December 9, 2013, www.faithstreet.com/onfaith/2013/12/09/honest-and-dishonest-bias/30059.

Chapter 14

"Reasonable Speech," *Post and Courier* (Charleston), September 27, 2002.

"Bad Neighbors," *Charleston City Paper,* January 7, 2009, www.charlestoncitypaper.com/charleston/letters-to-the-editor/Content?oid=1133664.

"Everybody's a Blasphemer," *On Faith,* January 4, 2010, www.faithstreet.com/onfaith/2010/01/04/everybodys-a-blasphemer/5042.

"Sticks and Stones," *On Faith,* February 16, 2010, www.faithstreet.com/onfaith/2010/02/16/sticks-and-stones/8028.

"Free Speech Trumps Firearms," *On Faith,* January 11, 2011, www.faithstreet.com/onfaith/2011/01/11/free-speech-trumps-firearms/102.

"In Support of Draw Muhammad Day," *On Faith,* May 3, 2010, www.faithstreet.com/onfaith/2010/05/03/draw-muhammad-day/8873.

"Freedom to Hate," *On Faith,* October 19, 2009, www.faithstreet.com/onfaith/2009/10/19/freedom-to-hate/3633.

"We Have a Religious Right to Be a Bigot," *Huffington Post*, April 6, 2015, www.huffingtonpost.com/herb-silverman/we-have-a-religious-right_b_6987720.html.

"Bad/Good Teachers," *The Humanist*, May-June, 2009, thehumanist.com/magazine/may-june-2009/first-person/badgood-teachers.

Chapter 15

"Patriotism, Religion, Obama," *Huffington Post*, May 5, 2015, www.huffingtonpost.com/herb-silverman/patriotism-religion obama_b_6783006.html.

"Is President Obama a Christian, and Does It Matter?" *Huffington Post*, August 7, 2015, www.huffingtonpost.com/herb-silverman/is-president-obama-a-chri_b_7939400.html.

"Do the Right Thing," *On Faith*, November 8, 2010, www.faithstreet.com/onfaith/2010/11/08/do-the-right-thing/1276.

"Herb Tea Party," *On Faith*, September 21, 2010, www.faithstreet.com/onfaith/2010/09/21/herb-tea-party/2231.

"Exceptional Arrogance," *On Faith*, November 29, 2010, www.faithstreet.com/onfaith/2010/11/29/exceptional-arrogance/6496.

"The Right to Blaspheme: For No God and Country," *On Faith*, June 19, 2013, www.faithstreet.com/onfaith/2013/06/19/the-right-to-blaspheme-for-no-god-and-country/11117.

"Nothing Says 'Divisible' Like 'Under God,'" *On Faith*, September 12, 2013, www.faithstreet.com/onfaith/2013/09/12/nothing-says-divisible-like-under-god/11599.

"'Under God' Is Not All That Needs to Change About the Pledge," *On Faith*, September 26, 2014, www.faithstreet.com/onfaith/2014/09/26/under-god-is-not-all-that-needs-to-change-about-the-pledge/34274.

Chapter 16

"Health Care a Priority, Not a Product," *On Faith*, August 18, 2009, www.faithstreet.com/onfaith/2009/08/18/when-to-hold-em-when-to-fold-em/1958.

"Quality of Life Panels," *On Faith*, November 3, 2009, www.faithstreet.com/onfaith/2009/11/03/quality-of-life-panels/5280.

"Spare Rods, Not Vaccines," *On Faith*, October 13, 2009, www.faithstreet.com/onfaith/2009/10/13/spare-rods-not-vaccines/3385.

"Separation of Church and Health," *On Faith*, January 24, 2011, www.faithstreet.com/onfaith/2011/01/24/separation-of-church-and-health/3708.

"Banning Circumcision Won't Change Reality for Children," *On Faith*, June 7, 2011, www.faithstreet.com/onfaith/2011/06/07/banning-circumcision-wont-change-reality-for-children/31494.

"Religion and Health," *Post and Courier* (Charleston), September 7, 2000.

Chapter 17

"Be Good, Accept Diversity, and Strive for Peace," *U.S. News*, December 21, 2011, www.usnews.com/debate-club/has-christmas-become-too-secular/be-good-accept-diversity-and-strive-for-peace.

"Being Nice," *Post and Courier* (Charleston).

"Holidays for Everyone," *On Faith*, November 23, 2009, www.faithstreet.com/onfaith/2009/11/23/holidays-for-everyone/2268.

Unfair Comments," *Post and Courier* (Charleston).

"War on Thanksgiving," *On Faith*, November 29, 2011, www.faithstreet.com/onfaith/2011/11/29/war-on-thanksgiving/31510.

"Happy Halloween to All Who Aren't Afraid of Harmless Fun," *On Faith*, October 27, 2014, www.faithstreet.com/onfaith/2014/10/27/war-on-halloween-christmas-jesus-zombies/34765.

"7 Tips for Atheists at Thanksgiving Dinner," *On Faith*, November 19, 2014, www.faithstreet.com/onfaith/2014/11/19/7-tips-for-atheists-at-thanksgiving-dinner/35105.

"7 Things Not to Say to the Atheist in Your Family," *On Faith*, December 17, 2014, www.faithstreet.com/onfaith/2014/12/17/7-things-not-to-say-to-the-atheist-in-your-family/35508.

"7 Ways to Talk to Your Family Atheist," *On Faith*, December 22, 2014, www.faithstreet.com/onfaith/2014/12/22/7-things-to-say-to-the-atheist-in-your-family/35582.

Chapter 18

"Laughter, the Best Islamic Medicine," *On Faith*, June 16, 2009, www.faithstreet.com/onfaith/2009/06/16/laughter-the-best-islamic-medicine/8322.

"Pluralism at Ground Zero," *On Faith*, September 10, 2011, www.faithstreet.com/onfaith/2011/09/10/pluralism-at-ground-zero/31930.

"A Very Brief History of Jews, Christians, and Muslims," *Huffington Post*, April 29, 2015, www.huffingtonpost.com/herb-silverman/a-very-brief-history-of-j_b_7161846.html.

"Theological Terrorism," *Huffington Post*, December 1, 2015, www.huffingtonpost.com/herb-silverman/theological-terrorism_b_8689202.html.

"To Show Solidarity with Muslims, I Spent a Day at a Local Mosque," *Friendly Atheist*, December 25, 2015, www.patheos.com/blogs/friendlyatheist/2015/12/25/to-show-solidarity-with-muslims-i-spent-a-day-at-a-local-mosque/.

"Israel and Saudi Arabia: America's Favorite Middle East Countries," *Huffington Post*, April 5, 2016, www.huffingtonpost.com/herb-silverman/israel-and-saudi-arabia-a_b_9609276.html.

"Islamo and Atheisto Phobia," *Huffington Post*, January 7, 2016, www.huffingtonpost.com/herb-silverman/islamo-and-atheisto-phobi_b_8930092.html.

"Onward Secular Peacemakers," *On Faith*, June 2, 2009, www.faithstreet.com/onfaith/2009/06/02/onward-secular-peacemakers/6507.

"We're All Stereotypes," *On Faith*, November 6, 2009, www.faithstreet.com/onfaith/2009/11/06/were-all-stereotypes/6661.

"Fashion, Freedom and Coercion," *On Faith*, June 24, 2009,www.faithstreet.com/onfaith/2009/06/24/a-bad-answer-and-a-worse-one/2853.

"Hate Your Neighbor, but Don't Forget to Say Grace," *On Faith*, February 22, 2011, www.faithstreet.com/onfaith/2011/02/22/hate-your-neighbor-but-dont-forget-to-say-grace/6977.

"Neither Catholic Nor Sharia Law," *On Faith*, June 29, 2011, www.faithstreet.com/onfaith/2011/06/29/neither-catholic-nor-sharia-law/31501.

"Theocratic State?" *Post and Courier* (Charleston), August 15, 2011, www.postandcourier.com/article/20110815/ARCHIVES/308159949.

"A Conservative Christian Engaged in a Christian War," *On Faith*, July 27, 2011, www.faithstreet.com/onfaith/2011/07/27/a-conservative-christian-engaged-in-a-christian-war/31490.

Chapter 19

"Whose Jews," *On Faith*, November 15, 2013, www.washingtonpost.com/blogs/on-faith/wp/2013/11/25/whose-jews/.

"Who Is a Jew? What Is a Christian?" *On Faith*, October 20, 2014, www.faithstreet.com/onfaith/2014/10/20/who-is-a-jew-what-is-a-christian/34645.

"Godless Jews," *Huffington Post*, November 6, 2015, www.huffingtonpost.com/herb-silverman/godless-jews_b_8479794.html.

"The Jew/Atheist Paradox," *Huffington Post*, November 16, 2015, www.huffingtonpost.com/herb-silverman/the-jewatheist-paradox_b_8575286.html.

"Humoristic Judaism," *Humanistic Judaism*, Summer/Autumn 2014.

"Five Reasons I Might Join the Ku Klux Klan," *On Faith*, December 2, 2014, www.faithstreet.com/onfaith/2014/12/02/five-reasons-i-might-join-the-ku-klux-klan/35252.

"God's Welfare Dilemma," *On Faith,* July 15, 2013, www.faithstreet.com/onfaith/2013/07/15/gods-welfare-dilemma/16867.

"Why I No Longer Support Israel," *Huffington Post,* March 16, 2015, www.huffingtonpost.com/herb-silverman/why-i-no-longer-support-i_b_6869098.html.

"My Passover Evolution," *On Faith,* March 29, 2013, www.faithstreet.com/onfaith/2013/03/29/my-passover-evolution/20103.

"A Godless Passover," *On Faith,* April 20, 2011, www.faithstreet.com/onfaith/2011/04/20/a-godless-passover/33089.

"High Holidays for Jewish Atheists," *On Faith,* September 6, 2013, www.faithstreet.com/onfaith/2013/09/06/high-holidays-for-jewish-atheists/10224.

"Jewish Atheists and Koufax Jews," *The Humanist,* September-October 2014, thehumanist.com/magazine/september-october-2014/humanist-living/jewish-atheists-and-koufax-jews.

Chapter 20

"Even Churches Need to Grow Up," *On Faith,* August 3, 2009, www.faithstreet.com/onfaith/2009/08/03/even-churches-need-to-grow-up/584.

"Gays Are Not An 'Uppity Minority,'" *Post and Courier* (Charleston).

"Boy Scouts Should Move to End All Discrimination," *Post and Courier* (Charleston), May 30, 2015, www.postandcourier.com/article/20150530/PC1002/150539924/1025.

"I'm Not Gay, But I Am Jealous," *On Faith,* May 26, 2015, www.faithstreet.com/onfaith/2015/05/26/im-not-gay-but-i-am-jealous/36937.

"Interfaith and Faithless," *Huffington Post,* August 14, 2016, www.huffingtonpost.com/entry/interfaith-and-faithless_us_57a8b15ce4b08f5371f1ab3b?

"The Bathroom War Between the States," *Huffington Post,* April 19, 2016, www.huffingtonpost.com/herb-silverman/the-bathroom-war-between-_b_9721290.html.

Chapter 21

"My Wife and Her Husbands," *On Faith,* July 27, 2009, www.faithstreet.com/onfaith/2009/07/27/my-wife-and-her-husbands/4728.

"Interfaithless Marriage Works, Especially for the Secular," *On Faith,* July 26, 2010, www.faithstreet.com/onfaith/2010/07/26/interfaithless-marriage-works/1362.

"Find Meaning in Marriage Without Religion," *On Faith,* December 6, 2010, www.faithstreet.com/onfaith/2010/12/06/what-really-matters/1978.

"An Atheist's Defense of Marriage Act," *On Faith*, August 5, 2015, www.faithstreet.com/onfaith/2013/08/05/an-atheists-defense-of-marriage-act/10893.

"The L-word," *On Faith,* February 14, 2011, www.faithstreet.com/onfaith/2011/02/14/the-l-word/671.

Chapter 22

"Humor Is in the Eye of the Beholder," *On Faith*, June 15, 2011, www.faithstreet.com/onfaith/2011/06/15/humor-is-in-the-eye-of-the-beholder/31496.

A Presidential Candidate Good for the Atheists," *Secular Nation.*

"We Should Judge Their Politics, Not Their Religion," *On Faith*, February 8, 2011, www.faithstreet.com/onfaith/2011/02/08/too-much-religion-in-politics/2700.

"Mixing Religion and Politics," *Huffington Post,* March 9, 2012, www.huffingtonpost.com/herb-silverman/mixing-religion-and-politics_b_1327255.html.

"Mitt Romney: A Reasonable Man?" *On Faith*, September 23, 2011, www.faithstreet.com/onfaith/2011/09/23/mitt-romney-a-reasonable-man/31934.

Chapter 23

"Still Hoping for a Secular Miracle," *On Faith*, June 2, 2011, www.faithstreet.com/onfaith/2011/06/02/still-hoping-for-a-secular-miracle/31492.

"Only Humans Can Solve Human Problems," *On Faith*, August 10, 2011, www.faithstreet.com/onfaith/2011/08/10/only-human-can-solve-human-problems/31278.

"My Plan Is God's Plan," *On Faith*, October 4, 2010, www.faithstreet.com/onfaith/2010/10/04/my-plan-is-gods-plan/3925.

"The Power of Positive Praying—Even for Atheists," *On Faith*, July 23, 2–13, www.faithstreet.com/onfaith/2013/07/23/the-power-of-positive-praying-even-for-atheists/16767.

"National Day of Non-Prayer?" *On Faith*, May 5, 2009, www.faithstreet.com/onfaith/2009/05/05/national-day-of-non-prayer/33083.

"A National Day of Reason?" *On Faith,* May 3, 2012, www.faithstreet.com/onfaith/2012/05/03/instead-of-a-national-day-of-prayer-do-we-need-a-national-day-of-reason/16888.

"An Atheist's Favorite National Day of Prayer," *Huffington Post*, May 9, 2014, www.huffingtonpost.com/herb-silverman/an-atheists-favorite-nati_b_5296306.html.

"Why the Supreme Court's Conservative and Liberal Judges Are All Greek to Me," *On Faith*, May 15, 2014, www.faithstreet.com/onfaith/2014/05/15/why-the-supreme-courts-conservative-and-liberal-judges-are-all-greek-to-me/32089.

"Non-Specific Deity," *Post and Courier* (Charleston).

Chapter 24

"How Would Jesus Vote?" *Huffington Post*, January 13, 2012, www.huffingtonpost.com/herb-silverman/how-would-jesus-vote-poli_b_1205316.html.

"Martin Luther King and the Republican Race For Righteousness," *Huffington Post*, March 18, 2012, www.huffingtonpost.com/herb-silverman/martin-luther-king-and-th_b_1211604.html.

"South Carolina Primary Humor, Intentional and Unintentional," *Huffington Post*, March 23, 2012, www.huffingtonpost.com/herb-silverman/south-carolina-primary-hu_b_1222620.html.

"Hypocritical Values," *On Faith*, March 30, 2011, www.faithstreet.com/onfaith/2011/03/30/hypocritical-values/33095.

"Who Is God's Candidate?" *Huffington Post*, September 23, 2015, www.huffingtonpost.com/herb-silverman/who-is-gods-candidate_b_8177582.html.

"Sharia, Christian, or Constitutional Law?" *Huffington Post*, July 20, 2016, www.huffingtonpost.com/herb-silverman/sharia-christian-or-const_b_11040526.html.

"My Brief Support for Marco Rubio," *Huffington Post*, February 29, 2016, www.huffingtonpost.com/herb-silverman/my-brief-support-for-marc_b_9341648.html.

"Politically Incorrect, Literally," *Huffington Post*, October 15, 2015, www.huffingtonpost.com/herb-silverman/politically-incorrect-lit_b_8293266.html.

"Are Secular Progressives Murderers?" *richarddawkins.net*, November 3, 2015, richarddawkins.net/2015/11/are-secular-progressives-murderers-2/.

"Did WikiLeaks Reveal I Was a Shill For Hillary Clinton?" *Huffington Post*, August 5, 2016, www.huffingtonpost.com/herb-silverman/did-wikileaks-reveal-i-wa_b_11306076.html

"Post-Election Healing: An Atheist's Perspective," *On Faith*, November 10, 2016, www.onfaith.co/commentary/post-election-healing-an-atheists-perspective.

Chapter 25

"How to Read (and Think) Like an Atheist," *On Faith*, June 24, 2013, www.faithstreet.com/onfaith/2013/06/24/how-to-read-and-think-like-an-atheist/10861.

"Religious Fiction: Isn't That Redundant?" *On Faith*, August 19, 2013, www.faithstreet.com/onfaith/2013/08/19/religious-fiction-isnt-that-redundant/12129.

"5 Books Atheists and Other Outsiders Should Read," *On Faith*, August 25, 2014, www.faithstreet.com/onfaith/2014/08/25/5-books-all-atheists-and-other-outsiders-should-read/33816.

"How Can a Made-Up Bible Still Be God's Word?" *On Faith*, January 28, 2015, www.faithstreet.com/onfaith/2015/01/28/how-can-a-made-up-bible-still-be-gods-word/35985.

"Church Invitation: An Atheist on American Anglicans and Amazing Grace," *On Faith*, April 9, 2014, www.faithstreet.com/onfaith/2014/04/09/church-invitation-an-atheists-experience-of-st-andrews-and-amazing-grace/31637.

"One of America's Best Kept Religious Secrets," *On Faith*, July 3, 2014, www.faithstreet.com/onfaith/2014/07/03/one-of-americas-best-kept-religious-secrets/32898.

"God Must be Proud of Atheists," *On Faith*, July 31, 2015, www.faithstreet.com/onfaith/2015/07/31/god-must-be-proud-of-atheists/37540.

"What's God Got to Do with It?" *On Faith*, December 25, 2009, www.faithstreet.com/onfaith/2009/12/25/whats-god-got-to-do-with-it/3985.

"Atheists Bad, Christians Good," *On Faith*, April 23, 2014, www.faithstreet.com/onfaith/2014/04/23/atheists-bad-christians-good-a-review-of-gods-not-dead/31790.

Chapter 26

"The Gould Standard," *Washington Post,* May 26, 2002.

"Science Is Not Democratic," *On Faith*, August 24, 2011, www.faithstreet.com/onfaith/2011/08/24/science-is-not-democratic/31449.

"The 'Stupid Party,'" *On Faith*, November 15, 2012, www.faithstreet.com/onfaith/2012/11/15/the-stupid-party/11993.

"Natural, Not Supernatural, Disasters," *On Faith*, January 19, 2010, www.faithstreet.com/onfaith/2010/01/19/natural-not-supernatural-disasters/1244.

"Hawking and the Pope," *On Faith*, September 8, 2010, www.faithstreet.com/onfaith/2010/09/08/hawking-and-the-pope/920.

"Yes, Mr. Hawking, Evidence Should Determine Belief," *On Faith*, May 17, 2011, www.faithstreet.com/onfaith/2011/05/17/yes-mr-hawking-evidence-should-determine-belief/31504.

"A Godless Apocalypse," *On Faith*, May 11, 2011, www.faithstreet.com/onfaith/2011/05/11/a-godless-apocalypse/11221.

"Perpetuating Ignorance," *On Faith*, November 29, 2012, www.faithstreet.com/onfaith/2012/11/29/perpetuating-ignorance/16954.

"Science Solution," *Post and Courier* (Charleston), April 22, 2010,www.postandcourier.com/article/20100422/ARCHIVES/304229970.

"How God Led Me to Mathematics and Then Turned Me into an Atheist," *Secular Nation*, first quarter 2004.

"God *IS* Great," *The Humanist,* November-December 2007, thehumanist.com/magazine/november-december-2007/up-front/god-is-great.

"Three Equals One," *Secular Nation*, second quarter 2003.

Chapter 27

"Inaugural Prayerfest No Godsend," *On Faith*, January 21, 2009, www.faithstreet.com/onfaith/2009/01/21/inaugural-prayerfest-no-godsen/3072.

"A United States for Nonbelievers?" *On Faith*, January 23, 2013, www.faithstreet.com/onfaith/2013/01/23/a-united-states-for-nonbelievers/10031.

"Why Atheists Should Embrace America's 'Godless' Constitution," *On Faith*, March 4, 2013, www.faithstreet.com/onfaith/2013/03/04/why-atheists-should-embrace-americas-godless-constitution/15776.

"Freedom from Religion," *Washington Post*, August 31, 2000.

"Taxation for Religious Discrimination," *On Faith*, September 21, 2009, www.faithstreet.com/onfaith/2009/09/21/taxation-for-religious-discrimination/954.

"All Taxpayers Are Created Equal," *On Faith*, March 8, 2010, www.faithstreet.com/onfaith/2010/03/08/all-taxpayers-are-created-equal/5291.

"A Few Kind Words For Satan," *Huffington Post*, March 12, 2014, www.huffingtonpost.com/herb-silverman/a-few-kind-words-for-sata_b_4941371.html.

"Is America a Christian Nation?" *Friendly Atheist*, January 26, 2010, www.patheos.com/blogs/friendlyatheist/2010/01/26/is-america-a-christian-nation/.

"Do Christian Conservatives Believe in the First Amendment?" *On Faith*, August 26, 2013, www.faithstreet.com/onfaith/2013/08/26/do-christian-conservatives-believe-in-the-first-amendment/10855.

"'In God We Trust,' When Politically Convenient," *On Faith*, November 2, 2011, www.faithstreet.com/onfaith/2011/11/02/in-god-we-trust-when-politically-convenient/31508.

"The Problem of Religious Privilege for Prisoners," *On Faith*, November 6, 2014, www.faithstreet.com/onfaith/2014/11/06/the-problem-with-religious-privilege-for-prisoners/34937.

"Matter of Prayer," *Post and Courier* (Charleston), www.postandcourier.com/20160716/160719535/letter-matter-of-prayer

"Three Wrongs Don't Make a Right," *On Faith*, July 6, 2009, www.faithstreet.com/onfaith/2009/07/06/three-wrongs-dont-make-a-right/2998.

"Vice President of Religion," *On Faith*, October 6, 2016, www.onfaith.co/commentary/vice-president-of-religion?utm_source=twitter&utm_medium=social&utm_campaign=share-explanation.

"From Jefferson to Trump," *On Faith*, October 25, 2016, www.onfaith.co/commentary/from-jefferson-to-trump.

Chapter 28

"Doing What Comes Naturally," *On Faith*, April 20, 2010, www.faithstreet.com/onfaith/2010/04/20/doing-what-comes-naturally/3784.

"Changing an Unchanging Church," *On Faith*, May 12, 2009, www.faithstreet.com/onfaith/2009/05/12/changing-an-unchanging-church/5304.

"The Elephant in the Notre Dame Auditorium," *On Faith*, May 18, 2009, www.faithstreet.com/onfaith/2009/05/18/the-elephant-in-the-notre-dame-auditorium/2921.

"7 Family Issues Pope Francis Should—But Won't—Discuss," *On Faith,* October 10, 2014, www.faithstreet.com/onfaith/2014/10/10/family-pope-francis-catholic-synod-women/34495.

"When Catholic Bishops Control Health Care for All of Us," *On Faith*, November 17, 2009, www.faithstreet.com/onfaith/2009/11/17/when-catholic-bishops-control-health-care-for-all-of-us/3964.

"Messy Path to Gay Progress," *On Faith*, June 22, 2011, www.faithstreet.com/onfaith/2011/06/22/the-messy-path-to-gay-progress/31499.

Chapter 29

One sentence sound bites without links.

Chapter 30

"A Christian Response: To What?" *Huffington Post,* June 5, 2015, www.huffingtonpost.com/herb-silverman/a-christian-response-to-w_b_7504686.html.

"Religious Beliefs," *Post and Courier* (Charleston), September 15, 2016, www.postandcourier.com/20160915/160919645/letter-religious-beliefs.

"Talking to 'The Other,'" *On Faith*, September 15, 2009, www.faithstreet.com/onfaith/2009/09/15/talking-to-the-other/7601.

"Rebel Flag Debate," *Post and Courier* (Charleston), January 15, 1995.

"Experiences with South Carolina Law," *Huffington Post*, April 14, 2015, www.huffingtonpost.com/herb-silverman/experiences-with-south-ca_b_7054412.html.

"Tragedy in South Carolina," *Huffington Post*, June 19, 2015, www.huffingtonpost.com/herb-silverman/tragedy-in-south-carolina_b_7616722.html.

"Spiritual Shift," *Post and Courier* (Charleston), July 15, 2015, www.postandcourier.com/article/20150715/PC1002/150719538/1025/.

"Heritage *and* Hate," *Huffington Post*, June 30, 2015, www.huffingtonpost.com/herb-silverman/heritage-and-hate_b_7697116.html.

"The Confederate Flag and the 10 Commandments," *Huffington Post*, July 15, 2015, www.huffingtonpost.com/herb-silverman/the-confederate-flag-and-_3_b_7804744.html.

"The NAACP and Me," *Huffington Post*, September 15, 2015, www.huffingtonpost.com/herb-silverman/the-naacp-and-me_b_8136402.html.

Chapter 31

"Male Problem or Millennial Problem," *On Faith*, July 21, 2009, www.faithstreet.com/onfaith/2009/07/21/male-problem-or-millennial-problem/33078.

"Religion's Outdated Notion of Gender," *On Faith*, April 11, 2011, www.faithstreet.com/onfaith/2011/04/11/religions-outdated-notion-of-gender/33091.

"Palin: A Pat Robertson Feminist," *On Faith*, May 17, 2010, www.faithstreet.com/onfaith/2010/05/17/palin-a-pat-robertson-feminist/9006.

"Opposite Games by Politicians," *On Faith*, March 1, 2011, www.faithstreet.com/onfaith/2011/03/01/opposite-games-by-politicians/4434.

"Finally, an Anti-Contraception Ruling I (Sort of) Support," *Huffington Post*, September 8, 2015, www.huffingtonpost.com/herb-silverman/finally-ananticontracept_b_8096562.html.

"My Complaint About Oprah," *On Faith*, May 27, 2011, www.faithstreet.com/onfaith/2011/05/27/my-complaint-about-oprah/31506.

"Pro-choice and Pro-life," *On Faith*, September 13, 2011, www.faithstreet.com/onfaith/2011/09/13/pro-choice-and-pro-life/31926.

ABOUT THE AUTHOR

Herb Silverman is Founder of the Secular Coalition for America and Distinguished Professor Emeritus of Mathematics at the College of Charleston. He ran for governor of South Carolina in 1990 to challenge a state law that required religious belief to hold public office. After an eight-year battle, Herb won a unanimous decision in the South Carolina Supreme Court, which struck down this religious test requirement. He is the author of *Candidate Without a Prayer: An Autobiography of a Jewish Atheist in the Bible Belt*. You can browse a collection of Herb's public speeches and debates at his website www.herbsilverman.com. He lives in Charleston, South Carolina.